CHANGING LEADERSHIP FOR CHANGING TIMES

CHANGING EDUCATION

Series Editors:
Professor Andy Hargreaves, Ontario Institute for Studies in Education
Professor Ivor Goodson, University of East Anglia

This authoritative series addresses the key issues raised by the unprecedented levels of educational change now facing schools and societies throughout the world.

The different directions of change can seem conflicting and are often contested. Decentralized systems of school self-management are accompanied by centralized systems of curriculum and assessment control. Moves to develop more authentic assessments are paralleled by the tightened imposition of standardized tests. Curriculum integration is being advocated in some places, more specialization and subject departmentalization in others.

These complex and contradictory cross-currents pose real challenges to theoretical and practical interpretation in many fields of education and constitute an important and intriguing agenda for educational change. *Changing Education* brings together leading international scholars who address these vital issues with authority and accessibility in areas where they are noted specialists. The series will commission books from all parts of the world in an attempt to cover the global and interlinked nature of current changes.

Published titles:

David Corson: *Changing Education for Diversity*
Gill Helsby: *Changing Teachers' Work*
Joe L. Kincheloe and Shirley R. Steinberg: *Changing Multiculturalism*
Colin Lankshear: *Changing Literacies*
Kenneth Leithwood, Doris Jantzi and Rosanne Steinbach: *Changing Leadership for Changing Times*
Louise Stoll and Dean Fink: *Changing Our Schools*

Titles in preparation include:

Bob Lingard: *Changing Educational Policy*
Carrie Paechter: *Changing School Subjects*
Peter Tomlinson: *Changing Approaches to Learning and Teaching*

CHANGING LEADERSHIP FOR CHANGING TIMES

KENNETH LEITHWOOD
DORIS JANTZI AND
ROSANNE STEINBACH

OPEN UNIVERSITY PRESS
Buckingham · Philadelphia

Open University Press
Celtic Court
22 Ballmoor
Buckingham
MK18 1XW

email: enquiries@openup.co.uk
world wide web: http://www.openup.co.uk

and
325 Chestnut Street
Philadelphia, PA 19106, USA

First Published 1999

A catalogue record of this book is available from the British Library

ISBN   0 335 19522 9 (pbk)   0 335 19523 7 (hbk)

Library of Congress Cataloging-in-Publication Data
Leithwood, Kenneth A.
     Changing leadership for changing times / Kenneth Leithwood, Doris Jantzi and Rosanne Steinbach.
          p.   cm. — (Changing education series.)
     Includes bibliographical references (p.) and index.
     ISBN 0-335-19523-7 (hardbound). — ISBN 0-335-19522-9 (pbk.)
     1. Educational leadership.   2. School management and organization.
     3. School improvement programs.   I. Jantzi, Doris.   II. Steinbach, Rosanne,
     1942–   .   III. Title.   IV. Series: Changing education.
     LB2805.L358   1999
     371.2—dc21   98-36636
                                                                                        CIP

Typeset by Type Study, Scarborough
Printed in Great Britain by St Edmundsbury Press, Bury St Edmunds, Suffolk

CONTENTS

SERIES EDITORS' PREFACE

Around the world, schools, and the societies of which they are a part, are confronting the most profound changes, the like of which have not been seen since the last great global movement of economic and educational restructuring more than a century ago. The fundamental forms of public education that were designed for an age of heavy manufacturing and mechanical industry are under challenge and fading fast as we move into a world of high technology, flexible workforces, more diverse school populations, downsized administrations and declining resources.

What is to follow is uncertain and unclear. The different directions of change can seem conflicting and are often contested. Decentralized systems of school self-management are accompanied by centralized systems of curriculum and assessment control. Moves to develop more authentic assessments are paralleled by the tightened imposition of standardized tests. Curriculum integration is being advocated in some places, more specialization and subject departmentalization in others.

These complex and contradictory cross-currents pose real challenges to theoretical and practical interpretation in many fields of education, and constitute an important and intriguing agenda for educational change – and for this series, which is intended to meet a deep-seated need among researchers and practitioners. International, social and technological changes require a profound and rapid response from the educational community. By establishing and interpreting the nature and scope of educational change, *Changing Leadership for Changing Times* will make a significant contribution to meeting this challenge.

Kenneth Leithwood is one of the world's leading and most long-standing researchers on educational leadership. His book, like many others, attests to the centrality of leadership issues in the educational change agenda. Without effective educational leadership, little positive educational change will happen, and still less of it will be sustained over time. If good learning depends on good teachers, good teaching ultimately depends on excellent leaders. But what constitutes effective educational leadership? How can we cultivate it? And is the leadership required to guide schools and students to higher levels of performance in complex times of rapid change, the same as that which was said to be valuable in more conventional and conservative schools? These are the kind of questions to which Kenneth Leithwood has dedicated a sustained research programme over many years.

The key concept which Leithwood addresses is that of transformational leadership. Adapted from the management and business literature, transformational leadership has been advocated by many in education, but seriously investigated by few. Through solid and systematic quantitative research and vivid, intensive case studies, Leithwood sets out the core components of transformational leadership, shows why they make a difference, and brings them to life in the words and actions of the secondary-school leaders and their schools that he and his team have studied.

The leadership literature of education is packed with spirited but often speculative advocacy. This literature is often strong on rhetoric but weak on evidence. Leithwood sets out the evidence on leadership strategies and styles that make a difference and does this in a way that makes the material practical and accessible. Educational leaders and aspiring leaders the world over who want to build their practice on a foundation of solid research that they can apply to their own work almost immediately, will find that this book stands head and shoulders above most of its competitors. Schools these days are being urged to use data about achievement and accountability more intelligently. This book enables and urges leaders to do just that in relation to their own practice, bringing evidence and imagination together to create leadership practices that really work in schools, that are fitted to the needs and demands of the new century.

ACKNOWLEDGEMENTS

We are pleased to have the opportunity to thank the many people who contributed to this book in a variety of ways. We are especially indebted to all the teachers and administrators (in particular the staffs at 'COSS', 'SOES', and 'Constantine High') who gave us their time and shared their expertise to help us unravel the mysteries of school leadership.

Several of the chapters have been liberally adapted from previous work with other colleagues. We are grateful for the opportunity to collaborate with Dan Duke, Diana Tomlinson, Maxine Genge, Tiiu Strauss, Sherrill Ryan, Alicia Fernandez, Teresa Menzies, Jennifer Leithwood, Byron Dart, Laurie Leonard and Lyn Sharratt.

We also appreciated the efforts of Vashty Hawkins, who made sure the finished product was properly formatted and paginated, while cheerfully coping with daily changes to the manuscript.

This book was based on research funded by the Social Sciences and Humanities Research Council of Canada, the Johann Jacobs Foundation (Switzerland) and the Ontario Ministry of Education through its block transfer grant to OISE/University of Toronto. We gratefully acknowledge their support.

part 1

THE CONTEXT FOR
CHANGING LEADERSHIP

one

CHANGING LEADERSHIP:
A MENU OF POSSIBILITIES

. . . we are coming to believe that leaders are those people who 'walk ahead', people who are genuinely committed to deep change in themselves and in their organizations. They lead through developing new skills, capabilities, and understandings. And they come from many places within the organization.

(Senge 1996: 45)

A book on leadership! 'Why,' you ask, 'do we need another book on leadership?' On the shelves in just one of our offices are 213 different such books already. The short answer is 'Times change', and productive leadership depends heavily on its fit with the social and organizational context in which it is exercised. So as times change, what works for leaders changes also.

This is not to deny that there are relatively enduring leadership qualities – qualities that travel well through time and across organizational contexts. But this is because some features of our times are a lot like features of earlier times. Many of us in schools today, for example, would resonate with the claim that, 'Never before have we had so little time in which to do so much', an assertion attributed to Franklin D. Roosevelt in the 1930s (Anderson 1989).

On the other hand, the observations about leadership by Peter Senge opening this chapter speak about, for example, approaches to leadership that productively respond to the complexity of the challenges faced today by many organizations, the radically altered expectations that employees bring to their work, and the considerably greater respect that has developed for the capacities of people throughout organizations to think productively about their missions and how they can be addressed. Senge's observations draw attention to relatively recent conceptions of leadership as something widely distributed throughout organizations, and to a central purpose of such leadership; the empowerment of others. This is not quite what Machiavelli had in mind when he proffered one of his general rules of leadership: 'whoever is responsible for another's becoming powerful ruins himself, because this power is brought into being either by ingenuity or by force, and both of these are suspect to the one who has become powerful' (Machiavelli 1981: 44).

So there is no final word on what is good leadership. We are simply trying to hit a moving target; maybe even get a little ahead of it. Granted, the qualities that are relatively enduring may become clearer in the process, but these qualities will never be more than the 'basic skills' of leadership. They will never tell us anything important about how to exercise outstanding leadership, because outstanding leadership is exquisitely sensitive to the context in which it is exercised.

This is a book about school leadership exercised in restructuring contexts, of the sort found in many different countries on virtually all continents today. Towards the end, it becomes a book about leadership for a kind of school that has yet to see the light of day. This is a school that we believe provides a defensible vision for leaders of today's schools, at least those in developed countries across the world. Read Chapter 13 and see what you think. By far the bulk of the book is based on evidence that has emerged over the past seven years of our research on leadership and school restructuring. This was research prompted by our dissatisfaction with the power of a model of instructional leadership to account for what was taking place in a number of Canadian restructuring schools that we were studying in the early 1990s.

Because productive leadership in those schools did not conform very closely to our understanding of instructional leadership, a model especially popular in North America, we began to search for something more satisfactory. What we ended up with was an approach to leadership usually referred to as 'transformational'. So the first section of this book begins by outlining a menu of current leadership models from which one might choose. Then we share our reasons for thinking that transformational leadership is a sensible point of departure for better understanding changing leadership for changing times.

The second section of the book describes the outcome of our efforts to unpack the meaning and understand the details of transformational leadership in schools, in particular. In the third section, we summarize a series of studies undertaken to both deepen and broaden this approach to school leadership. Chapters in this section reaffirm the impact of transformational approaches to leadership on many different aspects of schools. More importantly, in our view, they add up to a unique understanding of what forms of leadership will be helpful in educational organizations, not only tomorrow, but many years from now.

The meaning of leadership as a concept

Leadership as a concept and a set of practices has been the subject of an enormous quantity of popular and academic literature. Most of this literature is about particular approaches to, or models of, leadership – servant leadership or strategic leadership, for example. Leadership is a term used frequently in conversation both inside and outside organizations. Such everyday uses of the term are typically prefaced by such adjectives as 'good', 'effective', 'exemplary', 'poor' and 'terrible'. In neither the leadership literature nor in everyday uses of the term is attention given to the concept of leadership. This raises the question, 'At its root, what does "leadership" mean and, if we knew, would we be any better off?'

Arguably, a great deal has been learned about leadership over the past century. But this actually has not depended on any clear, agreed upon definition of the concept, as essential as this would seem at first glance. Indeed, Yukl argues that, 'It is neither feasible nor desirable at this point in the development of the discipline to attempt to resolve the controversies over the appropriate definition of leadership. Like all constructs in social sciences, the definition of leadership is arbitrary and very subjective. Some definitions are more useful than others, but there is no "correct" definition' (Yukl 1994: 4–5).

This observation has been echoed by other respected students of leadership (such as Bennis 1959). But others disagree. Clark and Clark, for example, argue that, 'You cannot talk about leaders with anyone until you agree on what you are talking about. That requires a definition of leadership and a criterion for leadership acts that can be agreed on' (Clark and Clark 1990: 20). In the same vein, Rost begins his analysis of leadership and leadership literature in non-school organizations by arguing that lack of attention to definition has been one of the main impediments to progress in the field. Indeed, he notes that 'over 60 percent of the authors who have written on leadership since about 1910 did not define leadership in their works' (Rost 1991: 6).

One wonders how so many smart people could have overlooked such an obvious issue. Or did they? More likely they were at least in implicit agreement with Lofti Zadeh, the father of fuzzy logic, who framed the Law of Incompatibility: 'As complexity rises, precise statements lose meaning and meaningful statements lose precision' (McNeil and Freiberger 1993: 43). As these authors go on to point out, the Law of Incompatibility captures a feature common to most complex disciplines; that is, they teem with complex concepts. Responding to worries over the lack of precision in defining the meaning of 'strategic management', for example, Thomas and Pruett ask: 'how much more precise are economists when they discuss "innovation" or "regulation", or psychologists when they talk about "intelligence"?' (1993: 4). Whereas simple concepts are typically open to crisp definition, complex concepts are usually defined vaguely. Perseverating on the development of a precise definition of a complex concept like leadership is likely to be counterproductive, following this line of reasoning.

Although Yukl pointed to lack of consensus about the precise meaning of leadership, he did discern a core of agreement across definitions very similar to what Bass (1981) detected a decade earlier. 'Most definitions of leadership', Yukl claimed, 'reflect the assumption that it involves a social influence process whereby intentional influence is exerted by one person [or group] over other people [or groups] to structure the activities and relationships in a group or organization' (1994: 3). Influence, then, seems to be a necessary part of most conceptions of leadership. This suggests that most of the variation in leadership concepts, types or models can be accounted for by differences in who exerts influence, the nature of that influence, the purpose for the exercise of influence and its outcomes. This is taken up in more detail in the conclusion to this chapter.

Developing a menu of approaches to school leadership

There is much yet to be learned about leadership, the different forms that it can take and the effects of these different forms. So the menu of approaches available today is undoubtedly smaller than the menu that will be available ten or twenty years from now. New approaches to leadership have evolved quite slowly over the past century and most contemporary approaches are evident, in one form or another, in the leadership literatures of 30, 40, and 50 years ago (Leithwood and Duke, in press). So a review of a representative sample of contemporary international literature concerning leadership in schools today is likely to identify the serious possibilities for some time to come. This section of the chapter describes six different approaches to school leadership identified through such a review.

The sample of literature included in the review consisted of all feature-length articles concerned with leadership published in four representative English-language educational administration journals. These journals were reviewed at least as far back as 1988. Two of the four journals selected for review, *Educational Administration Quarterly* (*EAQ*), and the *Journal of School Leadership* (*JSL*), publish work largely from North America. Papers in the *Journal of Educational Administration* (*JEA*) reflect perspectives from Australia, New Zealand and other countries, as well as North America, whereas *Educational Management and Administration* (*EMA*) primarily reflects contemporary thought on leadership in the United Kingdom. Because of the reputations of each of these journals, and the relatively broad theoretical perspectives they collectively reflect, it seems likely that most significant contemporary conceptions of leadership in the English-speaking world would find some expression in their contents.

Approximately eight volumes were reviewed for each journal, several less in the case of *JSL* because it was not established until 1991, and several more in the case of *EMA* so as to balance the almost exclusively North American perspectives reflected in *EAQ* and *JSL*. A total of 121 articles were identified. These were of several types, including descriptions of leadership theories, reviews of literature, empirical reports and critical analyses.

Twenty specific leadership concepts were explicitly mentioned in the articles. The most frequently mentioned specific concepts of leadership were instructional leadership, leadership styles and transformational leadership. Instructional leadership appeared almost exclusively in the North American journals and in papers written by North Americans. All four journals also contained papers about transformational leadership although it was most often mentioned in the North American journals. Mention of leadership styles was fairly evenly distributed across the journals. The next most frequently mentioned leadership concepts were moral leadership, managerial leadership and cultural leadership. Managerial leadership appeared exclusively in the UK journal. Some articles explicitly discussed as many as three or four such concepts (for example Walker 1989; Cusack 1993; Gronn 1996).

The focus of 54 articles was on leadership, but no attempt was made to label the form or model of leadership in question. Some of these articles supported multiple perspectives on leadership, while others treated leadership as a generally understood phenomenon without specific discussion of its meaning. There were also many instances in which an implicit leadership concept was evident, as, for example, Hayes's (1995) study of collaborative relationships (or 'shared leadership') in a British primary school, and Goldring's (1990) examination of principals' boundary spanning activities (or 'organizational leadership').

Each of the 20 separate leadership concepts was assigned to one of six broad categories, referred to subsequently as 'models'. Included in the six categories of approaches to school leadership are instructional, transformational, moral, participative, managerial and contingent leadership. These models, clustering together leadership concepts sharing the same primary focus and key assumptions, are described in the next six sections of the chapter.

Instructional leadership

Instructional leadership, a single, separate category, typically assumes that the critical focus for attention by leaders is the *behaviours of teachers as they engage in activities directly affecting the growth of students*. Many versions of this form of leadership focus, additionally, on other organizational variables (such as school culture) that are believed to have important consequences for such teacher behaviour. This has led Sheppard (1996) to distinguish between 'narrow' and 'broad' views of instructional leadership. Most conceptions of instructional leadership allocate authority and influence to formal administrative roles (usually the principal), assuming, as well, considerable influence through expert knowledge on the part of those occupying such roles.

Lack of explicit descriptions of instructional leadership (Foster 1986) make it difficult to assess the extent to which such leadership means the same thing to all those writing about it. Geltner and Shelton (1991) modified the term, referring to 'strategic instructional leadership', but offered no notion of what non-strategic instructional leadership might mean. Stalhammar (1994) used the term 'pedagogical leadership' and Kleine-Kracht (1993) differentiated between 'direct' and 'indirect' instructional leadership, noting that principals alone cannot fulfil all of a school's need for instructional leadership. Others argued that original beliefs concerning the principal as the primary or most important instructional leader required rethinking. Davidson (1992), for example, argued for the value of teachers serving as instructional leaders, while Floden *et al.* (1988) focused on district-level instructional leadership. And Achilles (1992) challenged the idea that instructional leadership (or any form of leadership for that matter) was necessarily a substitute for capable management.

Examples of extensively elaborated contemporary models of instructional leadership include Duke (1987), Smith and Andrews (1989), and Hallinger and his colleagues (Hallinger and Murphy 1985; Hallinger and McCary 1990; Hallinger 1992; Hallinger and Heck 1996). In each case, this model of leadership is described along multiple dimensions, each of which incorporates a number of practices, and evidence is reviewed concerning the effects of these practices on important outcomes. The most fully tested of these models, the one developed by Hallinger and his associates (for example Hallinger and Murphy 1985), consists of three broad categories of leadership practice: defining the school mission; managing the instructional program; and promoting school climate. Associated with these broad categories of practice are 21 more specific functions (such as supervising instruction). Using a teacher survey developed by Hallinger (1992), considerable empirical evidence has accumulated in support of the contribution that these leadership practices and functions make to student achievement and other types of outcomes (see Sheppard (1996) for a review of this evidence).

Transformational leadership

In addition to writing that refers explicitly to transformational leadership, included as part of this leadership category are writings about charismatic, visionary, cultural and empowering concepts of leadership. This form of leadership assumes that the central focus of leadership ought to be *the commitments and capacities of organizational members*. Higher levels of personal commitment to organizational goals and greater capacities for accomplishing those goals are assumed to result in extra effort and greater productivity. Authority and influence are not necessarily allocated to those occupying formal administrative positions, although much of the literature adopts their perspective. Rather, power is attributed by organization members to whomever is able to inspire their commitments to collective aspirations and the desire for personal and collective mastery of the capacities needed to accomplish such aspirations.

The literature offers varying interpretations of the concept of transformational leadership. Kowalski and Oates (1993), for instance, accepted Burns's (1978) original claim that transformational leadership represents the transcendence of self-interest by both leader and led. Dillard preferred Bennis's (1959) modified notion of 'transformative leadership – the ability of a person to "reach the souls of others in a fashion which raises human consciousness, builds meanings and inspires human intent that is the source of power" '(Dillard 1995: 560). Leithwood (1994) used another modification of Burns, this one based on Bass's (1985) two-factor theory, in which transactional and transformational leadership represent opposite ends of the leadership continuum. Bass maintained that the two actually can be complementary. Leithwood identified seven factors that make up transformational (and transactional) leadership. Hipp and Bredeson (1995), however, reduced the factors to five in their analysis of the relationship between leadership behaviours and teacher efficacy. Gronn (1996) noted the close relationship, in much current writing, between views of transformational and charismatic leadership, as well as the explicit omission of charisma from some current conceptions of transformational leadership.

The most fully developed model of transformational leadership in schools has been provided by Leithwood and his colleagues. This model conceptualizes such leadership along seven dimensions (described in more detail in subsequent chapters): building school vision; establishing school goals; providing intellectual stimulation; offering individualized support; modelling best practices and important organizational values; demonstrating high performance expectations; creating a productive school culture; and developing structures to foster participation in school decisions (Leithwood 1994).

A recent review of empirical research on transformational school leadership, described more extensively in Chapter 2, offers modest amounts of evidence for the contributions of such leadership to teacher-perceived student outcomes through its effects on a variety of teachers' psychological states that impact student learning (for example professional commitment, job satisfaction). There is also evidence that transformational leadership contributes to such organization-level effects as organizational learning and the development of a productive school climate (Leithwood 1996).

Moral leadership

As a category, moral leadership includes normative, political/democratic, and symbolic concepts of leadership. During the 1990s, the normative dimension of leadership has been one of the fastest growing areas of leadership study (Duke 1996). Those writing about moral leadership argue that values are a central part of all leadership and administrative practice (for example Evers and Lakomski 1991; Greenfield 1991; Bates 1993). Indeed, Hodgkinson, one of the best known proponents of this orientation to leadership, claims that 'values constitute the essential problem of leadership . . . If there are no value conflicts then there is no need for leadership' (1991: 11). Moral leadership assumes that the critical focus of leadership ought to be on *the values and ethics of leaders* themselves. So authority and influence are to be derived from defensible conceptions of what is right or good. Nevertheless, much of the writing about moral leadership, as in the case of transformational leadership, adopts the perspective of those in formal administrative roles.

The papers reviewed from the four journals illustrate quite different approaches to moral leadership. For example, Duignan and MacPherson (1993: 10), in discussing their concept of 'educative leadership', contended that leadership should be concerned with right and wrong, and not attitudes, styles or behaviours. Greenfield (1995) maintained that leadership entails five 'role demands' or 'situational imperatives', including the moral, instructional, political, managerial and social/interpersonal. Reitzug and Reeves (1992) argued that cultural leadership involves defining, strengthening, and articulating values, but warned that leaders may manipulate culture to further their own ends. Reitzug (1994) argued, further, that leadership is moral, but only under certain conditions. Lees argued that leadership in a democratic society entails a moral imperative to 'promote democracy, empowerment, and social justice' (1995: 225).

Among the issues of greatest concern to those exploring moral orientations to leadership are the nature of the values used by leaders in their decision making and how conflicts among values can be resolved. A brief synopsis of two distinctly different positions on these matters helps to illustrate the range of views evident in contemporary literature.

Perhaps the most widely known position has been developed by

Hodgkinson (1978, 1991). His 'analytic model of the value concept' includes three categories of values, distinguished from one another by their adequacy in justifying administrative choices. In general, the model recommends that leaders choose higher-level over lower-level values when confronted with value conflicts. Related to this general position, however, are refinements allowing for difficult cases to be addressed in authentic and morally responsible ways. The least adequate set of values are 'subrational', and encompass the leader's self-justifying preferences; manifestations of feeling and emotion. More defensible are a set of 'rational' values. Leaders using this set of values justify their choices based on either consensus among those affected, or an appeal to some future consequences of choice that are held to be desirable. The most defensible set of values on which to base decision making, according to this model, are 'transrational'. No particular set of values is associated with this category. Rather, Hodgkinson refers to such values as having a metaphysical grounding: they are principles that 'take the form of ethical codes, injunctions or commandments . . . their common feature is that they are unverifiable by the techniques of science and cannot be justified by merely logical argument' (1991: 99).

A quite different position on leaders' values and how value conflicts are to be resolved is political in its origin. In addition to a concern for specific sets of values, this perspective on moral leadership focuses on *the nature of the relationships among those within the organization, and the distribution of power between stakeholders both inside and outside the organization*. This perspective assumes that even though the formal organization may clearly specify power relationships, lines of communication and procedures for carrying out the organization's work, the informal organization may be quite different and may in fact provide a more authentic explanation for organizational activity. Forms of leadership referred to as 'democratic' or 'political' can equally well be placed in either moral or participative categories of leadership, since the central argument for participation is justified by democratic theory.

Ward's theoretical exploration of leadership applied to school administration illustrates this political or democratic perspective on moral leadership. It also clarifies public sources of legitimate leader values wider than those found only in the local community. As one member of an emerging 'new public administration', Ward argues that school administration 'is normative in orientation, embracing rather than ignoring the application of values in public policy, and hold[ing] an active role in policymaking' (1994: 8). Values central to this form of leadership are derived from democratic theory, and give credit to wide participation of organizational stakeholders as a reflection of the society in which we live. Public institutions such as schools cannot be governed or administered in ways that violate constitutionally enshrined rights and responsibilities, no matter how cumbersome

some might find those forms of governance and administration to be. This position appears to challenge the relative importance that Hodgkinson attributes to the rational value of consensus as compared with transrational values.

Participative leadership

The term 'participative leadership' was adopted from Yukl's (1994) description to encompass 'group', 'shared' and 'teacher' leadership. Participative leadership, examined in nine articles in the review, assumes that *the decision-making processes of the group* ought to be the central focus for leaders. One school of thought within this category of leadership argues for such participation on the grounds that it will enhance organizational effectiveness. A second school rests its case for participation on democratic principles such as those discussed in relation to moral leadership. Additional reasons for participation emerge in the context of site-based management approaches to participatory leadership. In the case of this form of leadership, authority and influence are available potentially to any legitimate stakeholder in the school based on their expert knowledge, their democratic right to choose and/or their critical role in implementing decisions.

Most of the articles included in our review associated participative leadership with enhanced organizational effectiveness. For example, evidence from Hayes's (1995) study in a single primary school demonstrated that the head's success in managing the government-driven change agenda depended on forging mutually beneficial relationships with all significant groups of internal and external stakeholders. Johnston and Pickersgill (1992) and Vandenberghe (1992) argued that the substantially increased demands placed on school leaders by changing contexts and expectations could best (or only) be met by moving towards forms of shared or team leadership. Citing such changes as increased complexity, uncertainty, ambiguity, workload and expectations for innovation, Murphy and Hallinger (1992) and Hallinger (1992) conclude that school leaders will need to adopt more participatory forms of leadership; forms of leadership that are more consultative, open and democratic, involving teachers and parents much more in school decision making.

Savery *et al.* (1992) illustrate approaches to participatory leadership driven largely by arguments for democratic processes. The framework for this study included seven categories of decision making (including school policy, student discipline) each of which incorporated from two to five more specific decision categories. Teachers were asked to indicate their preferences for five different types of participation in each decision category ranging from the principal making the decision to staff deciding for themselves. This study begins to illustrate what would be required to develop a fully specified model of participatory leadership in a school, viewed from a democratic perspective.

The centrepiece in a majority of the past decade's school restructuring initiatives, variously termed site-based management (SBM), local management of schools (LMS), or shared decision making (SDM), is arguably the most fully developed and widely advocated conception of participatory leadership available. Murphy and Beck (1995) suggest that SBM usually takes one of three forms: administration controlled SBM; professional controlled SBM; and community controlled SBM.

Administration controlled SBM is aimed at increasing accountability to the central district or board office for the efficient expenditure of resources, on the assumption that such efficiencies will eventually pay off for students. These efficiencies are to be realized by giving local school administrators greater authority and influence over such key decision areas as budget, personnel and curriculum. Advocates of this form of SBM reason that such authority, in combination with the incentive to make the best use of resources, ought to get more of the resources of the school into the direct service of students. To assist in accomplishing that objective, the principal may consult informally with teachers, parents, students or community representatives.

When professional controlled SBM is advocated, the goal is to make better use of the teachers' knowledge in such key decision areas as budget, curriculum and (occasionally) personnel. Basic to this form of SBM is the assumption that professionals closest to the student have the most relevant knowledge for making such decisions (Hess 1995), and that full participation in the decision-making process will increase their commitment to implementing whatever decisions are made. Participatory democracy, allowing employees greater decision-making power, is also presumed to lead to greater efficiency and effectiveness and better outcomes (Clune and White 1988; Mojkowski and Fleming 1988; David 1989).

Increased accountability to parents and the community at large, along with 'consumer satisfaction' are the central purposes for establishing community control forms of SBM (Malen *et al.* 1990; Wohlstetter 1990; Wohlstetter and McCurdy 1991; Bryk *et al.* 1993a; Wohlstetter and Mohrman 1993). The basic assumption giving rise to this form of SBM is that the curriculum of the school ought to directly reflect the values and preferences of parents and the local community (Wohlstetter and Odden 1992). School professionals, it is claimed, are typically not as responsive to such local values and preferences as they should be. Their responsiveness is greatly increased, however, when the authority to make decisions about curriculum, budget and personnel is in the hands of the parent and other community constituents of the school.

Managerial leadership

In addition to explicit concepts of management, this leadership category subsumes forms of leadership referred to in the literature as 'organizational' and 'transactional'. Managerial leadership assumes that the focus of leaders ought to be on *functions, tasks, or behaviours* and that if these functions are carried out competently the work of others in the organization will be facilitated. Most approaches to managerial leadership also assume that the behaviour of organizational members is largely rational. Authority and influence are allocated to formal positions in proportion to the status of those positions in the organizational hierarchy. The terms 'management' and 'manager' frequently appeared, especially in papers originating in the UK, but without explicit attempts to conceptualize their meanings.

Several studies published in the four journals characterized management as a form of leadership, to be replaced or supplemented in the face of present organizational challenges and the need for change (for example Hallinger 1992; Cusack 1993). Lesourd *et al.* (1992) contrasted 'managerial leadership' with 'visionary leadership', for example. Others assumed the utility of managerial tasks and inquired about how they had been intensified by recent changes (for example, Dunning 1993) or how they affected the quality of teachers' work lives (Rossmiller 1992). A number of other articles continued the long-standing debate (for example, Bennis and Nanus 1985) over the relationship between the concepts of leadership and management. Most of these articles (Whitaker *et al.* 1991; Achilles 1992; Bolman and Deal 1992; Atkinson and Wilmore 1993; Reilly 1993; Bolman and Deal 1994) treated leadership and management as distinct and, to some extent, competing concepts. But two articles (Reitzug and Reeves 1992; Leithwood 1994) regarded leadership and management as complementary concepts that should not be considered separately, a position supported by evidence from close analysis of the actual activities of formal school leaders (for example Kmetz and Willower 1982; Harvey 1986; Davies 1987). This evidence indicates that whatever influence these leaders exercise in their schools takes place through their responses to a host of often seemingly mundane tasks, which they face from day to day. As a minimum, school leaders need to adopt a 'bifocal' perspective (Deal and Peterson 1994) in carrying out their tasks.

To what does management refer, however, when it is treated as a unique form of school leadership in its own right? Those studies explicitly responding to this question illustrate a range of possibilities. For example, Rossmiller identified two broad functions: buffering the technical core (curriculum and instruction) of the school from excessive distractions and interruptions and smoothing 'input or output transitions [for example organizing support groups for students experiencing stress]' (1992: 143).

This study also described a number of sub-dimensions; specific ways in which principals carried out each of the two broad functions. In a second example with private-sector origins, managerial functions in the study by Myers and Murphy (1995) included six 'organizational control' mechanisms: supervision; input controls (for example teacher transfers); behaviour controls (for example job descriptions); output controls (student testing); selection/socialization; and environmental controls (community responsiveness). Goldring (1990) inquired about the 'boundary spanning' function of school principals. Caldwell argued that leaders of self-managing schools should engage in a cyclical process 'of goal-setting, needs identification, priority-setting, planning, budgeting, implementing, and evaluating in a manner which provides for the appropriate involvement of staff, and community' (1992: 16–17).

As Rost (1991) suggests, there is evidence of considerable support in the literature and among practicing leaders for managerial approaches to leadership, but this support and the meaning of such leadership often has to be inferred. As a whole, these functions convey an orientation to leadership similar to the orientation found in the classical management literature. This is quite different from the relatively entrepreneurial, creative and change-oriented view of leadership referred to as 'strategic management' in the non-school literature (for example Thomas and Pruett 1993). Those writing about educational leadership in the past decade appear to have incorporated such orientations in other, non-managerial models.

Contingent leadership

Included as part of this category are leadership 'styles' and leaders' 'problem-solving' processes (including 'reflective' and 'craft' views of leadership). This approach assumes that what is important is *how leaders respond to the unique organizational circumstances or problems that they face* as a consequence, for example, of the nature and preferences of co-workers, conditions of work and tasks to be undertaken. This approach to leadership assumes, as well, that there are wide variations in the contexts for leadership and that, to be effective, these contexts require different leadership responses. Also assumed by this approach to leadership is that individuals providing leadership, typically those in formal positions of authority, are capable of mastering a large repertoire of leadership practices. Their influence will depend, in large measure, on such mastery.

While sharing the same assumptions, the 'styles' and 'problem-solving' orientations to contingent leadership are otherwise quite distinct. Leadership styles have been the stimulus for extensive empirical investigation in both school and non-school organizations. Examples of earlier research include the Ohio State studies, which led to the widely used Leadership Behaviour Description Questionnaire, and subsequent work by investigators such as Blake and Mouton (1964) and Hersey and Blanchard (1977). Twelve studies included in this review made explicit reference to leadership style. Dimensions of leadership style investigated in these 12 studies varied considerably: task vs. relationships (Heller *et al.* 1993); managerial vs. visionary (Lesourd *et al.* 1992); initiating structure vs. consideration; autocratic vs. facilitative (Johnston 1986; Hoy and Brown 1988; Cheng 1991; Uwazurike 1991; Fenech 1994); male vs. female (Coleman 1996). Bredeson (1993) inquires about the relationship between an individual's leadership style and the role strains resulting from restructuring efforts in schools.

The literature on leadership styles focuses on overt leadership practice, attempting to define a relatively small number of coherent, effective patterns of such practice. In contrast, the literature on problem solving focuses on the internal cognitive and affective processes engaged in by leaders as they ponder the challenges facing them and decide how best to act. From this perspective, there is a virtually unlimited universe of leadership practices. Leaders choose or invent those patterns of practice that appear to make most sense to them in response to the challenges they are addressing. What leaders do depends on what they think.

Problem-solving orientations to leadership are of two types. Those describing leadership as a reflective or craft-like enterprise stress the importance of leaders' internal processes without attempting to explicitly model such processes. For example, Battersby (1987), Clark (1988) and Sergiovanni (1989) use Schön's (1983) concept of reflective practice, or knowing-in-action, to explore the limited utility to practising leaders of formal, scientific theory. Bredeson (1988) advocates the use of metaphors as stimulants for administrators' thinking and problem solving, whereas Willower (1994) invokes Dewey's method of inquiry as a frame to use in developing habits of reflection on the part of school leaders.

Also focused on leaders' thinking were articles explicitly framed by contemporary cognitive science models of such processes. Three of these studies appeared in a special issue of *EAQ* entitled: 'Cognitive perspectives on educational administration' (see also Hallinger *et al.* 1993). Leithwood and Hallinger (1993) and Leithwood (1995) argue for the usefulness of cognitive perspectives on leadership and outline what inquiry guided by such an orientation would entail. Allison and Allison (1993) invoke schema theory in their comparison of the domain-specific knowledge structures of novice and experienced school principals. Elsewhere, Allison (1996) reviews the literature on cognitive processes associated with problem interpretation and its application to the thinking of school leaders. Leithwood *et al.* (1993d) describe the problem-solving processes of superintendents within a framework that attends to those cognitive processes entailed in problem interpretation, goal setting, anticipating constraints, the use of personal values and principles (see also Moorhead and Nediger 1991), solution processes and mood or affect. Based on this framework, Leithwood and Steinbach (1995) offer the most comprehensive set of research results to date, exploring the nature of expert school leaders' problem-solving processes and their consequences for leadership practice.

Conclusion

Although the six leadership categories or models described in this chapter were presented as distinctly different approaches to leadership, they are by no means pure types. Table 1.1 summarizes similarities and differences among the models. It does so in relation to the four dimensions discussed earlier as key to a conception of leadership as the exercise of influence: who exerts influence, and what is the nature, purpose and outcome of that influence.

Contemporary leadership models vary in who is assumed to exercise influence, from only those in formal administrative roles (managerial and moral leadership), through typically, but not necessarily, those in formal leadership roles (instructional, transformational and contingent leadership), to the group, potentially including all those with a stake in the organization (participative leadership).

Each of the six models has as its premise a different, primary form or source of leadership influence, although secondary use of many sources of influence are likely in all models. Typically positional power and (invariably) expert knowledge about teaching and learning processes, are the sources of influence for instructional leadership. For transformational leadership, influence is exercised through motivational processes that elevate organizational members' aspirations for their work and inspire higher levels of commitment to the organization and its purposes. Influence is exercised by moral leadership through systems of moral values to which organizational members are encouraged to adhere. Participative leadership assumes mutual influence to flow from structured opportunities for members to interact together around issues important to the organization. Positional power, in combination with formal policies and procedures, is the source of influence exercised by managerial leadership. For those exercising contingent leadership, the primary sources of influence arise through matching leaders' behaviour closely to the needs of members, and through relatively expert problem-solving and decision-making processes.

The immediate, instrumental or short-term purpose for exercising influence (what was referred to earlier as the *focus* of leadership) is at least partly different for each model. In the case of instructional leadership, the

Table 1.1 The role of influence in alternative leadership models

Approaches to school leadership	Who exerts influence	Sources of influence	Purposes for influence	Outcomes of influence
Instructional	• Typically those in formal leadership roles, especially principals	• Expert knowledge • Typically positional power	• Enhance the effectiveness of teachers' classroom practices	• Increased student growth
Transformational	• Typically those in formal leadership roles, but not restricted to such persons	• Inspire higher levels of commitment and capacity among organization members	• Greater effort and productivity • Develop more skilled practice	• Increased capacity of organization to continuously improve
Moral	• Those in formal administrative roles	• Use of a system of moral values to guide organization decision making	• Increase sensitivity to the rightness of decisions • Increase participation in decisions	• Morally justified courses of action • Democratic schools
Participative	• The group (including non-administrative organization members)	• Interpersonal communication	• Increase participation in decisions	• Increased capacity of organization to respond productively to internal and external demands for change • More democratic organization

Table 1.1 continued

Approaches to school leadership	Who exerts influence	Sources of influence	Purposes for influence	Outcomes of influence
Managerial	• Those in formal administrative roles	• Positional power • Policies and procedures	• Ensure efficient completion of specified tasks by organization members	• Achieve formal goals of the organization
Contingent	• Typically those in formal leadership roles	• Matching leader behaviour to organization context • Expert problem-solving processes	• Better meet needs of organization members • More effective responses to organization's challenges	• Achieve formal goals of the organization • Increased capacity of organization to respond productively to internal and external demands for change

immediate purpose is to enhance the effectiveness of teachers' classroom practices. Transformational leadership aspires, more generally, to increase members' efforts on behalf of the organization, as well as to develop more skilled practice. Increasing sensitivity to the rightness of decisions and increased decisional participation among stakeholders are the immediate goals for moral leadership. Managerial leadership, on the other hand, tries to ensure efficient completion of clearly specified tasks by employees, whereas contingent leadership attempts to better support employees in their decision making and develop more effective responses to the organization's challenges.

The long-term purposes or intended outcomes of the six leadership models vary in breadth and in their acknowledgement of future challenges for change likely to be encountered by the organization. With respect to breadth, five of the models explicitly acknowledge the need to accomplish the official goals of the organization; some version of 'productivity'. Instructional leadership offers the narrowest and most static interpretation of productivity – student achievement, usually defined in relatively traditional terms. Managerial and contingent models of leadership interpret productivity more broadly to encompass achieving the official goals of the organization. Transformational, participative and contingent models assume the need for organizational goals to change and so view increased capacity for change as one of their central outcomes. Additionally, moral and participative leadership models aim for more democratic organizations, an outcome to be valued in its own right. Moral leadership advocates, in addition, morally justified courses of action toward goals that should be justifiable on moral grounds.

These six overlapping approaches to school leadership are among the most obvious starting points for addressing the leadership needs of schools as they respond to the challenges of today and tomorrow.

two

TRANSFORMATIONAL LEADERSHIP AS A PLACE TO BEGIN

Great leaders are bred from great causes, but leaders, at their best, also breed great causes. Sadly, for want of a cause, we too often create a crisis, which is not the same thing at all.

(Handy 1996: 9)

Chapter 1 outlined the 'menu' of approaches to leadership found in a sample of contemporary educational administration and leadership literature. This menu consisted of some 20 leadership concepts further classified into six models of school leadership: instructional, transformational, moral, participative, managerial and contingent. None of the selections on this menu, however, completely serves the purpose of this book, which is to offer a comprehensive approach to leadership that will help those in, and served by, current and future schools respond productively to the significant challenges facing them.

'Transformational leadership' comes closest to providing such an approach and will serve as a point of departure for developing what, in current social science jargon, might be termed a 'post-transformational' approach to leadership. A rationale for building on transformational approaches to leadership is offered in the next section of the chapter. This rationale will be relatively brief, because the reasons for this choice become more evident as the nature of transformational and 'post-transformational' leadership is unpacked in subsequent chapters.

The remaining sections of this chapter clarify the meaning of transformational leadership as it is reflected largely in the non-school literature, and summarize results of research on the dimensions and effects of such leadership in schools, specifically.

Why transformational leadership?

To serve the purposes established for it in this book, an approach to leadership must both be comprehensive and 'fit' the school context in which it is to be exercised. Let us consider what this means.

Comprehensiveness of perspective

One aspect of comprehensiveness, in reference to leadership, is reflected in Bolman and Deal's (1991) frames, or lenses, through which those exercising leadership interpret the challenges they face. They argue that many leaders customarily employ only one or two such frames in their problem solving. As a consequence, these leaders often fail to see and to address aspects of their problems that remain troublesome for their organizations. For example, Bolman and Deal (1991) report that principals typically do not employ political and symbolic frames in the interpretation of their problems. Structural and human resource frames alone shape their sense of what needs to be done in their schools. A comprehensive approach to leadership, given this argument, is one that explicitly draws leaders' attention to multiple dimensions of the school organization. This is an interpretation of comprehensiveness as *breadth of perspective*. The breadth of the approach to leadership outlined in this book will be evident in the dimensions of practice, described later in this chapter, typically used to define transformational leadership, and the additions and revisions to those dimensions introduced in Chapters 3–6.

A second aspect of comprehensiveness, in reference to leadership approaches, is *depth* or extent of development. This is what Argyris (1982) focuses attention on with his criteria for a 'comprehensive theory of management'. Such a theory, he claims, should be rigorously defined, include testable propositions about effective actions consistent with the theory, and produce consequences or outcomes that matter. This aspect of comprehensiveness is addressed throughout the remainder of the book.

Fit with context

As Leithwood and Duke (in press) have documented, each of the approaches to leadership outlined in Chapter 1 has a history. Each developed in a context of organizational and broader social goals, needs, norms, ideas, and expectations, which allowed one or several approaches to leadership to dominate, as an ideal, until such time as that context changed sufficiently as to more clearly favour yet another approach or approaches. Once each of these leadership approaches became widely recognized, they retained a following, long after losing their dominance. All six approaches to leadership (instructional, transformational, moral, participative, managerial, contingent) are reflected in current literature and practice.

By way of illustrating the influence of context on what are considered to be ideal forms of leadership, early forms of managerial leadership emerged in schools as part of the scientific management movement in the first two decades of this century. This movement aimed at bringing greater efficiency and accountability to growing urban school districts in the USA. By the 1930s, efficiency and accountability concerns had been overtaken by concerns about fairness in the workplace and the problem of developing democratic values in organizations that did not themselves behave according to democratic principles. Reinforced by newly emerging evidence from social psychology about the positive effects of employee participation in decision making, this new set of needs, norms, ideas and expectations gave rise to participatory forms of leadership as an ideal. All this happened very gradually.

Some specific leadership practices are helpful in almost all organizational contexts. It is almost always helpful to consider the views of other organizational members when making decisions, for example. But history has taught us, as the examples above begin to illustrate, that the meaningfulness of each approach to leadership is also significantly context dependent. Truly productive leadership depends not only on engaging in commonly helpful practices, it also depends on recognizing and responding to the unique challenges and features presented by particular types of organizational contexts (and each school also has its own unique challenges).

School restructuring undoubtedly frames the context for school leadership in the 1990s (Murphy 1991). Across virtually all parts of the developed world schools are being challenged, in the name of restructuring, to, for example, change their governance structures, open themselves to greater community influence, become more accountable, clarify their standards for content and performance and introduce related changes in their approaches to teaching and learning. Widespread school restructuring has arisen from a combination of such trends as economic retrenchment, neo-conservative ideologies and globalization of the market place.

As a way to illustrate the fit of transformational approaches to leadership with this restructuring context, four central features of that context are examined. In each case the relative suitability of transformational and instructional approaches to leadership are compared. Instructional approaches were selected for this comparison because of their dominance as an ideal form of school leadership over the past 15 years, at least in North

American school systems and literature (Beck and Murphy 1993). Instructional approaches to leadership are also quite similar to what is typically referred to as 'strong leadership' in the current European school effectiveness literature.

The means and ends for school restructuring are uncertain

Initial portraits of instructional leadership were, if not exclusively, then certainly heavily classroom-focused; they featured practices intended to directly influence classroom curriculum and instruction (Beck and Murphy 1993). Such classroom focus, as far as it went, was a reasonable response to both the dominant educational reform agenda of the time (one closely aligned with the effective schools movement) and the improbability of prevailing school administrator practices to push that agenda forward. Equity, the central goal for reform, was largely pursued in inner-city, urban elementary schools. Indicators of success in achieving the goal were defined in terms of advances in the basic maths and language skills achieved by socially disadvantaged children (for example Brookover *et al.* 1978). Direct forms of instruction, additionally legitimated by the then current 'process-product' research on teacher effectiveness, seemed uncontestably powerful in developing such skills. So it made sense for school administrators to advocate such instruction (not a hard sell to many teachers) and to supervise teachers closely to ensure its consistent implementation.

School restructuring is fundamentally different from the change agenda of the late 1970s and early 1980s. Much of that earlier change agenda was driven by the effective schools movement. Where this was not the case, implementing new texts or curricula one at a time was often the goal. The important implications for leadership, in relation to both sources of change, are found in the clarity (or illusion of clarity) that advocates had about the changes they wished to make. As Rowan (1990) argues, when the purposes for change are known and agreed upon and the practices required to accomplish those purposes can be clearly specified, one is likely to be successful using control-oriented strategies for change. And the original image of instructional leadership was, above all, aimed at control, as are the images of 'strong leadership' found in contemporary effective schools research.

In contrast, however, there is nothing clear about the purposes for school restructuring – higher order thinking or creating schools that are more responsive to the demands of the 21st century, for example. Nor are the initiatives required to accomplish these purposes, such as site-based management, teacher empowerment and teaching for understanding (Cohen *et al.* 1993), at all clear. Under these circumstances, 'commitment' rather than 'control' strategies are called for. These are strategies that help front-line school staffs to appreciate the reasons for change and that foster their commitment to developing, trying out and refining new practices until those purposes are accomplished (or until they change). Virtually all treatments of transformational leadership claim that among its more direct effects are employee motivation and commitment, leading to the kind of extra effort required for significant change (Yukl 1989).

School restructuring requires both first- and second-order changes

Instructional leadership (by definition) focuses attention on what school-improvement researchers refer to as 'first-order' changes; changes in core technology. These changes are necessary elements of any reform strategy likely to have pay-off for students. Within the school restructuring agenda, constructivist models of learning (Leinhardt 1991) and forms of instruction designed to teach for understanding are examples of first-order changes. But there is now an impressive accumulation of evidence demonstrating that an almost exclusive focus on first-order changes is an important part of the explanation for the failure of most change initiatives – especially failure to institutionalize such changes after their implementation (for example Fuhrman 1993; Fullan 1993).

Attention to second-order change is essential to the survival of first-order change. Otherwise, the resulting incoherence becomes unbearable and, like white blood cells, unchanged 'standard operating procedures' surround and kill off promising first-order changes. School restructuring is certainly about second-order change. That is what devolved decision making or site-based management is, for example. If anything, some manifestations of the school restructuring movement might be accused of forgetting about first-order changes. Second-order changes require a form of leadership that is sensitive to organization building: developing shared vision; creating productive work cultures; distributing leadership to others; and the like. While images of instructional leadership do not obviously press for attention to such matters, transformational forms of leadership are especially attuned to the influence of, for example, organizational structure and culture on the meaning people associate with their work and their willingness to risk change (for example Hunt 1991).

School restructuring is increasingly focused on secondary schools

Compared with 15 years ago, the focus of much more of the reform effort has shifted from elementary to secondary schools. Especially the case in North America, this is of consequence for images of school leadership because of the size and complexity of secondary schools and because of the nature of secondary school administrators' practices. The size of secondary schools challenges the feasibility of principals exercising the sort of direct influence on classroom practice envisaged in early views of instructional leadership. There are just too many teachers and classrooms for the time available. Additionally, the complexity of the secondary school curriculum and the amount of pedagogical content knowledge required for expert teaching and its development defies the sort of comprehensive appreciation that would be required for direct teacher supervision, even if it were feasible to find the time.

Instructional leadership images were not, at the outset, developed with secondary schools in mind, and there has been a surprising lack of research devoted to understanding effective leadership practices in secondary schools. So it is time the unique challenges of secondary school leadership were addressed more seriously. Transformational forms of leadership, emphasizing the empowerment of their colleagues, encourages secondary administrators to focus their energies on the capacities and motives of those in a position to offer 'direct' (Hunt 1991) leadership within their organizations, as distinct from front-line staff.

The professionalization of teaching is a centrepiece of the school restructuring agenda

This is not uniformly the case, as Bullock and Thomas (1997) point out. For example, recent changes appear to deprofessionalize the teacher by enhancing the role of non-professional groups in England, Wales and New Zealand. In the USA and parts of Canada, however, teacher professionalization is a reform goal. Such professionalization seems warranted for many reasons, among them: widespread failure of traditional forms of managerial leadership or administrative supervision to contribute to teacher development (for example Darling-Hammond and Sclan 1992); the promising effects reported for recent teacher leadership initiatives (for example Smylie and Brownlee-Conyers 1992); and the incentive to join the teaching ranks which such professionalization offers to highly talented prospective candidates (Ogawa 1993). Instructional leadership demands an active role in classroom practice based on high levels of pedagogical expertise. Because such leadership is exactly what the professionalization of teaching aims to turn over to teachers, other leadership contributions are required of leaders in non-teaching roles. Such contributions seem evident in forms of transformational leadership.

It is not surprising, given these four premises about restructuring, that it has become increasingly difficult to justify instructional leadership images for those in formal leadership roles – principals and superintendents, in particular. Indeed that image is now displaying all the signs of a dying paradigm.

Rather than being awkward afterthoughts, however, appendages glued on to the more recent images of instructional leadership (for example Kleine-Kracht 1993) are among the central dimensions of transformational leadership theory (Podsakoff *et al.* 1990). Such theory is, as a consequence, potentially more powerful and more elegant as a description of effective leadership in the context of school restructuring. Furthermore, the different but nevertheless relatively narrow foci of most other competing images of school leadership are also to be found among the dimensions of transformational leadership.

The meaning of transformational leadership

> Out of the varying motives of persons, out of the combat and competition between groups and between persons, out of the making of countless choices and the sharpening and steeling of purpose, arise the elevating forces of leadership and the achievement of intended change.
>
> (Burns 1978: 432)

The term transformational leadership has appeared with increasing frequency in writings about education since the late 1980s. Sometimes it has been used to signify an appropriate type of leadership for schools taking up the challenges of restructuring, which is now well underway in most developed countries throughout the world (Leithwood 1992). In this context, a common-sense, non-technical meaning of the term is often assumed. For example, the dictionary definition of 'to transform' is 'to change completely or essentially in composition or structure' (*Webster's Seventh New Collegiate Dictionary* 1971). So any leadership with this effect may be labelled transformational, no matter what specific practices it entails or even whether the changes wrought are desirable.

This chapter is not concerned with transformational leadership defined in this loose, common-sense fashion. It is concerned, rather, with a form of leadership by the same name that has been the subject of formal definition and systematic inquiry in non-school organizations for at least several decades. The small but rapidly growing body of evidence, which has emerged quite recently, inquiring about such leadership in elementary and secondary school settings is reviewed in this chapter. Much of this research takes the non-school literature on transformational leadership as a point of departure, both conceptually and methodologically. So it is important, at the outset, to appreciate the general nature of that literature.

Downton's (1973) study of rebel leadership is often cited as the beginning of systematic inquiry about transformational leadership in non-school organizations. However, charisma, often considered an integral part of transformational leadership, has substantially more distant origins – typically attributed to Max Weber's efforts almost five decades ago (for example Weber 1947).

James McGregor Burns's (1978) prize-winning book first drew

widespread attention to ideas explicitly associated with transformational leadership. Based on a sweeping historical analysis, Burns argued that most understandings of leadership not only overemphasized the role of power but held a faulty view of it as well. There were, he claimed, two essential aspects of power – motives or purposes and resources – each possessed not only by those exercising leadership but also by those experiencing it. The essence of leadership is to be found in the relationships between motives, resources, leaders, and followers: 'the most powerful influences consist of deeply human relationships in which two or more persons *engage* with one another' (Burns 1978: 11). Burns's distinction between transactional and transformational types of leadership hinges on this appreciation of power-as-relationships.

In contrast to transformational leadership, transactional leadership occurs when one person takes initiative in making contact with others for the purpose of exchanging valued things (economic, political or psychological 'things', for example). Each person in the exchange understands that they bring related motives to the bargaining process and that these motives can be advanced by maintaining that process. But because of the nature of the motives at issue, those involved are not bound together in any continuing, mutual pursuit of higher purposes. With this form of leadership, motives or purposes may well be met using the existing resources of those involved in the exchange. Neither purposes nor resources are changed, however.

Transformational leadership entails not only a change in the purposes and resources of those involved in the leader–follower relationship, but an elevation of both – a change 'for the better'. With respect to motives or purposes, 'transforming leadership ultimately becomes *moral* in that it raises the level of human conduct and ethical aspiration of both leader and led, and thus has a transforming effect on both' (Burns 1978: 20). This form of leadership, according to Burns's view, also aims to enhance the resources of both leader and led by raising their levels of commitment to mutual purposes and by further developing their capacities for achieving those purposes.

Burns's seminal work provided a solid conceptional footing on which to build the distinction between transactional and transformational types of leadership; it also illustrated the meaning of these forms of leadership in many different contexts. Not to be found in this work, however, was a testable model of leadership practices or any empirical evidence of their effects. The prodigious efforts of Bass and his associates have been largely in response to these limitations. Bass's (1985) book, *Leadership and performance beyond expectations*, provided an impressive compendium of survey research evidence about the effects of one model of transformational leadership. Among the most important features of this model are the dimensions of leadership practice it includes and the proposed relationships among these dimensions.

Bass and his colleagues define transformational leadership as including charisma or idealized influence, inspirational motivation, intellectual stimulation and individualized consideration, referred to in more recent publications as the four 'i's (for example Bass and Avolio 1993, 1994). In addition to these dimensions of transformational leadership, three dimensions define the meaning of transactional leadership: contingent reward; management-by-exception; and a *laissez-faire* or 'hands off' form of leadership.

Whereas Burns considered transformational and transactional practices as opposite ends of the leadership continuum (essentially more and less effective forms of leadership), Bass offers a quite different conception, a 'two-factor theory' of leadership; transactional and transformational forms of leadership, in his view, build on one another (for example Howell and Avolio 1991; Bass and Avolio 1993). Transactional practices foster ongoing work by attending to the basic needs of organizational members. Such practices do little to bring about changes in the organization, however. For this to occur, members must also experience transformational practices. Enhanced commitment and the extra effort usually required for change, it is claimed, are consequences of this experience.

Transactional practices were the traditional focus of attention for leadership theorists until the early 1980s. Disillusionment with the outcomes of that focus, however, gave rise to a number of alternative approaches, among them transformational leadership. These approaches have been referred to collectively by Bryman (1992), Sims and Lorenzi (1992) and others, as the 'new leadership paradigm'. Empirical studies of transformational leadership, reflecting this pessimism with transactional practices, often give them minimum attention. This is the case with Podsakoff *et al.* (1990) for example. While Podsakoff and his associates adopted a quite limited conception of transactional leadership for their research, they offered arguably the most comprehensive set of transformational leadership dimensions available at that point, dimensions based on a synthesis of seven prior perspectives on transformational leadership. These dimensions, used to organize parts of the subsequent review in this chapter, include: identifying and articulating a vision; fostering the acceptance of group goals; providing an appropriate model; high performance expectations; providing individual support; providing intellectual stimulation; contingent reward; and management-by-exception.

Remaining sections of this chapter and central sections of the next four chapters rely on a synthesis of research evidence about facets of transformational leadership specifically in schools. This synthesis of evidence was provided by an exhaustive sample of 34 published and unpublished (primarily theses), English language, empirical and formal case studies conducted in elementary and secondary school organizations up to about 1995. A more exhaustive and more technical analysis of them can be found in

Leithwood *et al.* (1996b). Of these 34 studies, most were concerned with the leadership of school principals (22 studies), but described transformational leadership offered by those in a number of other educational leadership roles, as well. These other roles included superintendents and other central-office staff (5), some combination of school and district roles (4) and multiple roles across schools and districts (2). One study examined multiple roles, not only in schools but in other organizations too.

Dimensions of transformational leadership in schools

Of the 34 studies, 21 provided evidence about specific dimensions of transformational leadership relevant to school contexts; these included six qualitative and 15 quantitative studies. For each of these studies, the leadership dimensions explicitly referred to by the author(s) were identified and the effects reported. A total of 12 dimensions of transformational leadership were enquired about in the 21 studies. All but two of these dimensions can be found in the research literature on transformational leadership in non-school settings.

Culture building and *structuring* are unique to school-based research. Although these dimensions are found primarily in a series of studies carried out by us (Leithwood and Jantzi 1990; Leithwood and Steinbach 1991; Silins 1994b), their relevance to leadership in schools is also reflected in the work of others. *Culture building* is prominent in studies by Kendrick (1988), Helm (1989), Darling (1990), Sashkin and Sashkin (1990), Skalbeck (1991), and Vandenburghe and Staessens (1991). *Structuring*, including the involvement of staff in decision making, for example, is identified as an important leadership practice by Helm (1989) and Roberts (1985).

These 21 studies were also useful in assessing the extent to which each leadership dimension originating in non-school settings has been found to be relevant to school settings. Using information from these studies, judgements of relevance depended on: the total number of studies providing data about the dimension (although there is no non-arbitrary way of establishing a minimum number, more studies add certainty to the judgement); the average number of significant positive relationships reported across studies between a leadership dimension and an outcome or dependent measure (many studies include multiple dependent measures); and the number of non-significant and significant negative relationships reported.

Clearly relevant to schools, given the evidence from these studies, are leadership dimensions that have been the object of a relatively large number of studies, and in which an overwhelming proportion of significant positive relationships have been reported. Meeting this standard are: *transformational leadership as a composite; charisma/inspiration/vision; intellectual stimulation;* and *individual consideration*.

Management-by-exception, the object of many studies reporting a high proportion of significant negative relationships, is the only leadership dimension clearly not relevant to schools.

Of the remaining dimensions, *contingent reward* and *transactional leadership as a composite* have been relatively well studied but results are conflicting, possibly suggesting that their effects vary more across different contexts than do the effects of other dimensions.

Structuring and *culture building* have been too little studied for a judgement of relevance to be made; the sparse results are promising, however. *High performance expectations* and *modelling* show signs of behaving like *contingent reward*, but the amount of evidence is sparse. And finally, *goal consensus* shows signs of being clearly relevant to schools, but more evidence is still needed to make that judgement with reasonable certainty.

Transformational leadership effects in schools

Evidence about the effects of these dimensions of transformational school leadership was provided by 20 of the 34 studies included in the Leithwood *et al.* (1996b) review. The 13 different types of effects that have been studied are listed in Table 2.1. These are grouped into effects on students, effects on perceptions of leaders, effects on the behaviour of followers, effects on followers' psychological states and organizational-level effects. Table 2.1 describes the number of studies in which evidence is reported about each effect. This table also describes the number of positive relationships found between each outcome and the total set of transformational dimensions included in the studies. Also reported in Table 2.1 is the total number of relationships reported to be negative or not significant (in the case of the 15 quantitative studies, 'significant' means statistically significant). The remainder of this section examines evidence related to each effect, in turn: how the effect was defined and measured; the weight of the evidence in support of the effect; and those leadership dimensions that demonstrably contributed to the effect.

Effects on students

The effects on students of transformational school leadership are likely to be mediated by teachers and others. This may account for why there is only a modest amount of formal evidence concerning such effects. The complexity of analyses required to determine the indirect effects of transformational leadership on students may also account for the limited evidence. In spite of the compelling theoretical and other reasons for advocating transformational leadership in schools at the present time and in the not too distant future, there is still considerable work to be done in clarifying empirically

Table 2.1 Effects of transformational leadership (total number of studies = 20)

Types of effects or outcomes measured	Number of studies (N = 20)	Total positive*	Total NS or negative*
Effects on students			
1 Teachers' perceptions of student effects	6	5	1
2 Student participation and identification	3	0	2
Effects on perceptions of leaders			
3 Perceptions of leader effectiveness	3	15	4
4 Satisfaction with leader(s) and style	5	16	5
Effects on behaviour of followers			
5 Extra effort	2	5	2
6 Organizational citizenship behaviour	1	1	3
Effects on followers' psychological states			
7 Commitment	5	12	10
8 Developmental press	3	12	6
9 Control press	1	5	3
10 Morale/job satisfaction	1	1	0
Organization-level effects			
11 Organizational learning	1	5	1
12 Organizational improvement/effectiveness	7	35	16
13 Organizational climate and culture	7	14	1

* Many studies reported associations between an outcome and multiple dimensions of transformational leadership.

the effects of this form of leadership on students. Nevertheless, the demands on schools cannot await the outcome of such research. It is also important to point out that the evidence of direct effects on students of alternative leadership models, including those commonly used in schools at present, is also quite meagre. For example, Hallinger and Heck (1996) have reported evidence concerning instructional leadership effects in some detail, and offer reasons why this research probably underestimates instructional leadership effects on students.

Our own studies offer the only evidence that is available about student effects. Six of our studies inquired about the relationship between transformational school leadership and an outcome they termed 'teacher-perceived student outcomes' (Leithwood *et al.* 1991a, 1993a, 1993b; Silins 1992, 1994a; Silins and Leithwood 1994). This outcome was measured through items on a survey that asked teachers to estimate the effects on students of various innovative practices being implemented in their classrooms. These practices were usually the product of school-wide initiatives, which were often promoted (or at least supported) by those in formal school-leader roles. While teacher perceptions offer indirect evidence of student effects, there is substantial evidence of high correlations between such evidence and direct measures of student achievement such as those provided by standardized tests (Egan and Archer 1985). Based on similar data-analysis techniques, five of our six studies reported significant indirect effects of transformational school leadership on teacher-perceived student outcomes.

We have also completed three studies inquiring about the effects of transformational school leadership on an outcome we called 'student participation in, and identification with, school' (Leithwood *et al.* 1993a, 1993c, 1997a). This outcome is derived from Finn's theory of factors explaining variation in student retention rates (Finn 1989; Finn and Cox 1992). Responses to the instrument developed for this research were provided by three samples of elementary and secondary school students ($N = 3700, 3557$ and 2045). These studies found weak direct and significant indirect effects of transformational school leadership on student participation in and identification with school.

Effects on perceptions of leaders

Three studies, two carried out in the USA and one in New Zealand, examined transformational leadership effects on perceptions of leader effectiveness and satisfaction with the leader (Bass 1985; King 1989; Kirby *et al.* 1992). Data from leaders at both school and district levels were collected in these studies, all of which used a version of Bass's (1988) Multifactor Leadership Questionnaire (MLQ). In addition to measuring aspects of transformational leadership, the MLQ includes a two-item scale measuring respondents' satisfaction with their leader and a four-item scale measuring perceptions of the leader's effectiveness.

These studies report largely consistent results in relation to both sets of effects. Positive relationships are reported between transformational and transactional dimensions as a whole. Among the specific leadership dimensions, these effects were most strongly related to *charisma/vision/inspiration, intellectual stimulation, individual consideration* and *contingent reward*. Non-significant relationships were reported in respect to *management-by-exception*. *Laissez-faire* leadership was negatively related to both perceptions of leader effectiveness and satisfaction with the leader.

Two additional studies (Koh 1990; Orr 1990) reported significant positive relationships among transformational leadership as a composite, transactional leadership as a composite, and satisfaction with the leader. Although Koh (1990) included Bass's MLQ among the instruments in his study of Singapore principals, he used a subscale of the Index of Organizational Reactions (Smith 1976) to measure satisfaction with leaders. Orr (1990) developed two new instruments for his study of US superintendents.

Included in the instrument used to collect data from those working with superintendents was a two-item scale asking for a rating of the superintendent's performance.

Effect on behaviours of followers

Three studies (Bass 1985; Koh 1990; Orr 1990) inquired about the effects of transformational leadership on two types of colleague (follower) behaviours: the extent to which colleagues are prepared to engage in extra effort on behalf of their organization; and 'organizational citizenship behaviour'. Two of these studies were about superintendents (Orr's US study) or other central administrators (Bass's New Zealand study); Koh (1990) studied Singapore principals.

Bass (1985) assessed 'extra effort' using responses of followers to a three-item scale included in the MLQ. These same three items were used by Orr (1990) to collect data from both superintendents and their immediate subordinates. Both studies report significant positive relationships between transformational leadership and colleagues' extra effort. In the Bass study, extra effort mostly was accounted for by *charisma/inspiration/vision, intellectual stimulation* and *individual consideration*. *Contingent reward* and *management-by-exception* had non-significant and negative correlations, respectively, with extra effort. Orr (1990) reported positive correlations between extra effort and transformational and transactional leadership considered as composites.

Organizational citizenship behaviour, one of the outcome variables in Koh's (1990) study, was measured using an adapted version of a questionnaire originally developed by Smith *et al.* (1983); 16 items formed three subscales measuring altruism, compliance and non-compliance with leaders' suggestions. Transformational leadership as a composite was significantly but negatively related to non-compliance. This means, as Koh explains, that, 'The more the principals were perceived as transformational, the lower will be the teacher's tendency to take undeserved breaks, make unnecessary phone calls, and so forth' (1990: 113). Positively related to non-compliance were active and passive *management-by-exception*. No significant correlations were evident with *contingent reward*.

Effect on followers' psychological states

There is evidence from five studies (four quantitative) that transformational leadership influences four psychological states of those who experience such leadership, those states being: commitment; developmental press (changes in teachers' attitudes and/or behaviour); control press (the tendency for teachers to feel that they must adhere to central demands for orderliness and structure); and satisfaction. Several forms of commitment served as outcome variables in these studies, including teacher commitment to change (Leithwood *et al.* 1993c, 1994), and organizational commitment (Koh 1990; Skalbeck 1991). Considered to be part of this category of studies as well is Smith's (1989) study of teacher work motivation.

Evidence reported in our own two studies was collected from 534 intermediate and secondary teachers in a large sample of schools in one Canadian province and from 168 teachers in nine secondary schools in a second province. Both of these studies tested a model in which transformational leadership, as well as sets of other in-school and out-of-school conditions were treated as independent variables. A multi-scale, multi-item survey of transformational school leadership, developed and refined in our earlier work, was used to collect evidence about six dimensions of transformational leadership. Dependent variables, measured with items in the same survey, were four categories of psychological processes that were identified in the social-psychological literature as giving rise to teachers' commitment to change. Transformational leadership, as a composite, had significant direct and indirect effects on teachers' commitment to change. These effects were accounted for most strongly by *vision building, high performance expectations, developing consensus about group goals* and *intellectual stimulation.*

Koh (1990) measured organizational commitment with the widely used, 15 item Organizational Commitment Questionnaire (OCQ) developed by Mowday *et al.* (1979). This instrument describes respondents' loyalty and attachment to an organization, their agreement with its purposes and values and their willingness to expend extra effort. Koh found that transactional leadership explained much more of the variation in organizational commitment than did transformational leadership.

Skalbeck's (1991) qualitative study enquired about the transformational practices of one elementary school principal and the extent to which these practices influenced teachers' commitment to the school's mission and vision. Leadership practices accounting for such commitment can be classified as *individual support, culture building* and *contingent reward.*

Using Bass's MLQ as a measure of 100 superintendents' transformational leadership, Smith (1989) also collected evidence about the work motivation of about 100 principals associated with these superintendents. The questionnaire measuring such motivation was based on the work of Herzberg (1959) and others. *Intellectual stimulation* was the dimension of transformational leadership best predicting principals' work motivation.

One quantitative (Leithwood *et al.* 1991b) and two qualitative (Leithwood and Jantzi 1990; Skalbeck 1991) studies reported effects of transformational leadership on the 'developmental press' created among those experiencing such leadership. Leithwood *et al.* (1991b) measured transformational leadership using a version of the instrument described above; developmental press was defined as changes in teachers' attitudes, and school or classroom behaviour. Data about both sets of variables were provided by 291 elementary school teachers and 43 principals in two Canadian provinces. Dimensions of transformational leadership significantly related to developmental press included *vision building, developing consensus about group goals, individual consideration* and *intellectual stimulation*. A dimension termed 'leadership pressure' had non-significant relationships with developmental press.

Skalbeck's (1991) study of a single principal suggested that the stimulus for growth among teachers (developmental press) was a function of the principal's *vision-building* initiatives and the *collegial culture* she was able to build among teaching staff. Interviews with 133 teachers from nine elementary and three secondary schools provided the data for a study by Leithwood and Jantzi (1990). *Vision building, culture building, developing consensus about group goals, intellectual stimulation* and *individual consideration* made substantial contributions to teachers' change initiatives in these schools; neither *modelling* nor *contingent reward* had such effects.

Only King's (1989) study provides evidence about the relationship between 'control press' and transformational leadership (measured using Bass's MLQ). Control press, one of two higher-order factors measured in this study with the 80-item Organizational Climate Index (Stern and Steinhoff 1965), is indicative of 'an organizational environment that emphasized high levels of orderliness and structure. The environment is work-oriented, rather than people oriented' (King 1989: 94). Contrary to expectation, King found that transformational leadership explained substantially more variation in control press than did transactional leadership. *Charisma/inspiration/vision, intellectual stimulation* and *individual consideration* accounted for most of this variation.

Helm's (1989) qualitative study of principals' leadership in US Catholic elementary schools was the only source of data about the effects of transformational leadership on teacher morale. Aspects of leadership contributing to teacher morale included warm, informal, positive relationships between principals and teachers (*individual consideration*) and the creation of opportunities for shared decision making and leadership (*structuring*).

Organization-level effects

Included among organization-level effects of transformational leadership that have been studied are organizational (collective or group) learning, organizational improvement and effectiveness and organizational climate and culture. We examined the effects of transformational leadership on organizational learning (Leithwood *et al.* 1995) in the context of secondary school improvement efforts. These efforts were partly in response to a major reform initiated in one Canadian province. Conditions giving rise to such learning were extracted from the literature. Both quantitative and qualitative data were collected from school staff about the extent to which these conditions prevailed in their schools and whether and how school leaders influenced these conditions. Organizational learning was defined as an increase in the collective capacity of organizational members to better accomplish the purposes of the school. Transformational leadership practices were helpful in fostering organizational learning; in particular, *vision building, individual support, intellectual stimulation, modelling, culture building* and *holding high performance expectations*.

Seven studies report more evidence about the relationship between transformational leadership and organizational improvement and effectiveness than any other set of outcomes. Most of these studies come from one line of our own research (Leithwood *et al.* 1991a, 1992b, 1993b,c; Silins 1992, 1994a), the context for which was essentially the same as in the study of organizational learning described above. Both qualitative and quantitative evidence from these studies suggest that transformational leadership is a powerful stimulant to improvement. *Vision building, developing consensus about group goals, providing intellectual stimulation and individual support, culture building* and *contingent reward* were the leadership dimensions that most accounted for this stimulation.

Two other studies also offer evidence relevant to transformational leadership and organizational effectiveness and improvement. Kendrick's (1988) case study of her own leadership in one school over a five-year period makes a compelling case for the contribution of an evolving set of transformational leadership practices. Koh (1990), using evidence from the Index of Perceived Organizational Effectiveness (Mott 1972), did not find support for the contribution of transformational over transactional leadership.

The contributions of transformational leadership to organizational climate and culture have been assessed in seven studies. Qualitative studies by Kendrick (1988), Helm (1989), Leithwood and Jantzi (1990), and Vandenburghe and Staessens (1991) report generally positive contributions. In the case of culture, these studies provide extended descriptions of what it means to offer 'symbolic leadership'; such practices help define the meaning of *culture building* as a distinct dimension of transformational leadership.

In three quantitative studies, measures used to describe climate and culture included the School Work Culture Profile (Darling 1990), the Organizational Climate Index (King 1989) and the Leader Behaviour Questionnaire (Sashkin and Sashkin 1990). Each instrument measures something a bit different. Nevertheless, the studies all provide reasonably strong support for the claim that transformational leadership contributes to more desirable school cultures and climates.

Summary and conclusion

Twenty studies provided evidence about the effects of transformational leadership on several different categories of outcomes. Transformational approaches to leadership have significant indirect effects on teachers' perceptions of student effects as well as on other, more conventional student outcome measures. Their direct effects on student outcomes are modest but important. This approach to leadership is strongly related to satisfaction with the leader and positive perceptions of the leader's effectiveness. While it is also related to the willingness of organizational members to engage in extra effort, it is weakly or negatively associated with most aspects of organizational citizenship behaviour.

Psychological states of followers, including their organizational commitment and perceptions of both a developmental and control press in the school environment, are significantly and positively associated with transformational leadership. Organization-level effects are also positively associated with such leadership. These leadership practices explain significant variation in organizational learning, teachers' perceptions of school improvement and effectiveness, and productive school cultures and climate.

On the face of it, this body of evidence seems to provide only modest empirical support for using transformational approaches as a foundation on which to build a model of leadership for present and future schools. But let's put this evidence in perspective. Hallinger and Heck (1996), for example, were able to locate a total of only 40 empirical studies of the principal's role in school effectiveness. These studies covered many different approaches to leadership and the authors claimed to be 'reasonably confident that [their] article has captured most of the empirical studies of principal effects disseminated internationally between 1980 and 1995' (Hallinger and Heck 1996: 10). Results of their review provided moderate support for, especially, the indirect effects of principal leadership on students; such effects as those reported in relation to transformational leadership, for example. So on empirical grounds, there is probably as much support for the effects of transformational leadership as for any of the other approaches on the menu, if not more.

Evidence provided by 21 studies supports the use in schools of seven dimensions of transformational leadership originally proposed for non-school settings. This support is especially strong in the case of three of these dimensions: *charisma/inspiration/vision*, *intellectual stimulation* and *individual consideration*. In the case of four dimensions, *contingent reward*, *high performance expectations*, *goal consensus* and *modelling*, evidence in support of their use is either meagre but promising or ambiguous and further inquiry is needed. One dimension, *management-by-exception* (attending to an aspect of the organization only when something exceptional or unusual occurs), clearly can be dismissed as having no productive contribution to make to schools. Two dimensions unique to school-based research on transformational leadership have been proposed: *culture building* and *structuring*. Although there is only meagre direct evidence of their value in the 21 studies, substantial supporting evidence is available for them outside the framework of transformational leadership theory.

These dimensions show the comprehensive breadth of transformational leadership theory. Using Bolman and Deal's (1991) frames for comparison, for example, transformational leadership theory explicitly incorporates both structural and symbolic frames in its *structuring* and *culture-building* dimensions. Human resource perspectives are well represented in the dimensions *providing individualized support, modelling, demonstrating high performance expectations* and *providing intellectual stimulation*. Bolman and Deal's (1991) political perspectives are captured in those practices associated with *vision building* and *goal setting*. A new dimension added to those described to this point, *school–community relations* (see Chapter 6) also acknowledges the importance of viewing the challenges encountered in schools through a political lens.

The next four chapters of the book describe in more detail, and illustrate using a case study, specific practices associated with the dimensions of transformational school leadership. For this purpose, the leadership dimensions will be organized into four categories. One category, labelled 'setting directions', includes vision building, goal consensus and the development of high performance expectations (Chapter 4). A second category, labelled 'developing people', encompasses the provision of individualized support, intellectual stimulation and the modelling of values and practices important to the mission and culture of the school (Chapter 5).

Chapter 6 focuses on those practices associated with 'organizing'. This label includes both culture building and structuring, with the treatment of structuring extended to include building relationships with the school community. This is a responsibility of considerable importance to school leaders involved in restructuring but not addressed in prior treatments of transformational leadership.

TRANSFORMATIONAL
SCHOOL LEADERSHIP

three

TRANSFORMATIONAL LEADERSHIP AT CENTRAL ONTARIO SECONDARY SCHOOL

This chapter introduces a case of exemplary leadership that will be used throughout the following three chapters to illustrate leadership practices well suited to changing times for schools. Leadership practices described and illustrated in these chapters include many elements associated with traditional conceptions of transformational leadership. But our research, as well as research by others, has given rise to significant modifications and extensions of this form of leadership as it is usually described. These modifications and extensions better reflect the unique contexts of school as distinct from other sorts of organizations, especially schools in the midst of significant restructuring.

This chapter introduces a school in which some of our case-study research was carried out, and continues to be carried out. It has been given a fictitious name, Central Ontario Secondary School (COSS), as have all the people associated with it. But it is a real school that has experienced significant change and improvement over the past ten years. This has been due, in no small measure, to the leadership of its principal and vice-principals, especially in the early years. While the leadership provided by administrators remains exceptional to this day, it is now more widely distributed throughout the school and the community.

COSS shares features common to secondary schools found in many national contexts. It is a large comprehensive school with a diverse student population, a significant proportion of which is quite needy. It has a well trained staff, a large percentage of which have many years of teaching experience. And it was subject to the oversight of a district school board, most directly, and a provincial ministry of education from a greater distance. Unlike secondary schools in some other national contexts, however, at the time of the study COSS was just beginning to experience the 'joys' and stresses of province-wide exams and some other accountability tools much more fully implemented in other countries. There was no uniform policy in the district or province about parental involvement in school decision making, although one was being formed. During the period of most of our research, school funding remained relatively stable, and quasi-market strategies intended to increase the competitiveness of schools were not much in evidence, a context quite different from the one facing schools in the UK or New Zealand, for example.

This chapter describes the school, the administrators and the staff as a whole. It describes the nature of the challenges faced by the school when the principal and one especially talented vice-principal first arrived in 1988 and 1989 respectively (at the time of writing, that vice-principal, after two years in another school, had returned as principal). Also introduced in this chapter are the programmatic responses of the school to those challenges, focusing especially on the 1988 to 1993 period. The administrators' orientation to leadership is previewed briefly. Chapters 4–6 draw on the COSS case to illustrate productive leadership practices for changing times.

Central Ontario Secondary School (COSS)

> When I got here, I was trying to make this into an inviting school. There was a lot of hostility in the halls. For instance, I recall one of the first days I was here I used to stand at the entry and just say 'Hi' to the kids. One girl said something like, 'I don't talk to principals, I hate principals and my whole family hates principals. So leave me alone.' And that was the way I was greeted. And this is an extreme case, but a lot of the other kids would avert their heads when they saw me coming down the hall because they didn't want to come in contact with the principal. And I kept saying 'Hi' to them and eventually it got better.
>
> (Principal)

> I've only been here for four years. The change in the last couple of years . . . [has] probably been in helping the kids to cope with what's going on in the world around them. I think when I first came here, the focus was more on academics and sports and that kind of regular stuff. We've become a lot more pragmatic. We've become . . . risk-takers. I think it's partly that there's a really solid base between the community and the school. The administrators have made an effort to consciously go out and seek supports, and people work together as a team. The school gets involved in the community. The community gets involved in the school. I think it's that partnership between school and community.
>
> (Teacher)

The problem at COSS: eroding social capital

A central justification for using COSS to illustrate the practices associated with transformational school leadership is the nature of the problem faced by the administrators and staff in the school, which is also experienced in many developed countries. Today's secondary schools are often troubled institutions. Employers, colleges and universities, parents and students all bring their own expectations to these organizations. Those expectations are often diverse, if not in direct conflict with one another. Among the most intractable circumstances are those faced by secondary schools such as COSS, which are attempting to address such diverse expectations while serving communities and students with above average levels of social instability.

These circumstances typically conspire in such schools to produce unusual levels of disinterest in academic work, vandalism, non-attendance, lack of discipline and dropping out. Problems of this sort, however, are simply one subset, faced most directly by schools, of a much larger set reported by the media almost daily: instances of gross and hostile student disregard not only for schools but the rights and dignity of adults and other students. Children are 'swarmed'; drugs and alcohol and even guns are a routine part of some student subcultures; and part-time jobs take precedence over school in many students' lives. Many children spend less time in school than they do vicariously experiencing the problematic values often portrayed on television and through rock videos. Overworked and overstressed parents have precious little time to spend with their children. This is not a comprehensive list.

Perhaps the most potent explanation for why high levels of social instability have these consequences, especially in combination with economic hardship, is to be found in Coleman's (1987) concept of 'social capital'. In Coleman's terms, social capital in the raising of children 'is the norms, the social networks and the relationships between adults and children that are of value for the child's growing up' (1987: 37). Social capital is reflected, for example, by the presence of adults in the home and the range of exchanges between children and parents or other members of the community about academic, social, economic and personal matters. Such social capital equips children with the attitudes and dispositions toward personal effort, and the realistic but robust self-concepts required for them to benefit from the opportunities, demands and rewards provided by good schools.

Schools, as institutions apart from families and their surrounding communities, stand no chance whatsoever of making a dent in the problems these symptoms point to (Mathews 1997). Although each of these problems has multiple causes, their prominence is partly a consequence of reduced levels of attention by parents or, as Coleman explains, of the 'downward migration of the point at which parental authority is released' (1987: 35). Over the past two decades, in particular, schools have been the object of an incredible amount of criticism for failing to meet the needs of today's and tomorrow's youth. The target has been a safe one for politicians in need of a platform and for other reformers, even though many of their criticisms have been misguided and fraudulent (Berliner and Biddle 1996). Schools do not bite back. Rarely are schools in a position to respond vigorously. Although a quasi-monopoly, they are entirely dependent on public support for their continuing existence. Nor do they have the 'slack' resources required to adequately document their contributions in ways that would satisfy their critics.

Over the same two decades of school criticism, of course, the so-called 'traditional' nuclear and extended family unit has continued its rapid decline. Whatever one might think about the other effects of the two parent, single income family and its attendant trappings, it was well designed for raising children. And schools were designed in symbiotic relationship with that traditional family unit. However, many families have gradually backed away from their part of the deal. Schools have often tried to fill the vacuum, but their basic characteristics, mission and resources have appeared to place a ceiling on what they can do.

But the critical question is this. If schools do not fill this vacuum in the provision of social capital to children, who will? The most likely answer is 'no one' – and that is not an answer most people are prepared to tolerate. So the way forward that appears to hold the greatest promise is to return to the school as the institution offering the greatest hope, but return to it with a much more respectful and empathetic posture than is common in the popular critiques of schooling, with much greater appreciation for the truly 'wicked' nature of the problems that society has asked its schools to address, and with some sense of appreciation for how remarkably dedicated are the staffs of most schools to attempting to solve these problems, given half a chance. We also need to return to schools with a more even-handed perspective on just how they do perform their designated mission for society *judged in comparison with any of the other professions*, not some Utopian ideal, ungrounded in what can realistically be expected of organized mortals. We then need to identify existing schools that have responded in exceptionally productive ways to the challenge of providing their students with both the social capital they might otherwise lack, and the education that builds on the foundation provided by that capital. These schools, their staffs and their leaders have much to teach us.

There are three important questions on which studies of schools like COSS can shed light. What is it that schools can do to serve the needs of students and communities characterized by social instability and its attendant problems? How do these schools change in order to serve such needs? What forms of leadership are helpful in bringing about such changes? These were the general questions addressed by our case-study research in COSS and, of course, the last of these questions receives most of the attention in the next three chapters. A summary of what was learned from our research with respect to the first two questions is outlined in the remaining sections of this chapter.

The community served by COSS

COSS is a comprehensive school located in a rural township in central Ontario, Canada. It is part of a large school district including over 125 elementary and secondary schools. The township in which the school is located covers 290 square kilometres of picturesque, rolling countryside in which are located three communities with a total of 29,000 residents. At the time we began our study, the kinds of problems that exist in any community seemed to be particularly intense and concentrated in this township. Unemployment was very high and many students came from low income families. Although this community represented only 4 per cent of the population of the larger region of which it was a part, it had 25 per cent of the welfare cases. There were higher occurrences of spousal abuse and such psychological problems as personality disorders, alcoholism and suicide than in other areas. Violence and crime were significant concerns within the community. The poverty and lack of jobs led to, and aggravated, existing tensions. Social services were not available locally and there were virtually no medical or psychiatric facilities in the immediate area.

At the time of our initial data collection, December 1991 to May 1992, COSS served 1300 students in a rural/small town setting with approximately 80 per cent of students being bused to school. Programmes were offered at basic, general and advanced 'levels', designations then required by Ontario curriculum policy. Roughly 60 per cent of students took basic and general level courses.

Until about 1988, the school was a fairly accurate reflection of its community with a high incidence of violence (five or six fights daily) and erratic attendance. Between 1980 and 1988, the average annual graduation rate was approximately 50 per cent. Students loitered in hallways, smoked in stairwells and used foul language indiscriminately. The school also had high teacher and administrator turnover. 'The administration, principals and vice-principals, have changed every year since 1985. There's only been one year since 1980 when the team has been the same' (principal). This had contributed to low staff commitment and poor relations with administration. 'Most of the people,' noted the principal at the time of our study, 'have gotten nice promotions out of being here for a while. So if you're a vice-principal, [and] you stay here for two years and you survive it, you either go to a principalship or to a superintendency. The last two principals became superintendents after two years in the job.' The general attitude of the students and community toward the school was quite negative and there was very little parental support or involvement.

Between 1988, when the principal and vice-principal featured in our study arrived, and 1993, the graduation rate changed dramatically. It was 55 per cent in 1989, 62 per cent in 1990, 66 per cent in 1991, 72 per cent in 1992, and 80 per cent in 1993.

A brief note on method

This study began quite serendipitously. While working with the COSS principal in an entirely different context, he expressed enthusiasm for what his school was doing and invited us to visit the school. After a half-day informal visit, it was clear that, indeed, some remarkable things were happening. So we made a return visit, at which time we decided that the school's efforts ought to be more widely shared with others.

Over the course of a series of subsequent visits, scheduled interviews were conducted with the principal and two vice-principals, with 18 teachers and department heads, nine students, the principal's secretary, the childcare supervisor, and the head caretaker. In addition, we attended several meetings and assemblies, roamed the halls, spoke with several classes of students and tried to absorb, in an unstructured way, some of the culture of the school. All 34 scheduled interviews were tape recorded and transcribed. These data then were analysed by several different people and groups. The first analysis was carried out by a graduate student, who wrote an early report on the COSS case. Subsequently, these data were revisited by two other teams of graduate students, who developed their own independent descriptions of the COSS case.

Given the nature of the school's work and the focus of the case study, the lack of data directly from parents and other community members is regrettable. Had the focus of the case been clearer to us at the outset and had we not had to 'steal' resources from elsewhere to do the study, we most certainly would have collected information from such people. Nevertheless, we believe that much of what is important to learn from the case is clearly revealed in the available data.

The change process at COSS

One of the important lessons to be learned from the COSS case concerns the relationship between the content and process of change. COSS implemented a large bundle of quite specific changes in its programmes, policies and practices and an important reason for success at COSS appeared to be *the clarity of the content of each change; clarity in terms of purposes, procedures materials and the like.* No one we spoke to ever complained that the changes being made in the school were vague or abstract, or hard for them to understand or impractical, a charge often made by teachers in response to many changes initiated external to schools. The importance of this lesson has also been learned on a much larger scale in the case of the New American Schools Project (Bodily 1996).

On the other hand, there was a kind of seamlessness to the changes created, it appears, by a widely shared understanding of the problems that they were designed to solve. This seamlessness is a far cry from school improvement initiatives that depend on the linear implementation of one 'innovation' at a time (usually one considered important by a person or people external to the school). Seamlessness, in the COSS case, means that the changes spun off or flowed 'naturally' or reasonably from one another, as some problems were addressed and others crept on to the agenda for attention. In order to understand the work of COSS staff, it is important to appreciate that sense of seamlessness.

The change processes touched on here were designed largely by the principal and vice-principal. Clearly, they understood how to approach school change effectively.

Key changes at COSS

A brief synopsis of the content of key changes made at COSS helps illustrate just how carefully they were rooted in the problems of the school and how they built on one another. These changes proved to be powerful responses to the issues facing COSS and most directly account for COSS's success.

Cooperative education programmes

Initially this programme was intended for students normally enrolled in basic-level courses. Based on the premise that such students could do very well at school given an appropriately designed programme, the curriculum was redesigned into a series of two-week, self-contained modules. Students were evaluated at the end of each module. Students enrolled in the program were divided into two cohorts; while one cohort was at school, the other was in the workplace. This meant that participating employers could always rely on a person being available to them.

Attendance policies

In September 1988 COSS implemented a '5-10-15' attendance system. After five absences from a class, a letter was sent home informing parents/guardians. After ten absences, a letter was sent home and the student was given an assignment equivalent to about ten hours work. At 15 absences, the student was removed from the course. In September 1989, the policy was tightened up to become a '3-6-9' attendance system.

Behaviour policies and practices
In the autumn of 1988, COSS began suspending students for fighting (no matter who started the fight). Initially this policy was applied to the school building and grounds. As the fighting began to move off school grounds, students were suspended for fighting during school hours wherever the fighting occurred (usually the local arcade). Subsequently, the policy became one of 'zero tolerance for anything that is antisocial' (including foul language).

The buses
More than 80 per cent of the student population travelled to school by bus. Normal bus schedules effectively eliminated the possibility of most of the students becoming involved in extracurricular activities at the school. So the school initiated a late bus (5:00 p.m.) schedule in addition. Having promised the late bus to the student council in a May 1988 meeting, prior to the start of this principal's tenure, it was implemented on the first day of school in September 1988. In 1993 the school purchased its own bus without any funding from the school district.

The childcare centre
In September 1989, a childcare centre was added to COSS, primarily to serve its student-mothers who wished to complete their high-school education after having children. Students received credit for working in the centre and enrolled in regular courses in the school as well.

The 'Let's graduate [name of township]' initiative
COSS staff recognized the crucial role played by students' families in shaping students' attitudes toward school and the importance of successfully completing secondary school. But more than half of the parents of COSS students had less than a grade ten education and did not provide role models that would encourage their children to graduate. The 'Let's graduate [name of township]' initiative was aimed at these parents; it encouraged *them* to return to school and successfully complete their diplomas. The school provided credit night-school opportunities in several locations and places in the re-entry programme (below). Information about this initiative was disseminated widely throughout the community.

Re-entry policies and programmes
Some time around September 1990, a programme was begun for previously registered students who had dropped out of school and wished to re-enter. This special programme of support consisted of a class held in the first period each day, for which students received an English credit (the remainder of the

day was spent in regular classes). The objectives of the programme were to build up re-entering students' study skills and life skills. A 're-entry team' of teachers interviewed students when they applied to re-enter and tightly monitored their progress in school.

Homework policy

A more systematic procedure for assigning and assessing homework was initiated school wide, with all students. This procedure was widely publicized to parents and students and provided parents with considerable training in helping their children with homework.

Cooperative learning strategies

Because a straight lecture style of teaching is not suitable for many students, cooperative learning became a focus for professional development. Due to a combination of pressure and support from administration, most teachers now incorporate group work into their lessons.

Social service coordination

In order to make social services other than education more accessible to the local community, COSS allocated space in the school building to seven other social agencies.

Satellite programmes (1990)

Since the population centre for the township was a town 15 kilometres away from the school, many parents could not attend night-school classes at the school (through lack of transportation, poor weather, time and so on). In an attempt to reach out to and foster closer ties with the community, satellite programmes were taught in the library in the town, beginning with literacy classes. These have since been expanded to include other courses.

Native language programme

In an attempt to encourage First Nation students to stay in school, a native studies programme was established in 1989. The second stage of this venture was the creation of a native-language programme in 1991.

First Nations Study Centre (1993)

Opened on 5 June 1993, with a successful pow-wow in the courtyard of COSS, this is the third phase of the effort to help native students feel they belong at the school and to encourage a feeling of pride in their heritage. Housed in the library, there is a collection of materials for anyone interested in learning more about the people of the First Nations. In November 1993 a native art exhibition was held.

Women's shelter (1992)
This initiative was a response to the amount of physical abuse against women in the community. COSS's role was to provide support through fund-raising, consciousness raising and political mediation. As part of their coursework, woodworking students helped to build 36 cabinets for the shelter; there is a plaque thanking them. Two women from the staff serve on the board of directors.

These changes at COSS most directly accounted for its success. They were an especially powerful response to issues facing COSS, tackling, as they did, each issue head on and in a way that demonstrated exquisite sensitivity to the context in which solutions had to be found. Which brings us to another lesson. COSS's changes were powerful in a context; in other contexts (even schools with similar types of students, for example) these changes might well be less useful. *At least partly unique solutions are likely to be required for success in almost any school. What is important about such solutions is the directness with which they address the school's problems or mission.* This is an old but often overlooked lesson.

An introduction to COSS leadership

Site-based management, self-managing schools, teacher leadership and team problem solving: all these initiatives illustrate the considerable value currently attached to widely distributing leadership throughout the organization. Evidence from quite diverse sources provides compelling support for this valuation, but this in no way diminishes the importance of the leadership provided by those in formal administrative roles. This was especially evident at COSS.

Indeed, perhaps the most important single lesson to be learned from COSS is that people in formal leadership roles are capable of enormous influence on the success of their schools. While empirical evidence of this influence has accumulated for some time (for example Leithwood *et al.* 1990; Hallinger and Heck 1996), COSS provides an especially dramatic illustration of such evidence. Particularly noteworthy was the leadership provided by the principal and two vice-principals, although department heads also made significant contributions.

When the principal and one of the vice-principals were asked to describe their leadership at COSS 'in a nutshell', this is what they said:

> I think it's very easy-going. It's not formal, it's friendly – I hope it's not intimidating. I try to talk to every teacher every day, at least for a second or two. People drop in all the time. I drop into classes all the time. I'm all over the school. It's not unusual for me to be seen in the halls by the

kids or teachers. Or to be in a classroom. If I walk into a classroom, it's not the inspector is here. It's more casual. I don't think there's any confusion in people's minds of what my responsibilities are. I'm not familiar with the people but I think [I am] friendly and casual and receptive, I hope.

(Principal)

It's very positive. I think all of us have an open-door policy. We are in a facilitative role. 'Let us know what we can do to help you do your job better, more effectively. What can we do, how can we work together to solve a problem?' But not with the administration solving it for them. The administration works through teachers to solve the problem.

(Vice-principal)

These personal descriptions focus on accessibility and stress the importance of trust and good communication between staff and students and those in formal leadership roles. These were themes repeated again and again by teachers when remarking on the leadership that they experienced from the principal and vice-principals:

The atmosphere in the classrooms, the atmosphere in the halls, and the staff room and our staff meetings [is friendly]. When you're walking down the hall, . . . [people are] smiling, they're not grumpy. Those types of things . . . [people are] approachable. You're not afraid to say 'Good morning' to somebody, because they have a smile on their face and they're approachable, and if they're approachable for you, they are also approachable for the kids.

(Teacher)

However, this emphasis on warmth, openness and caring is a misleadingly simple view of what the principal and vice-principals did in providing leadership. What it seems to capture is the overall 'style' with which those leaders engaged in a set of practices captured in more detail in subsequent chapters. But this is not to dismiss its value. Rather, a caring, open and inviting style is a prerequisite for exercising more specific, goal-directed leadership practices in schools. Substantial evidence for this claim is provided in a series of quantitative studies carried out as part of the research programme on which this book is based (for example Leithwood 1994). This may be the case because of the interpersonal intensity of the job of school leader and the discretion normally available to teachers in choosing the decision areas of the school in which to participate. As Smylie's (1990) study suggested, when teachers perceive this open, caring style in their principals they are willing to participate in even administrative-type decisions in the school, decisions they normally eschew as unconnected to their jobs.

Summary and conclusion

COSS found itself face to face with what may be the quintessential problem confronting secondary schools today: declining social capital among its student body, in combination with rising public expectations and increased educational requirements in the workplace. The changes introduced at COSS in response to this problem during the period 1988 to 1993, and the ways in which they were introduced, illustrate the nature of effective leadership practices in the context of this problem. Such practices, a considerably adapted version of transformational leadership, receive considerable support from our larger research programme. This form of leadership was demonstrated especially by the principal and one of the vice-principals, both of whom joined the school in the 1988–89 period.

Chapters 4–6 describe more specifically the nature of these leadership practices. Leadership at COSS is used to illustrate practices that have been identified in a comprehensive review of research on transformational school leadership (Leithwood *et al.* 1996b), the results of which will also be summarized in these chapters.

four

SETTING DIRECTIONS: VISIONS, GOALS AND HIGH EXPECTATIONS

... powerful leaders of the past and present were dreamers and visionaries. They were people who looked beyond the confines of space and time to transcend the traditional boundaries of either their positions or their organizations.

(Roueche *et al.* 1989: 109)

Direction setting, as we noted in the first chapter, is one of only two basic attributes (the other is influence) common to many otherwise diverse, generic definitions of leadership. The direction-setting leadership practices outlined in this chapter account for a very high proportion of the overall effects of school leadership in restructuring contexts. For example, in a series of seven quantitative studies concerning the nature and effects of transformational school leadership (summarized in Leithwood 1994), we found that direction-setting practices explained approximately 50 per cent of the effects of such leadership. These were effects on such outcomes as teachers' commitment to change in the school, the extent of teachers' individual and collective learning and teachers' opinions concerning the extent of their students' learning.

In this chapter, direction setting is considered to be most explicitly a function of three categories of practices:

- building a shared vision;
- developing consensus about goals;
- creating high performance expectations.

The remainder of this chapter describes some of the background thinking giving rise to each category, identifies research-based leadership practices associated with the category and illustrates a sample of such practices.

Because direction setting, in one form or another, is part of almost all leadership theories, there is a substantial literature devoted to describing these practices, explaining why they are important and advocating greater use of them by those exercising leadership. In this chapter we assume that, by itself, a statement of directions for a school (an official vision or mission statement, for example) may serve some short-term political ends. But it is quite unlikely to influence what those in the school actually do unless there also is strong, widespread commitment to those directions on their part. The changing times in which schools find themselves are likely to require substantial departures from business as usual, so it is important to consider how direction-setting processes can be designed to create such commitment. This problem is examined in greater depth in Chapter 9.

Building a shared vision

Background and research-based practices

'A vision', according to Nanus, 'is a realistic, credible, attractive future for your organization' (1992: 8). Included among those leadership practices relevant to developing such vision are not only practices aimed explicitly and directly at building a shared vision, but also practices giving rise to organizational members' inspiration and attributions of charisma. Evidence concerning charisma and inspiration largely describes attributions made by 'followers' about the qualities of those believed to be charismatic or inspirational. In contrast, evidence about vision building describes specific behaviours engaged in by leaders with their colleagues, a focus adopted in this description.

Charisma and inspiration

There is an extensively developed literature on charismatic leadership, in its own right, which substantially overlaps the literature on transformational leadership. For the purposes of this chapter, transformational leadership is not considered to be synonymous with charisma, although charisma is often considered to be an important part of such leadership. Furthermore, efforts to inquire about charismatic leadership predate research about transformational concepts by many decades. For example, Weber's early (1947) work usefully distinguished alternative forms of power on which authority might be based. These include legal, traditional and personal forms, the last being the form underpinning charismatic leadership. Personal power, Weber claimed, grows out of perceptions that leaders possess valuable expertise, as well as other unique attributes and characteristics.

The term *perceived* is crucial to the concept of charisma. Most contemporary views stress the attributions of followers concerning their leaders (for example Conger and Kanungo 1987). If followers do not 'feel' leadership there isn't any. Such perceptions arise in the context of particular kinds of social relationships, in which, 'by virtue of both the extraordinary qualities that followers attribute to the leader and the latter's mission, the charismatic leader is regarded by his or her followers with a mixture of reverence, unflinching dedication and awe' (Bryman 1992: 41). They are inspired by their leader.

Charismatic attributions are a consequence of what leaders do as well as the circumstances in which followers find themselves. Reflecting these different sources, Boal and Bryson (1988) argue that there are actually two types of charismatic leaders; 'visionary' and 'crisis-produced'. The power of visionary, charismatic leaders is to be found in the attractiveness or inspirational quality of the missions that they espouse and the willingness of others to believe in those missions. From the perspective of motivational theory, then, visionary charismatics influence the nature of the personal goals motivating the behaviour of followers. Followers will aspire to more ambitious or perhaps even morally more defensible goals than would be the case in the absence of visionary charisma.

Crisis-produced charismatic leaders, on the other hand, are products of a set of circumstances that potential followers feel unable to cope with. Charisma is attributed to people who are perceived to offer a way of at least beginning to deal with those circumstances. From a motivational perspective, crisis-produced charismatic leadership enhances followers' context beliefs; it increases followers' estimates of the likelihood of support for their change efforts through the actions of those awarded leadership status. Such attributions of charisma continue as long as those perceptions continue. Leadership attributions are not bipolar, however. Charisma may vary in intensity and may be dispersed beyond single individuals to groups and even to whole organizations.

The experience of charisma, according to the studies of school leadership reviewed by Leithwood *et al.* (1996b), generates both increased optimism among colleagues about the future and enthusiasm about work. Charismatic school leaders are perceived to exercise power in socially positive ways. They create trust among colleagues in their ability to overcome any obstacle and are a source of pride to have as associates. Colleagues consider these leaders to be symbols of success and accomplishment, and to have unusual insights about what is really important to attend to; they are highly respected by colleagues.

Vision

A leader who assists his or her colleagues in identifying and articulating a vision, whether or not attributed with charisma, engages in behaviours aimed 'at identifying new opportunities for his or her organization – and developing, articulating, and inspiring others with his or her vision of the future' (Podsakoff *et al.* 1990: 112). Such behaviour is not only central to theories of charisma, it is a critical part of the explanation offered by many leadership theorists for leaders' effects. Nanus, for example, begins his book, *Visionary leadership*, with the claim that 'There is no more powerful engine driving an organization toward excellence and long-range success than an attractive, worthwhile, and achievable vision of the future, widely shared' (1992: 3). And, Nanus says, 'That's it! That's the main message of this book; everything else is details' (1992: 3).

To the extent that vision is required for planning, its roots can be found in classical theories of management developed by Barnard, Krech and Crutchfield, among others, at least four decades ago (Bass 1981).

Eight research-based leadership practices at the school level associated with vision building were identified in the Leithwood *et al.* (1996b) review of research on transformational school leadership. These included

- helping to provide colleagues with an overall sense of purpose;
- initiating processes (retreats, and so on) that engage staff in the collective development of a shared vision;
- espousing a vision for the school but not in a way that pre-empts others from expressing their vision;
- exciting colleagues with visions of what they may be able to accomplish if they work together to change their practices;
- helping clarify the meaning of the school's vision in terms of its practical implications for programmes and instruction;
- assisting staff in understanding the relationship between external initiatives for change and the school's vision;
- assisting staff in understanding the larger social mission of which their vision of the school is a part, a social mission that may include such important end values as equality, justice and integrity;
- using all available opportunities to communicate the school's vision to staff, students, parents and other members of the school community.

Vision-building behaviours identified primarily in studies of superintendents include:

- developing a district mission statement and constantly using it with staff in communication and decision making;
- creating a shared vision for the district in which most district members believe;
- using research in decision making and planning;
- being sensitive to the views of the community, parents, board and staff about directions for the district;
- willingness to take risks in order to bring about change;

- incorporating considerations of the district's past and present in developing plans for the future.

Vision building at COSS

Changes introduced at COSS during the five-year period of our study were guided by a compelling and increasingly explicit vision of what the school wanted to become. Development of this vision occurred informally and opportunistically at the outset, and was driven by the principal and his vision. Once the school had begun to understand the principal's vision and its potential importance for their work, a more formal, participatory, vision-building process was initiated.

Informal vision-building practices

Most comments about development of the school's vision by teachers in our interviews concerned the principal. These comments, first of all, endorsed the value of the principal having a clear vision. As one teacher said, 'I think that one of the most important jobs of a principal is to have vision. Because if he doesn't have vision the rest of us are following a blind man.' Another teacher noted, further, 'He has some vision of his own and sometimes that vision is shared by staff and sometimes it's not, but that's being the principal. He is what I expect a principal would be; talks very strongly about the school, pats it on the back, [and is] very conscious of the public relations part which I think, in promoting a school, is a forte.'

Teachers also noted, as a positive aspect of the principal's contribution, the content of his vision. 'His vision,' said one, 'is just to get the school right. Now it's got a terrible reputation in the neighbourhood. He's trying to fix that up and trying to do things that people will respect the school for.' Another teacher said, when asked about the principal's priorities, 'Students, always, always. He's very responsive to the students. Teachers? I think it depends on the teacher and the approach – which makes sense. If a teacher comes in and demands something, he's not going to be as open. But he's great in terms of responses. He's supportive.'

Important in the principal's 'informal' approach to vision building, was the consistency he demonstrated between his vision and his actions. Explained one teacher,

if the student is here not to get an education, if the student is just here to socialize, the student no longer will be here. The student is kicked out. He does make sure that the student is here for an education. However he is also very good if I'm looking at a specific student and I'm more concerned about that particular student's particular need as far as additional services. He's willing to still run with that particular area. So I can have a student enrolled where I'm looking specifically at the [social] needs of that particular kid and not necessarily educational needs.

Another teacher explained, 'I think it's the same, if we say interactive learning for students and support; I think there's the thing. He's looking for support for students that need it and support for staff that need it. And support for the community if it needs it. I can always see there's a consistency.'

The principal's vision eventually seemed to be widely shared by staff. Undoubtedly the formal process of vision building (described below) had much to do with this. Nevertheless, there is an unmistakable impression from teachers that the principal was the keeper of the vision and, from their perspective, that was as it ought to be. Noted one teacher, 'The principal definitely has a vision. He does give specific direction and he'll make sure that we're still in tune with where we want to go. But he's willing to sit back and let the staff run.'

The formal vision-building process

A clear, widely shared sense of purpose is a central part of the explanation for what COSS accomplished. This sense of purpose, initiated by the principal informally and opportunistically, eventually was further developed, modified and captured in a formal, written statement of vision and goals. The process of arriving at the statement was created and managed primarily by one of the vice-principals. Five aspects of this process were especially important in understanding COSS's success.

First, development of a formal vision statement followed rather than preceded a considerable amount of early work aimed at school improvement. As Fullan (1991) has argued, this increased the probability that the school's 'official' vision and goals would be an authentic reflection of the problems it was attempting to cope with, rather than merely an idealistic, but contextually insensitive, statement of direction for 'Everyschool'.

Too often official vision and goal statements are viewed by staffs as bureaucratic necessities of no direct consequence for their immediate work. Only when the purposes of the school and the internalized professional purposes of individual staff members are one and the same is there much chance of realizing the school's purposes. The meaningfulness of COSS's official vision for teachers was evident in the way they talked about it in their own terms. 'The direction is really trying to make this even more a community school than it is today,' said one teacher. 'I think that's really where we were ten years ago and you know, I think we're getting closer and closer all the time. People are no longer having difficulty walking into the school.' As this teacher further pointed out,

An adult, age 55, has no problem coming into the school and taking courses here. There isn't a problem with somebody coming back and taking night school courses so that they can get their diploma. The 'Let's Graduate' programme has really emphasized that. I really feel the community is feeling more comfortable. The majority of people in this community have gone to this school because people don't leave this particular area. If they drop out, they stay in it. Or if they graduate they stay in it. That's the difficulty. We're a very closed community, and if we don't address those needs we're going to put up with those needs ten years from now. That was really what we saw years and years ago. So if we fail the student or the student drops out at age fifteen, we know we're going to have to still deal with that particular person in the community. Or if they need education, they're going to come back at age thirty-five and we still have to educate them.

'Our primary goal,' explained another teacher more concisely, 'is to graduate every student who comes in here, which we know is unrealistic, but that's the goal. And we work fairly hard towards that end and I think we have made some progress towards that.' 'Our programmes,' suggested this teacher, 'are geared so that the students have the expectation of succeeding and are not faced with failure every day when they come into the classroom.'

A further illustration of how the school's official purposes had been internalized was provided by one of the vice-principals. '[The school is trying to place] much more emphasis on graduation,' he pointed out,

much more emphasis on using your four years productively. Stronger emphasis on the fact that if you're not interested in school and you're sixteen, then leave and come back. There's a very structured process for re-entry to ensure that people know that they can come back and they are expected to come back. But the constant is, 'Don't waste our time, or your own. If you're not really interested in school, leave, we'll welcome you back any time. You can try again.' And things are in place to help that.

Furthermore, noted the vice-principal, '[for] students who are having difficulty, staff appear to bend over backwards to try and make sure that nothing is standing in the way of getting that credit except themselves. So there's lots of opportunity to get their thirty credits and feel successful about themselves.'

A second important feature of vision development at COSS was that the formal vision statement emerged from sustained, collective staff deliberation that spanned a considerable period of time. One vice-principal was in charge of this process. 'The development,' explained one teacher, 'was through staff meetings, heads meetings. We talked about this. We developed some ideas, a framework to work within, and then we came up with a statement.' Furthermore, as this teacher noted, 'every year we focus in on one thing [relevant to the vision]. This year it might be trying to get students to respect each other, conduct in the halls, words that should be used and shouldn't be used, appropriateness of language. It's very clear to the students when the teachers this year have been really working on that particular aspect. So it was developed as a staff.'

The initial process of vision and goal development took about a year. 'By the end of that first year,' explained the principal, 'we had developed a vision statement which everybody accepted. We dedicated one PD [professional development] day to pulling parts of that, of the vision statement, out as our priorities for each year, and they have been very successful.'

A third important feature of the vision building was that the formal statement of purpose was used quite directly by the school to solve problems concerning priorities and the distribution of scarce resources. This is evident in the previous remarks of both the teacher and principal. As further illustration, one vice-principal explained that 'A year ago, we wanted to get in a lot more cooperative learning, because we wanted to gain this oasis, of the school, kids cooperating, learning, working with each other. So out of our vision statement, there's "we learn by cooperating". We got speakers in, we got resources in, and taught people how to use cooperative learning in the classrooms.' This process, according to the vice-principal, 'had a major impact in a relatively short time'.

He went on to observe that

> Our major challenges now are to get our student population as a whole up to speed, in terms of work ethic and working so that they graduate on time. And that is a major challenge. Our effective drop-out rate at this school is about 19 per cent. Now when I say 'effective drop-out rate', we're on provincial average with 32–33 per cent of our students leaving school. But about a third of them come back to school. Our non-graduation rate is up around 40 per cent. That means we've got a number of kids who are here for four or five years, but they don't graduate. They don't accumulate enough credits to graduate.

One priority for action to meet this challenge was homework, a current priority when we spoke with the principal: 'all kids must have homework in grade nine and ten in every subject. It's a dramatic departure from the past.' He also pointed out that 'last semester, we talked about use of foul language, and courtesy in the halls, and just by insisting on it over and over again, all the teachers being on board, we feel that the flavour of the school has changed . . . kids are friendly, they say "Hi" to you. Very rarely do we now hear foul language in the halls, whereas before kids couldn't say a complete sentence without it. And now kids are stopping other kids from using bad language.'

As these examples indicate, the official statement of vision and goals established at COSS had very practical and quite immediate uses for staff, unlike such statements in many other schools.

Also an important feature of the vision-building process, the formal statement of purpose was the product of many individual visions, not only the formal leaders' visions. As we have already seen, the principal came to COSS with his own sense of what needed to be done and was considered the keeper of the vision by many. Nevertheless, he acknowledged the importance of what the rest of the staff brought to the vision-building process. 'I give 100 per cent support to it,' he explained, 'but I don't want it to be perceived as my vision. It's a staff vision that I support and I think there's a difference there. I think they all know that I support everything [that is in our vision statement], because if I didn't, if I couldn't live with any part of it, I would tell them . . . There's a committee that has worked on this and is more or less in charge of keeping us on track, and I think that's great.'

Finally, there was nothing static about the school's vision once it was developed. It was revisited and revised on a regular basis and so served as a stimulus for assessing progress and a point of departure for establishing new priorities. 'At the end of the school year,' described one staff member,

we get a process started that will be coming up in the next staff meeting. We'll be having a brainstorming session. We'll look at the vision statement and pick off the one or two items that we may want to discuss in terms of the goals for next year. For this year, we wanted to keep our vision statement references to treating each other with respect and communication. There was concern that the kids were not communicating appropriately in the halls, and so we had a staff initiative for the first semester. Not to crack down on swearing but rather a staff initiative to teach the kids how to communicate in a socially acceptable manner. It was very successful, if you wander through the halls here, you don't hear the swearing. And it's probably one of the only high schools in Ontario that that can happen.

In sum, COSS's success is partly explained by the content of its vision and both the formal and informal processes used in its development. Important in particular was the clarity of the vision, its meaningfulness to individual staff members, and the collaborative, unhurried and shared nature of the process used in its development. Also important was the direct and practical use of the vision in determining school priorities, and its evolving nature.

Developing consensus about goals

Background and research-based practices

Vision building and the development of consensus about goals are closely related sets of leadership practices. This was evident in the description of vision building at COSS. The conceptual difference lies in the time frame and the scope of concern of the direction-setting activities that both sets of practices entail. Vision building is intended to create a fundamental, ambitious sense of purpose, one likely to be pursued over many years. Developing a consensus on goals focuses organizational members on what will need to be accomplished in the short term, this year, in order to move towards the vision.

Transformational approaches to developing consensus about goals include behaviours 'aimed at promoting cooperation among employees and getting them to work together toward a common goal' (Podsakoff *et al.* 1990: 112). Goal-setting activities fostered by leaders are motivational to the extent that they increase the clarity of goals and the perception of goals as challenging but achievable. The promotion of cooperative goals may positively influence teachers' beliefs about the support available to them for change in their own school context, as well.

Goal setting is also part of an approach to leadership, pursued vigorously in the 1950s and 1960s, that focused on style or behaviour. This approach awarded substantial importance to the leader's 'initiation of structure' as a means to help define followers' tasks (for example Halpin 1957). Goal-setting practices were pivotal to the initiation of structure. Furthermore, the determination of objectives and the maintenance of goal direction were among the central functions of leadership identified even earlier by classical management and behavioural theorists (Bass 1981). Contemporary social cognitive theories of leadership continue to ascribe substantial importance to goals and to goal setting (Sims and Lorenzi 1992), awarding special attention to questions about how goals are set and what is the effect of variation in such processes.

Identified by those studies included in the Leithwood *et al.* (1996b) review of transformational school leadership were ten specific practices aimed at goal setting, typically on the part of school principals:

- providing staff with a process through which to establish school goals and to regularly review those goals; this is likely to be a 'problem-solving' process and to include careful diagnosis of the school's context;
- expecting teams of teachers (for example, departments) and individuals to regularly engage in goal setting and reviewing progress toward those goals;
- assisting staff in developing consistency between school visions and both group and individual goals;

- working towards the development of consensus about school and group goals and the priority to be awarded such goals;
- frequently referring to school goals and making explicit use of them when decisions are being made about changes in the school;
- encouraging teachers, as part of goal setting, to establish and review individual professional growth goals;
- having ongoing discussions with individual teachers about their professional growth goals;
- clearly acknowledging the compatibility of teachers' and school's goals when such is the case;
- expressing one's own views about school goals and priorities;
- acting as an important resource in helping colleagues achieve their individual and school goals.

Three additional behaviours were identified in studies of superintendents:

- influencing others to accept district goals;
- focusing on intra-system development;
- empowering others through goal-setting initiatives.

Developing consensus about goals at COSS

The vision-building process at COSS was also instrumental in identifying more specific goals and priorities for the school. Additionally, the vision itself provided a framework for teachers in thinking about other, quite specific, goals that they should be pursuing with their students. The personally meaningful nature of that vision made teachers focus directly on the needs of their students as the source of their goals. So programme and instructional change became a serious focus for COSS staff, one almost indistinguishable from goal setting. Unlike in many other schools, this focus was stimulated not by government policy or advocacy from some other external source, but rather by the need to respond much more effectively to the school's students as defined by the school vision, as teachers understood it. 'We are trying to address the drop-out rate and therefore we have to make sure that we change the way we teach,' explained one teacher. 'We no longer can stand at the front and lecture. That's definitely not appropriate and definitely not meeting the needs of our particular student body. We are looking at a lot of group work. We're looking at a lot of [student] presentations. We're looking at a lot of interpersonal skills.' Observed this teacher,

> When you're looking at people who have difficulty in our system, they don't have a lot of interpersonal skills. They could be a failure here or they could be a failure out in the community because they don't have a lot of social skills. I would say over 90 per cent [of our teachers are skilled in the use of a variety of teaching strategies], I would say the

majority of teachers. If they're not, they are probably having an extremely difficult time and probably are dying.

According to this teacher,

> Either they're going to transfer out of here, because that's not in tune with what's happening in the school, or they're going to be alienated and probably retire. It's just too difficult, to not address the needs, because the majority of students today are going to vote with their feet. And they're going to walk, leave the particular class. And I can't see why they shouldn't. Either we address where some of these people are coming from or we change so that we can look at those specific needs.

Teachers described some of the changes they are making in their instruction and what it feels like to be involved in such changes. The interactive learning, the cooperative learning, has been really pushed, according to one experienced teacher. 'And so the heads are trying to encourage this "go-down-and-get-your-elbows-dirty" approach. I personally tried a few risk takings with some of the group type stuff I have never done before. And evaluation, like peer evaluation, peer evaluation of teachers, this is all really rolling, at least in the science department and I feel throughout the school.' This teacher also was of the opinion that 'the younger people coming in from the faculty, they're bringing this with them. So I think it pervades the school. And I think no matter how many workshops you go to, what you need is support while you're trying it. I think if you really wanted to dive in, you'd need support of somebody who was confident with it.'

Another experienced teacher explained, 'I've always used a variety of methods. The students are really involved, but I set the curriculum, I set the programme, I decide what's going to happen in the classroom.' But now, he said,

> I would prefer it that they come up with some ideas about where we should go, see that it happens. I think I haven't really reconciled my own feelings about order and quiet in the classroom and letting people control their own learning. I try really hard to listen to them and I check in with them and then I do the evaluation at the end of every semester and say, 'what did you think, what could be changed?' I just don't think I'm doing my job unless they get a chance to say what's going on.

'But,' according to this teacher, 'it takes a certain amount of courage, because you're opening yourself up for criticism.'

Not all staff held this optimistic view of classroom practices, however. 'I don't find them [colleagues] that skilled,' said a new teacher.

> I find you mainly get the Socratic method, and I was told [that] by somebody in administration last year, because I was trying to

implement cooperative learning and trying to do a variety of things. This year, it was evaluation. I mean, I hear remarks that it's a lazy person's way to teach and things like that, but it actually took a lot more work. Last year I read about all different learning styles and teaching styles and things and you're realizing the importance of reaching the widest number of students.

According to this teacher, 'for us, [newer teachers] we're not set in Socratics, so it's really easy for us to learn everything.'

Instructional development, in sum, was a central part of the change agenda at COSS. It was a goal of new and experienced teachers alike, not because of a government mandate or some other external call for change, but because the nature of their students demanded it. Such change was not an easy business, but there were substantial opportunities to learn new instructional techniques at COSS as a consequence of those culture-related and teacher-development processes described later.

Considerable programme development was also underway in the school, again in direct response to student needs. A flavour of such development is evident in the remarks of several teachers and administrators. 'Right now,' said one teacher, 'we have a native language course going throughout both semesters. The teachers are all Ojibway, native culture is addressed, specifically Ojibway because it's catering to our clientele who are the Ojibways from [name of island]. So it has the component of culture and also the component of the language itself. The thing is on [name of island], it's becoming a lost language. That was one of the fears until the last two or three years.' Furthermore, explained this teacher,

> I came from a generation where the Ojibway language was spoken in the home, but it was not taught to the children. My parents felt that there was no need to teach the language to us, because it served no purpose educationally speaking. In fact my father thought it would be a detriment to our learning if we were taught the Ojibway language ... he came from a very strict schooling system where he was reprimanded for using his mother tongue. It's very difficult finding a qualified language teacher to teach and who's willing to be in an area like this – somewhat isolated but so close to [city]. You know, [city] seems to get them first before we have a chance too.

Also concerned with programme development, one administrator noted,

> We have a human relations course for the gifted. We have a rather large gifted programme. We have a trainable retarded programme that is life-skills based. And these students are quite disadvantaged, so we offer social adjustment support to deal with slow learners. We have a wide range, we have every programme that's in any school in the region. It

requires a lot of resources and a lot of time to supply that type of programme – and also follow up in terms of paperwork. It's a real challenge and as the community changes, so do the programmes.

'The alternative education department,' explained one teacher,

is working with adults in the re-entry programme doing interviews, setting them up with appropriate timetables, tutoring, social–emotional support, and then running the night school programme. I have been in the alternate ed department plus running a night school. I've got my finger on most of the people coming in, basically they have to go through our interview process and convince us that, hey, I need another chance. And if they're only in here to keep warm, we give them alternatives.

'We're developing a programme right now for high-risk kids at the grade nine level and offering a credit for it,' noted yet another teacher.

It's personal life management and the name of the course is Life-Long Learning. It's really new, based on the personal life-management document. So we're dealing with entrepreneurship, talking about a token economy. That's all department based . . . Each person in our department has put together a two-week module per unit, and we're going to be sharing that in a few days. And that's going to be a focus course for us next year in September. And we will be dealing with all students, not just [special needs] students, and I think really that's been the focus recently, that we deal with the whole population.

In sum, the principal lesson to be learned from the COSS story regarding the development of consensus about school goals is the importance of using the school's own students' needs and characteristics, within the framework provided by a meaningful vision, as the starting point for change.

Creating high performance expectations

Background and research-based practices

From a transformational perspective, encouraging high performance expectation entails practices that 'demonstrate the leader's expectations for excellence, quality, and/or high performance on the part of followers' (Podsakoff *et al*. 1990: 112). Expectations of this sort by school leaders will be motivational as they help teachers to see the challenging nature of the goals being pursued in their school. Such expectations also may sharpen teachers' perceptions of the gap between what the school aspires to and what is presently being accomplished. Done well, expressions of high expectations should also result in perceptions among teachers that what is being expected is also feasible.

Leadership practices that help to create high performance expectations among staff are also consistent with what House and his colleagues termed 'achievement-oriented leadership' in their path–goal theory. According to this theory, the effects of such expectations are contingent on both selected personal characteristics of followers and the environment in which they are working (for example House and Mitchell 1974).

Those studies in the Leithwood *et al.* (1996b) review of transformational school leadership that enquired about this dimension of leadership identified a total of six specific practices:

- expecting staff to be innovative, hard working and professional; these qualities are included among the criteria used in hiring staff;
- demonstrating an unflagging commitment to the welfare of students;
- often espousing norms of excellence and quality of service;
- not accepting second-rate performance from anyone;
- establishing flexible boundaries for what people do, thus permitting freedom of judgement and action within the context of overall school goals and plans;
- being clear about one's own views of what is right and good.

Studies of superintendents identified two additional practices:

- openly valuing justice, community, democracy, excellence and equality;
- expressing commitment to effective educational goals for students.

Creating high performance expectations at COSS

The COSS principal, in particular, was noted by staff to have high expectations for them, as well as for students. His vision demonstrated such expectations for students; they were all expected to graduate, regardless of their circumstances. His high expectations for teachers were expressed in at least three distinct ways. One of these ways was through expressions of confidence in staff. As one teacher said, 'The fact that he has confidence in what we're doing certainly makes us have confidence in what we're doing. He's not constantly interfering with it and at the same time if there is a need to talk to him, he's always available.' The principal also expressed high expectations through his assumption of careful planning on the part of staff. 'He would ask me,' explained one teacher, ' "what's your five-year plan?" Which to me makes it clear [that] I have to spell it out.'

High expectations also were manifest in the principal's expectation that teachers themselves would exercise the leadership to follow through on issues mutually considered to be important. 'He's probably impatient,' suggested one teacher. 'When he sees something is going, he'll go on to the next. If you're looking at leadership all the way through, he probably expects people to pick up a role and run with it. At meetings, he's very impatient. He's not willing to go ahead and sit day after day in meetings.' The experience of this teacher with the principal suggested that 'if you have a meeting and you don't get the main topics on the table in the first ten minutes, you're out of luck. And that's not a major problem providing you have a staff that supports that.' Said this teacher, 'I think some staff have difficulty with that. They would like some more direction, and they work perhaps better with somebody else who is a little more willing to do all of the paperwork that's involved. He's willing to look at concepts, ideas, put everybody on board and then go to something else.'

Conclusion

Setting directions is an absolutely key task for leaders, and transformational leaders perform that task in ways that give special meaning to those directions for each member of the school. 'Special meaning' in this case includes personal agreement with the importance of those directions, a sense that the directions have considerable value or moral weight, and motivation to develop whatever new capacities might be required to successfully progress towards them.

Organizational directions acquire such authentic meaning only through processes that are relatively extended, and that permit considerable individual reflection, as well as dialogue and discussion among school members.

five

DEVELOPING PEOPLE: INDIVIDUALIZED SUPPORT, INTELLECTUAL STIMULATION AND MODELLING

... organizations do not exist and cannot be imbued with action potential: all organizations are in fact only a series of interlocking routines, habituated action patterns that bring the same people together around the same activities in the same time and places.

(Westley 1990: 339)

This chapter identifies and illustrates transformational school leadership practices that contribute directly or indirectly to the development of the teachers' dispositions, motivations, bodies of knowledge and skills that are required to create a set of shared directions for the school and to pursue them successfully. There are three categories or dimensions of such practice: providing individualized support; creating intellectual stimulation; and modelling practices and values important for the school.

Our own empirical, quantitative evidence, summarized in Leithwood (1994), suggests that, by themselves, these dimensions of practice contribute less to explanations of variation in leadership effects than do the direction-setting dimensions (described in Chapter 4) considered alone. Nevertheless, the same evidence suggests that their contribution is still quite significant. And, such quantitative data aside, it is simply unreasonable to argue that building the capacities of people to identify and pursue shared directions is not a critical leadership task. Indeed, as the quotation opening the chapter suggests, this focus on people prevents us from reifying the organization. While individuals may act collectively as well as individually, people *are* the organization. Everything else we associate with the concept of an organization (for example structures, policies, routines) must be interpreted through the emotions, beliefs, values and behaviours of people.

Providing individualized support

Background and research-based practices

This dimension of transformational leadership encompasses behaviour indicating that the leader respects followers and is concerned about their personal feelings and needs (Podsakoff *et al.* 1990: 112).

Individualized support may be motivational in assuring teachers that the problems they are likely to encounter while changing their practices will be taken seriously by those in leadership roles, and efforts will be made to help them through those problems. This dimension of leadership closely parallels the central role of leaders in being considerate of their colleagues' aspirations and feelings, in the 'style' approaches to leadership: 'the extent to which leaders promote camaraderie, mutual trust, liking and respect in the relationship between themselves and their subordinates' (Bryman 1992: 5).

Fourteen studies included in the Leithwood *et al.* (1996b) review of transformational school leadership literature identified a total of twenty specific leadership practices associated with several distinct facets of the provision of individualized support. One facet, involving the *equitable, humane and considerate treatment of one's colleagues*, included the following practices:

- treating everyone equally; not showing favouritism towards individuals or groups;
- having an 'open-door' policy;
- being approachable, accessible and welcoming;
- protecting teachers from excessive intrusions on their classroom work;
- giving personal attention to colleagues who seem neglected by others;
- being thoughtful about the personal needs of staff.

A second facet of individualized support identified in our review of literature was the provision of *support for the personal, professional development of staff*. This included such practices as:

- encouraging individual staff members to try new practices consistent with their interests;
- as often as possible, responding positively to staff members' initiatives for change;
- as often as possible, providing money for professional development and other needed resources in support of changes agreed on by staff;
- providing coaching for those staff members who need it.

Individualized support also requires leaders *to develop close knowledge of their individual colleagues.* Evidence from our review of research suggests that this can be done by:

- getting to know individual teachers well enough to understand their problems and to be aware of their particular skills and interests; listening carefully to staff's ideas;
- having the 'pulse' of the school and building on the individual interests of teachers, often as the starting point for school change.

Support is also expressed through *recognition of good work and effort.* Transformational leaders:

- provide recognition for staff work in the form of individual praise or 'pats on the back';
- are specific about what is being praised as 'good work';
- offer personal encouragement to individuals for good performance;
- demonstrate confidence in colleagues' ability to perform at their best.

Finally, individualized support is reflected in transformational leaders' *approaches to change.* These leaders:

- follow through on decisions made jointly with teachers;
- explicitly share teachers' legitimate cautions about proceeding quickly toward implementing new practices, thus demonstrating sensitivity to the real problems of implementation faced by teachers;
- take individual teachers' opinions into consideration when initiating actions that may affect their work;
- instil, in staff, a sense of belonging to the school.

Two studies of superintendents' individual support (Buck 1989; Smith 1989) added nothing beyond those behaviours already described.

Included as part of individualized support, for our purposes, is what is frequently referred to in the literature as 'contingent reward'. As defined by Avolio and Bass, contingent reward occurs when the leader 'is seen as frequently telling subordinates what to do to achieve a desired reward for their efforts' (1988: 35). This leadership dimension is typically viewed as transactional. But the possibility of providing informative feedback about performance in order to enhance teachers' sense of professional self-efficacy, as well as contributing to their day-to-day sense of job satisfaction, makes this set of leadership practices potentially transforming, as well.

Contingent reward draws heavily on ideas central to path–goal theory (for example, House and Mitchell 1974), which itself draws extensively on behaviourist approaches to motivation.

Although ten studies in our research review enquired about this dimension of leadership, only a small number of specific practices were identified. Those practices include:

- assuring staff members that they can get what they want personally in exchange for their efforts;
- paying personal compliments to staff when they do outstanding work;
- frequently acknowledging good performance;
- providing public recognition for good work.

Providing individualized support at COSS

By far the largest proportion of interview responses from teachers about administrator–leaders at COSS concerned the supportive nature of the principal and vice-principals; an expected extension of the emphasis we noted earlier on openness and warmth. These responses described administrators who were highly attentive to the needs of students, community and teachers (probably in that order), in a variety of different ways. 'I would describe it [the principal's attitude] as very supportive and respectful,' said one teacher. 'I know there are people that get mad. But on the whole I would say it's very respectful. I've never had so much trust put in me to handle it in my own way, and make the decision [myself].' As another teacher explained, 'This administrative team . . . has worked really hard on staff relationships. They really want the staff to feel free to talk to them, and they in kind [feel free to talk to us]. I think they come across as being nice first and your boss second.' 'I've worked for lots of administrators,' said this teacher, 'but I think it's easier to respect people who are kind and who are very nice. I think it really helps if you get a diversity within the team and they all have different strengths and you can kind of know which would be the expert on any given matter.'

In the same vein a third teacher explained, '[The principal] comes and he talks to us and finds out how we're feeling about what we're doing and, I think, in a lot of ways [is] trying to make sure that we're happy. And if we aren't, he wants to know. There's not this hierarchy [where] we have to go first to our head and then all the way up the ladder to the principal. I find he's got an open-door policy and that makes me very happy.' Another of this teacher's colleagues agreed. 'I think the fact that he has an open-door policy [is helpful] . . . that he welcomes ideas, and that he welcomes involvement. That he sets up committees and processes that say what you think is important.' She added, 'He listens to the kids; when they say something, he listens. Even if it's a grade nine kid who needs to see him, he has time. And I think that says, "Yeah, you're important". I think all of these things support his vision.'

Illustrating the supportive practices of the administration further, a teacher noted, 'I had an emergency just now. And of course I go running in to [the principal] with this, and he's just, "Don't worry about it. It's okay. Everything's taken care of. Give me the details." He's very supportive.'

Feeling some sympathy for the principal, this teacher reflected that, 'Actually I think he maybe sets himself up too much. People go to him for personal problems or school problems or whatever. And it's great. It's nice. But I think he loads himself up sometimes.'

Another teacher especially valued the principal's relationship with students. 'I've seen kids come up to him and obviously they've talked to him before,' explained this teacher. 'For one reason or another they don't have any money and don't have any lunch and don't have any food and he just gives out food. He's very approachable, doesn't go through his secretary. He does it personally himself. If a teacher has a problem, he's very humane about it – his treatment of the person, technical things aren't as important to him as people [are].'

To sum up, 'individualized support' by the COSS principal was manifest in many different ways and was extended to all staff, students and community members. It was evident in formal policy – an open-door policy. It was evident in his creation of the impression that he was approachable. And it was clear in the warm, interpersonal style he demonstrated in his relations with students.

Creating intellectual stimulation

Background and research-based practices

Leadership practice that 'challenge[s] followers to re-examine some of their work and to rethink how it can be performed' (Podsakoff *et al.* 1990: 112) is the meaning of intellectual stimulation in the transformational leadership literature. Leadership initiatives potentially having this effect might take many forms. Such initiatives can be quite informal and modest, for example, asking a teacher why he or she continues to use a routine that has become an unthinking, but not very useful, part of his or her repertoire. An example of a somewhat more extensive but still informal initiative aimed at intellectual stimulation would be attempting to persuade a teacher that he or she has the capacity and support to attempt new grouping practices or to take on new professional challenges, such as leading a school team, providing some professional development to colleagues or mentoring a novice teacher. A more formal and extensive example of intellectual stimulation would be engaging staff in the planning and implementation of a several-year professional development programme coordinated with the school improvement plan.

Much of what organizational learning theorists have to say about leadership could be used to expand on the meaning of this dimension of leadership. Senge, for example, argues that a leader's task is 'to bring to the surface and challenge prevailing mental models, and to foster more systemic patterns of thinking – leaders are responsible for learning' (1990: 9). Argyris and Schön (1978) urge leaders to encourage their colleagues to question taken-for-granted assumptions about their work, to engage in 'double loop' learning. To the extent that leaders' own intellectual resources have a bearing on their abilities to provide such intellectual stimulation, cognitive resource theory (for example Fiedler and Garcia 1987) may also be helpful in better understanding the nature and effects of those practices included as part of this leadership dimension. How school leaders are able to facilitate the development of teachers' individual and collective professional knowledge and skill is explored in considerably more depth in Chapters 10 and 11.

Fourteen studies included in the Leithwood *et al.* (1996b) review of research provided evidence concerning practices aimed at intellectual stimulation. Four basic strategies were identified. One strategy was *to change those school norms that might constrain the thinking of staff*. This was accomplished by:

- removing penalties for making mistakes as part of efforts toward professional and school improvement;
- embracing and sometimes generating conflict as a way of clarifying alternative courses of action available to the school;
- requiring colleagues to support opinions with good reasons;
- insisting on careful thought before action.

A second (but related) strategy used by transformational school leaders was *to challenge the status quo* by:

- directly challenging the basic assumptions of staff about their work as well as unsubstantiated or questionable beliefs and practices;
- encouraging staff to evaluate their practices and refine them as needed;
- encouraging colleagues to re-examine some of their basic assumptions about their work; determining the problems inherent in the way things are;
- stimulating colleagues to think more deeply about what they are doing for their students.

Encouraging new initiatives, a third strategy, entailed such practices as:

- encouraging staff to try new practices without using pressure;
- encouraging staff to pursue their own goals for professional learning;
- helping staff to make personal sense of change;
- providing the necessary resources to support staff participation in change initiatives.

A fourth strategy aimed at intellectual stimulation reported in the research on transformational school leaders was *to bring their colleagues into contact with new ideas*. This was done by:

- stimulating the search for and discussion of new ideas and information relevant to school directions;
- seeking out new ideas by visiting other schools, attending conferences and passing on these new ideas to staff;
- inviting teachers to share their expertise with their colleagues;
- consistently seeking out and communicating productive activities taking place within the school;
- providing information helpful to staff in thinking of ways to implement new practices.

Intellectual stimulation at COSS

Leadership practices aimed at the provision of intellectual stimulation of staff were evident in the consistent attention to such stimulation in both the everyday work of teachers and in the more formal teacher development processes used at COSS.

Intellectual stimulation in everyday work

Comments by teachers about the provision of intellectual stimulation by the school's formal leaders were usually in reference to the principal. These responses identified very direct forms of stimulation initiated by the principal. 'He is always pulling out things [ministry guidelines],' noted one teacher, 'and I think he does shake people up when he thinks there's a need'. According to this teacher, the principal 'would be trying to continue to educate people, because a lot of the time people maybe aren't up on ministry lore or they don't know all the backup points that they should know'.

But intellectual stimulation was also provided indirectly. Offering an example of this, one teacher noted that the principal 'invites people to be on committees, he invites people to talk to him. He's got a lot of ideas on his own. He says, "Great, go ahead", or "Here's a committee that's already doing something similar, would you like to sit with them?"' Intellectual stimulation was provided by the principal opportunistically, as well. 'I notice that the principal's job has changed,' observed one teacher, '. . . more people come to him as a resource.'

Unlike many administrators, this principal found ways of avoiding immersion in 'administrivia' so as to provide this intellectual stimulation. One teacher saw this as his not 'doing a lot of the nuts and bolts of things. He's an idea guy. He runs relatively well with new ideas. His shortcoming probably is that he doesn't like doing the nuts and bolts of a lot of things . . . [so they are done by] teachers, mainly department heads, and he really relies fairly heavily on his other administration. He delegates a lot. He hands quite a bit over.'

Formal teacher development processes

Widespread commitment by school staff to an ambitious vision and set of goals for a school constitutes a powerful incentive for teacher development, an incentive present at COSS as we have already observed. But incentive must be accompanied by opportunity if teacher development is actually to occur. How, then, was opportunity provided at COSS? To be clear at the outset, infusing the school with lots of new money for professional development was not one of the answers. 'Funding is really low right now,' observed one teacher, 'and that's the board. There isn't money coming into the school and they don't have it to divvy up. Professional development they try when they can, and they try to divide up the money they get in a fair way.' In a similar vein, one department head said, 'Looking at the budget restraints, we have some difficulty. If I want[ed] to send somebody to a particular conference, I'd probably have some difficulty coming up with the money.'

Nevertheless, opportunity was provided in four ways. First, such opportunity was partly *a function of the strong and persistent encouragement of administrators*. One teacher observed, 'They've brought in a lot more cooperative learning and a lot more of the changing focus of left brain, right brain. They bombarded us with a lot of things to shake you up so you don't laminate your daybook and carry on. People are being jolted out of complacency.' Said another teacher, 'The administration has been very good in allowing a lot of individual growth. And they really want people to pick specific goals and see if they can meet them.' This teacher predicted, 'If there was more money, there would be no question, we'd be going to a lot more conferences. We would be going to a lot more programmes outside of our own school or outside of our own board.' And yet another teacher noted, 'We're encouraged to join committees, board-wide, school-wide. We're encouraged to follow our own professional development, to reserve our own teaching area in terms of our own careers. We have meetings once a month in our staffroom to discuss how the school is going. We have Monday morning update meetings. We also have in-house PD days.' This teacher was of the opinion that such activity 'builds a stronger climate in the school in terms of relationships between staff. I'm not afraid to go to the math department head and say I need some help here. There is always a linkup. For example, I've gone to three conferences this year on dealing with abused kids – dealing with young offenders.' From this teacher's experience, 'what happens is the administration will put a flyer in my mailbox and say, I think you should consider going to that type of conference. It's my decision whether I go, but I think it's a positive thing that they think highly enough of me to send me.' These remarks also suggest that while PD money was scarce, it was not entirely absent. Administrators were able to find such money when school priorities were to be addressed directly.

Second, *formal teacher development activities at COSS were also often driven by strong teacher commitment.* As one teacher explained, 'I think it goes back to personality, if you love it enough, you want to stay up to date. You do activities that reinforce your job. When you're not there you are thinking about it enough at all times that you do bring things in and share it because it's what you talk about.' When such commitment existed, individual teacher initiative often created opportunities that did not require extra resources.

Third, COSS's vision and the initiatives required to move towards the vision served as the main context for teacher learning and *the normal conduct of business in the school was designed to foster such learning.* Noted one teacher, '[At] our staff meetings, we always have a chunk of time where it's on professional development, whether it's a new type of learning technique, resources. Our last staff meeting was about AIDS.' Said another, 'We're 50 kilometres from any other school and 75 kilometres from the city. So we don't have access to a lot of things, so we have to look within. The administration has been good in giving us time.'

Finally, while COSS's problems served as the primary and most authentic context for teacher learning, the administration and staff were open to and actively sought out useful ideas externally as well as internally. 'At staff meetings we're actually encouraged by administration to go out and do,' noted a teacher,

> like they'll say, 'This is coming up, it'll be a great experience for you to do this.' Any time something comes up, they let me know. We are encouraged by the head of our department, actually, to attend [regional committee meetings]. We could take a half day and our classes would be covered for us. You're always pushed. Financially, they give you some money for it. If you have to go to a conference [and] it costs three hundred [dollars], they cover some of it for you.

This attitude of openness to external ideas was modelled by COSS administration. For example, as part-time staff members at the local university, the principal and one vice-principal had major, long-standing commitments to the training of aspiring school administrators. This was an activity that the principal and vice-principal believed fostered their own professional growth as much as that of the teacher-students.

Altogether, opportunities for teacher development at COSS were a function of strong and persistent encouragement by administrators, and the commitment of staff members to a school vision that demanded learning on their part to be achieved. The way in which daily business in the school was conducted, so as to allow for different styles of learning, with openness to useful ideas from external as well as internal sources, also provided opportunities for teacher development.

Modelling important values and practices

Background and research-based practices

This dimension of transformational leadership includes practices 'that set[s] an example for employees to follow that is consistent with the values the leader espouses' (Podsakoff *et al.* 1990: 112). Theoretically, such practices may enhance teachers' beliefs about their own capacities; their sense of self-efficacy. Modelling may also contribute to teachers' day-to-day enthusiasm for their work by helping to create perceptions of a dynamic and changing job.

Earlier trait theories of leadership (Hunt *et al.* 1988; Bryman 1992) identified a handful of relatively robust personal characteristics of leaders, the impact of which can be explained, in part, through their modelling effects: for example, energy, honesty, integrity, self-confidence, initiative and persistence.

Our review of research provided information about specific practices included in this dimension, all of which entail the leader acting as a role model, leading by doing rather than only by telling. Some of these practices model *the transformational leader's general commitment to the school organization*:

- becoming involved in all aspects of school activity;
- working alongside teachers to plan special events;
- displaying energy and enthusiasm for own work.

Other practices model *commitment to professional growth*:

- responding constructively to unrequested feedback about one's leadership practices;
- requesting feedback from staff about one's work;
- demonstrating a willingness to change one's practices in light of new understandings.

Yet other practices seem intended *to enhance the quality of both group and individual problem-solving processes*:

- demonstrating, through school decision-making processes, the value of examining problems from multiple perspectives;
- modelling problem-solving techniques that others can adapt for their own work.

Finally, transformational school leaders also engage in practices intended *to reinforce key values*: the basic values of respect for others; trust in the judgement of one's colleagues; integrity; and even the instrumental value of punctuality.

Models provided by leaders at COSS

Speaking about not only the principal, but also about several other administrators at COSS, one teacher described them as 'really willing to take risks. I don't know how many administrators would be willing to put a daycare in the school. We just had a really successful white ribbon campaign in the school and [the principal] was involved with the women's shelter.' Noted another teacher, '[The principal is] always positive with us and he's very visible in the school. The kids also feel comfortable with just approaching him in the halls or talking to him. He's a person of this school. If somebody has to go out somewhere and he's here and he can't get anyone on call, he'll do the supervision for you. He rolls up his sleeves and gets in there with everybody else.'

These two teachers' remarks focus on the modelling of risk-taking behaviour and an attitude concerning shared responsibility for the school's mission, both of which were important aspects of the school's culture.

Conclusion

The dispositions, motivations, emotions, bodies of knowledge and skills of people who belong to the school are the lenses through which the 'non-people' parts of the school are interpreted. Policies, resources, structures and the like exist only to shape or influence the thoughts, decisions and eventually the behaviours of these people. Leadership is exercised directly as those in leadership roles engage in those interpersonal practices referred to in this chapter as individualized support, intellectual stimulation and modelling. Indirect forms of leadership focus on changing the 'non-people' parts of the school; a matter we take up in the next chapter.

six

REDESIGNING THE ORGANIZATION: CULTURE, STRUCTURE, POLICY AND COMMUNITY RELATIONSHIPS

> . . . the only thing of real importance that leaders do is to create and manage culture and . . . the unique talent of leaders is their ability to work with culture.
>
> (Schein 1985: 5)

You may recall that, in Chapter 4, Nanus (1992) was quoted as claiming about the same amount of importance for vision as Schein claims here for culture. The moral of the story is that leadership cannot be reduced to just one 'key' thing. There is, however, an enormous body of evidence to suggest that much of a school's success depends on its organizational culture. This is not to say, however, that all leaders need to do for success is focus directly on changing the norms, beliefs, values and assumptions shared widely by members of the organization (a definition of culture suggested by Schein 1985). These components of culture are rarely formed or changed in a direct way. People do not change their values, for example, by simply being told that they should. Rather, norms, beliefs, values and assumptions are usually the product of repeated experiences extended over a lengthy period of time in combination with implicit or explicit reflections on both the nature of those experiences and the extent to which they were personally satisfying. They may even be the product of a shared vision, to keep Nanus happy.

In the case of teachers, many of these culture-producing experiences take place in the classroom and have little or nothing to do directly with those in formal school leader roles. Such experiences are framed indirectly, however, by many aspects of the school that are touched directly by those in formal school leader roles. This chapter begins with an examination of transformational leadership practices directly influencing school culture. Then our attention turns to three sets of leadership practices that significantly frame teachers' classroom experiences, and thereby indirectly influence school culture. These are practices for creating shared decision-making processes, developing and implementing school policies and fostering productive school–community relationships.

Culture building

Background and research-based practices

The culture of a school, as we have noted already, includes the norms, beliefs, values and assumptions shared by members of the school. And, as we also noted earlier, considerable evidence suggests that school culture, defined in this way, explains a large amount of the variation in school effects (for example Little 1982; Nias *et al.* 1989). This explanation includes not only the *content* of the culture (for example, student-focused norms are associated with 'effective' cultures), but its *strength* and *form* as well. The culture among professionals in schools is typically characterized as weak (little consensus) and isolated (Fieman-Nemser and Floden 1986), whereas strong, collaborative school cultures contribute more substantially to school improvement initiatives. Recent research not specifically framed by concepts of transformational leadership has argued for the importance of culture building and described relevant leadership practices (Deal and Peterson 1990; Cunningham and Gresso 1993).

Culture building by transformational leaders includes behaviours aimed at developing school norms, beliefs, values and assumptions that are student-centred and support continuing professional growth by teachers. Such behaviours also encourage collaborative problem solving when that is likely to be profitable. They have the potential to enhance teachers' motivation to change through their influence on teachers' beliefs about the social support available to them in their school ('We're all in this together'); they may be motivational, as well, through enhanced self-efficacy resulting from the professional growth fostered by close working relationships with peers.

Four studies identified in our review of transformational school leadership practices (Leithwood *et al.* 1996b) provided descriptions of culture-building practices (Helm 1989; Leithwood and Jantzi 1990; Skalbeck 1991; Leithwood *et al.* 1993c) on the part of school leaders. Some of these behaviours aimed at *strengthening* the school culture by:

• clarifying the school's vision in relation to collaborative work and the care and respect with which students were to be treated;

- reinforcing, with staff, norms of excellence for their own work and the work of students;
- using every opportunity to focus attention on, and to publicly communicate, the school's vision and goals;
- using symbols and rituals to express cultural values in the context of social occasions in which most staff participate;
- confronting conflict openly and acting to resolve it through the use of shared values;
- using slogans and motivational phrases repeatedly;
- using bureaucratic mechanisms to support cultural values and a collaborative form of culture (for example, hiring staff who share school vision, norms and values);
- assisting staff to clarify shared beliefs and values and to act in accordance with such beliefs and values;
- acting in a manner consistent with those beliefs and values shared within the school.

Other behaviours were aimed at the *form* of the school's culture, in particular the desire for it to be collaborative. These behaviours included:

- sharing power and responsibility with others;
- working to eliminate 'boundaries' between administrators and teachers and between other groups in the school;
- providing opportunities and resources for collaborative staff work (for example, creating projects in which collaboration clearly is a useful method of working).

There is little evidence available concerning the direct culture-building practices of transformational district-level leaders. Coleman and LaRocque offer some relatively rare and important insights about such practices, however. Based on their study of leadership in two high-performing districts, they concluded that the senior administrators in these districts 'valued collaborative approaches to solving professional problems, and also strongly valued accountability to the community [two issues addressed below]. This meant they asserted achievement and other goals at every gathering of teachers. Thus every meeting was a kind of bargaining session, and the issue of "what do we value" was always on the table' (1990: 194).

Culture building at COSS

Most COSS staff appeared to share many of the same norms, beliefs, values and assumptions. This is not surprising given the criteria used by the principal for selecting the large number of relatively recently appointed members of staff. Evidence suggests that this strong culture was a more powerful means of ensuring consistent action by staff in the direction of the school's vision than was any set of formal policies, rules or regulations. 'The teachers who come here and bond with the kids give an awful lot,' observed one teacher. 'So some of the people that you work with are just incredible, they just give so much . . . another thirty hours on top of the forty hours you put in, just extra-curricularly. And then you have to go home and do your course preparation, and you come in on weekends.' 'It's a real small-town community,' from this teacher's perspective, 'and it has very specific needs. I think all of us have to be not only teachers; we have to be friends. And a lot of teachers are.' The content of this culture was also highly consistent with the school's mission, as many previously quoted passages by teachers indicate.

Whereas many secondary schools, in particular, have what Hargreaves (1990) refers to as a form of culture that is either isolated (individual) or balkanized (collaboration only in small units), collaboration at COSS extended, for some matters, to school-wide collaboration among staff. This was evident in the plethora of *ad hoc* committees that formed to solve school-wide problems. Much collaboration also occurred, at least in some departments. 'I get a lot of help from people, especially in my department, obviously,' noted one teacher, for example. 'We share our lesson plans, we share ideas for lessons, everything.' Another teacher observed,

> The English department is a really large department. We have about 18 teachers and we have two main offices that we use, so we are in daily contact with each other. We have course meetings. We, just on a casual basis, discuss any problems that we have or anything that works really well, and if you have prepared some sort of handout for the students, then you just, as a matter of course, would give a copy to the other teachers who teach that course. We have regular department meetings and also staff meetings and so on. That's one of the things I like about this school, actually, we cooperate really well and work hard together.

Also in a department context, one teacher noted, 'I may say, who has had this student? How did he do last year? What's his skill . . . his strengths . . . his weaknesses? How can I get through to this kid? Did you get through? That's the nice thing. That's a big change for us.' As this last remark indicates, such collaboration was relatively new and seems likely to have contributed to the success of COSS through the effects on teachers' professional development. Department-level collaboration, however, did not often extend to teachers observing one another teach; one of the hardest-to-develop forms of collaboration (Leithwood and Jantzi 1990).

Altogether, contributing to COSS's success was the development of a culture among staff characterized by:

- considerable sharing of norms, beliefs, values and assumptions;
- culture content consistent with the school's mission (for example, norms of service to students);
- collaborative work extensively in departments and, when necessary, across the school as a whole.

Except for hiring like-minded staff, the specific leadership practices that fostered such culture were not so obvious in our case-study data. However, we expect it had a lot to do with the openness of the administrators themselves, and their modelling of cooperative and collaborative practices. Easily as important, the strengthening of the culture was significantly but indirectly stimulated by the organizational context of teachers' work created by the formal school leaders; this is described in the remaining sections of this chapter.

Creating and maintaining shared decision-making structures and processes

Background and research-based practices

This dimension of transformational leadership includes practices aimed at providing both informal and formal opportunities for members of the school to participate in decision making about issues that affect them and about which their knowledge is crucial. Also part of this dimension are leadership practices that create discretion and autonomy for teachers to use their expertise to greatest effect. Empowering teachers in these ways contributes to their motivation to change by enhancing beliefs about the extent to which their working context will support their best efforts to implement new practices in their classrooms and schools.

Our review of research on transformational school leadership (Leithwood et al. 1996b) identified the following practices for creating and maintaining shared decision-making processes:

- distributing the responsibility and power for leadership widely throughout the school;
- sharing decision-making power with staff;
- allowing staff to manage their own decision-making committees;
- taking staff opinion into account when making decisions;
- ensuring effective, group problem solving during meetings of staff;
- providing autonomy for teachers (groups, individuals) in their decisions;
- altering working conditions so that staff have collaborative planning time and time to seek out information needed for planning and decision making;

- ensuring adequate involvement in decision making related to new initiatives in the school;
- creating opportunities for staff development.

As with direct, culture-building leadership practices, there is little evidence about the practices of district-level leaders in building and maintaining shared decision-making processes. Roberts' (1985) case study of a female superintendent, one of the few studies available, indicated that she:

- designed an infrastructure in the district (formal and informal) to support change initiatives;
- hired and replaced staff to reflect changes in the district and the talent of district employees;
- developed joint expectations for the work of district and school staffs, and allowed considerable discretion in how these expectations were achieved;
- employed participative management.

Shared decision-making structures and processes in COSS

Seven aspects of organizational structure and decision-making processes appeared to contribute significantly to COSS's success.

First, structure in COSS clearly was in service to the vision and no particular structure was considered to have value as an end in itself. Second, decision making at COSS was a highly collaborative process most of the time, a process that, nevertheless, managed to avoid the pitfalls of being too time consuming or unrealistic in its expectations for amounts of participation. This was the case not only for school-wide decisions but also for department-level decision making. At the school level, one teacher explained that 'if you want to be a part of decision making, you're more than welcome in this school. I think a lot of teachers maybe perceive that they're not involved. But my perception is that they haven't taken the responsibility for being involved, if they're not. I think they're waiting for someone to ask them.' Noted this teacher, 'There's always, in any group of people, a minority who like to complain without doing anything about it – maybe 20 per cent. There are also people who don't like certain things. There's a whole lot of tolerance on our staff for people's idiosyncrasies.'

On the same issue, another teacher claimed that 'decisions aren't made in isolation. Actually we come and talk to any of our administrators so that they get a feel of what's going on. And so they sort of know what direction we're wanting to go [in], but they have to make the ultimate decisions.' This teacher claimed, however, that 'we are asked our opinions and if there's major decisions we'll strike a committee, and usually an administrator is on some of the committees so that it's a strong relationship there. Certainly there are times when we can have input, but there are also times when administration has to say "I'm sorry. For our school and where we want to go, this is the right decision." And they say the reasons why.'

Department decision making was also conducted in a highly collaborative and often spontaneous fashion. 'Department structure is very important in this school,' explained one vice-principal.

> The department heads really play quite a role in ensuring consistency of programme and consistency of approach to the students and to the classroom. We're very lucky because we have a one-hour common lunch, and if you go into the staff dining room or the staffroom, two-thirds of the time they are talking about what they have been doing successfully. [They are] a staff that takes very much an ownership of their own professionalism, and yet if you talk to them individually, I don't think they recognize it. But they do talk professionally about what they are doing and how they approach things, and where they want to go. And they work collaboratively, first as a department and then as a school.

Collaborative decision making was fostered in part by the principal's and vice-principals' willingness to delegate considerable authority to others, a third important aspect of decision making at COSS. 'That makes for a good working atmosphere,' in the view of one department head. '[The administration] allows you to do that, and they don't have to have their finger on everything. They would like to be kept abreast of what's going on but they're not the type of people [who] need to know exactly what's going on every second of the day. And that's important for risk takers, because they need to know that they're going to be backed up, but they also need to know that they can change for the positive.'

Said the principal,

> Any committees that come out, the teachers, I hope, feel that they have the ability and the power to make very strong recommendations. And I more or less leave them alone; I feed them information. In most cases I have a pretty good idea of what's going on with all these committees. And I'm satisfied that they're all focused, but I certainly don't want to be the one to make every decision for them. It's not my goal, also I don't have enough energy to be on every committee.

Decision-making processes and structures were also viewed as learning opportunities for staff; small contributions toward shaping COSS in the direction of a 'learning organization'. 'This year,' explained the principal, 'we're trying to have a significant proportion of every staff meeting to be for professional development, where people work in small groups, and discuss issues. A couple of them this year have been devoted to the transition years.'

Fifth, decision-making structures were kept quite flexible, targeted and problem oriented. Decision making did not have the inertia and lumbering quality of organizations tied up in their structures. On the contrary, COSS structures were often models of swiftness and evolution. For example, one of the vice-principals described the 'update meeting', which, he explained, began

in the start of the September that I came. I initiated that. There's free coffee. And staff got together after the weekend. And when we started the update meetings, if there were ten items on the agenda . . . [the principal] or myself or the other vice-principal at the time would probably have seven of the items. Now this morning was quite typical. [The principal] had three items, I didn't have any, and there were about eight items where people just sort of put it on the agenda. Somebody who has a project that's running, for example the person who was spearheading the Teen Sexuality Day, would stand up, and in about two or three minutes would just lay out what Teen Sexuality Day was and who it involved. A lot of stuff has been covered in a memo already but it's better to hear it. The meeting is an informal means of celebrating a lot of things and sharing a lot of things. We have very few items there now and the staff has a lot of items to share amongst each other. It is exactly what we're trying to accomplish in terms of this collaborative, empowered staff that takes ownership for projects. If they need people to help with it, they'll say. It's just a very flat kind of hierarchy to a staff if you like.

As another example, 'We often have little mini-committees developed if an issue comes up, and as often as possible try to make it something where staff are making the decisions. Committees come and go, and we don't have any long-standing ones necessarily. It depends on the issue that's coming up,' said a vice-principal. There were, at COSS, a lot of committees according to this vice-principal, 'and just about every decision is made by a committee. It's not a standing committee. What there will be [is] a committee of people who will work on a project, for example, get that project up and running, see it through, and then after it's over, disband.' The vice-principal explained, further,

whenever there's a major decision made by staff, they get involved tremendously. We don't say we want five people or four people or twelve people, we say anybody interested in being on the committee? Now over the course of time, it's very interesting that we get most of the staff, over about a cycle of two years, on one committee or another. Committees will present their workings, as a recommendation in draft form for the staff. Ratification is not by vote but rather by consensus.

Decision making by consensus at COSS, however, should not be construed as decision making in the absence of debate and disagreement. Critical scrutiny of decision alternatives was a norm encouraged by most staff. One teacher noted that

> any time that anything is brought to heads meetings and staff meetings and so on, if they haven't done some back-up work first it's very tough to make any headway at all. You almost have to thrash it out and go through all the steps and you can't skip any. If you do, if you just go straight to the end and say, 'well we know you all agree on this', they never do. I find this staff will say, 'Do we have any choice? Or are we just being given this?' I think people really are quick to pick up when someone has decided it already for you. Any inclination of that and they'd be chucked out pretty fast.

Finally, COSS administration worked hard at being efficient about their nevertheless collaborative decision-making processes. Explaining how he managed staff meetings, for example, the principal said,

> I tell them when the start time is and when the end time is. I time each item; I don't run over without asking their permission. I keep them to an hour and ten minutes in length. I don't believe staff meetings are productive after an hour and a half. In nine out of ten cases, we stick to the time. If we're not done, I'll ask permission for another ten minutes. I think I've asked twice and both times I got it, but people know they'll be out of here by [a] quarter to five, if they have kids to pick up or whatever. I respect their time, and I expect them to respect my time on that. We have discussion items, we have information items, and I think because we have an outline of how long it should take people limit themselves to that, and everybody has input into the meetings as much as possible.

He went on to explain,

> I give them a lot of information, the heads especially, I don't keep anything from them. Everything I know about, you know, staffing or budgeting or whatever, I'll feed to them and they very often would rather I handled it, and I will, but I want them to know what I'm doing at every step of the way. And I think they like that. They feed it on to their staff. So when we get to the staff meeting, it's usually the second time around that they've heard it. They've had a chance to think it over. And when they're making a suggestion, it's usually a really good, positive addition. And that's the kind of thing that's really positive, rather than just handing out information, which I try to avoid.

Altogether, contributing to COSS's success was an orientation toward organizational structure and decision making captured in such phrases as:

- structure-serving vision;
- collaborative but realistic;
- delegated authority and responsibility;
- problems as learning opportunities;
- flexible, targeted and problem-oriented;
- analytic;
- efficient.

Other leadership practices influencing school culture

Two other aspects of leadership are especially important in framing the experiences of teachers and thus indirectly shaping school culture. These are practices associated with school policy development and implementation, and the creation of productive relationships with the community. Our review of research on transformational school leadership failed to identify research-based practices concerning either of these matters. Current conceptions of transformational leadership appear to be blind to their importance, although much has been written about both areas in other literature. We conclude this chapter, therefore, only by describing how these matters were approached at COSS. While we cannot claim that these practices can be applied widely with the same effect, there are important lessons in the case.

Developing and implementing policies at COSS

Many of the changes made at COSS were in its policies. Some of these changes were in support of other, more program-oriented changes; and some were designed to have a direct impact on students. COSS's approach to school policy provides us with a forceful illustration of how experiences of students outside the formal teaching programme in classrooms can be shaped so as to contribute significantly to development of the school's educational goals. Three aspects of COSS policies and policy making are especially instructive.

First, policy development at COSS was clearly aimed at improving the school's contribution to student growth, as evident in the school's vision, and not (as in some schools) staff comfort. This is illustrated well by the policy guiding responses to students who complained about 'personality conflicts' with teachers and requested a change of teacher. These students' requests were usually accommodated! As one teacher explained,

> I don't always agree with it. But [the administrators] do that because if
> a student seems to be having significant problems with a certain teacher,

the student will be retimetabled to give that student every opportunity to succeed at that course, as opposed to saying, well the kid's going to have to learn to deal with this person, and if the kid fails, well, too bad . . . I see that kind of accommodation as supporting the goal of graduating all the students. I don't always agree with that, but on the other hand, it is consistent with the goal.

Further explaining the student orientation of COSS policies, another teacher said, 'I think our goal is to get kids in the right programmes and make sure timetables are fair without a lot of disruption. Attendance is an issue. And making kids accountable for being here. We have the 5-10-15 absence system and it has its pros and cons and it's frustrating because every student who really wants to can find loopholes in anything. But I think we're trying to work towards developing communication.' From this teacher's perspective,

the basic goal of a lot of teachers I know is that if students are away we say to them, 'We missed you yesterday, where were you?' So you're putting the onus on the kid to be accountable for himself. I think [the administrators] work towards retention and I think they're trying to make kids accountable. But we have such diverse programmes and diverse types of students that it is very hard finding a system that works for everyone. I think the policies are there to work towards retention and making students accountable.

Teacher hiring practices at COSS provided another striking example of the pursuit of vision and goals through school policy and how it was implemented, in particular by the principal. 'I think a lot of it is, that [the principal] does a really good job of hiring,' noted one teacher. 'He hires people who are hard-working, intelligent and caring . . . they take the job very seriously.'

Shedding more light on how hiring policies were implemented at COSS, a department head explained,

In fact because of my association with the English department and hiring on a regular basis, I probably get to see how [the principal] approaches the hiring. And [he] hires teachers before he hires them into slots. So if he interviews someone who he thinks is compatible with the goals and who will be an excellent teacher, he'll hire that person whether or not he has a specific position . . . If I had felt strongly about someone, he would have said, if you really want this person, fine, we'll hire this person.

According to this department head, 'the hiring definitely is consistent with the philosophies of the school and the kind of people that we want here'.

This approach to hiring was much appreciated. As one teacher said, 'I guess . . . who you pick to teach your kids . . . is the ultimate leadership. People are very keen, people are very committed, have a lot of [practical] background. Not just textbook background. The new teachers especially, who come into the school. They have significant experience and passion for what they are teaching. So the kids are feeling proud about going to the school.'

A second important aspect of COSS policy is that they were often self-consciously informed by the results of carefully examined evidence. This was the case in devising the school's homework policy, for example. Explained one vice-principal, 'There's a lot of research that will show you that the most effective way is to assign a little bit of homework in every subject, every night, and check it the next day. And, we have a school-wide initiative this semester for everybody [to give] homework, and to check it the next day.' And, he predicted, 'It will have a dramatic effect upon student performance . . . It's easy to monitor whether it's being successful, all you have to do is come down to one of the rooms and watch the kids coming off the buses. Last year, this time, they came off the buses with nothing in their hands. Now they've got their books. And we expect the average performance across the school to do what research suggests happens at every other place.'

Third, the implementation, evaluation and refining of policies at COSS was of just as much importance as was the initial development of policy. Administrators, in particular, persistently followed through to ensure policies had their desired effect rather than merely assuming such effects in the rush to get on to the next problem. This meant that even when policies in their original form missed the mark, they eventually became effective. A lengthy description by a vice-principal concerning attendance policy makes this point well.

> When I came here there was a 5-10-15 day absence policy. This meant that after 15 days absence the kids were removed from the class. The difficulty with the clear-cut and simple 5-10-15 day attendance policy is that you always have to make exceptions for the kids who are legitimately absent because of illness. And staff were hesitant to report all the absences. I started looking into ways of taking a lot of the onerous aspects of it away from the teachers and getting it down to the office and making us be the bad guys and the teachers be the good guys. All teachers have to do now is mark who's absent on a scan card and they go to period-by-period attendance. So now we have an accurate track of when kids are in and when kids are absent. They understand because of illness, doctor's notes, we're going to support you for the chunk of absences. Parallel to it, there's a 3-6-9 invalid absence policy. What it essentially says is after seven or eight skips, we get the message that you don't want to be in class, and we'll take you out. By removing the

onerous aspect of attendance from the teachers, they have bought into it and now we have pretty accurate attendance records. And the teachers get an update every day as to who's missing their class and why they were missing it, period by period. There's an example of how things that [the principal] started and I kind of came in behind and piggy-backed just what he was doing with a slightly different approach.

About this same policy, one teacher believed that 'the attendance policy is always going to be a problem. And they've redone this attendance policy over and over again to see if they can make it work. [To see if they can] encourage the kids to come to school. They're always revamping these things to try and fit in with the kids' goals. I don't think it ever stops. If they get something that works for a year, the next year they change it because there's a new set of kids coming in.'

Altogether, policies and their administration at COSS appeared to contribute to COSS success because:

- school policies were clearly aimed at fostering student growth and the school's vision;
- the content of school policies was informed by carefully examined evidence;
- as much attention was devoted to the implementation, evaluation and refinement of school policies as was given to their initial development.

Building relationships with the community at COSS

According to one of the vice-principals, COSS is 'a full-service school. We service the entire community of [township]. And we have just about every programme you can imagine from trainable retarded to multiply handicapped kids to everything in between; shops to Ontario Academic Credits (OACs) to cosmetology to food prep to electronics labs. We've got every course probably that is run in any school. We are full-service because we serve our community. That's our mandate, and that's what we deliver.'

COSS is an especially important exemplar with respect to school–community relationships. The parent community was composed of two distinct groups. On the one hand was a middle-class, commuter population of parents. As described by one teacher, this was 'a working population that commutes for so far. They get up and leave at six in the morning and get home at six or seven at night. They're just not up for meetings. Plus they are taking kids to swimming and ballet and running them to hockey games.' And, on the other hand, there was a population of low-income families with significant social problems. 'The kids we're dealing with,' explained one teacher, 'are also dealing with some really difficult personal situations complicated by low income. A lot of students . . . are coming from restructured families or from families who are single parent. We have an awful lot of students who seem to have to deal with their problems independent of support from their family. I think you can sure understand why educational priorities aren't always that high because the kids are really dealing with major personal problems.'

Neither parent population offered much potential for developing the kind of close school–parent partnership often advocated by current school restructuring enthusiasts. So, as one teacher noted, 'we don't have parents in and out of the school all the time. We don't have a huge group of people who support the school on a regular basis in that way. But they seem pretty much aware – when something's happening, they come.' COSS is instructive, then, because it managed to forge strong links with the community in spite of very limited time commitments to the school by parents. Rather than attempting to develop a 'partnership' with the community, COSS simply became very client-oriented. This meant learning from many sources what its clients' needs were and responding to those needs with well defined programmes. The nature of the response is particularly evident in relation to students from disadvantaged families. COSS staff explain several of those responses. One teacher said,

I know [that at] the schools further south in the region, if the kids need any help they go themselves. Here, the need is so great that they bring the community services to the school. They have social services coming here twice a week. They have a health nurse, who comes in if the kids are pregnant. We have a girl from the family health centre. The one from [centre name] is for kids who are over sixteen or over eighteen who have to move out of their home. Otherwise the kids have to go all the way down to [a town in the district].

Another teacher explained,

With a lot of our programmes, we use a lot of resources from the community. We have addiction services in the school, we have family life counsellors in the school, we have social services . . . [coming] directly into the school, so we have a lot of those people. We have the probation officer coming in. A lot of my students need social assistance, so we make sure that we have those people from the community coming in. Because the closest office is [town]. And it makes it very difficult. The [welfare] worker still comes into the schools so we don't have to have the students spend the day going over to [another town] or spend the day going out to [town]. We have them come in and we call them out of class and they are serviced. And we do that with all the counselling services. The person who coordinates that is the guidance secretary.

Furthermore, noted another teacher, 'Our cooperative work with support services is very integrated into the guidance services with the use of the family life counsellor, for example, [being] a really important aspect of service available. She is dealing with the really needy students that we wouldn't have been able to serve ourselves.'

As these three teachers explained, one type of response at COSS consisted of bringing a wide array of social services to the school. Another type of response involved significant adjustments in the way individual teachers thought about their jobs. For example, 'Once I adopted a new paradigm,' explained one teacher,

> once I began to realize that the world probably will go on without . . . [my subject area], I began to look at it being more from a point of [view of] people rather than subject area. Here I began to realize there was more of a people focus, and then we'll work on what subject we're teaching. During my second year I got my feet wet teaching those basic kids, the ones that needed the help and were rough and had bad language, and all the terrible things, but by the end of the year, 'You're cool sir, you're alright.'

Said this teacher, 'I think that was the big hump I had to get over, that people have something good in them, no matter how much we get mad. And I think that was probably the stepping stone that I had to take.'

COSS succeeded, in part, because it developed relationships with its parent community characterized by:

- high sensitivity and responsiveness to that community's needs;
- realistically modest expectations for its direct involvement in school affairs;
- a modification, by teachers, in their approaches to the instruction of students in acknowledgement of students' family circumstances and the school's vision for those students.

Conclusion

The nature, strength and form of a school's professional culture play a large part in its contribution to students, and transformational school leaders have many ways of influencing that culture – some direct, others indirect. In drawing attention to at least a sample of the school culture, we have asserted a role for decision-making structures, policy and relationships with the community that helps define the unique nature of transformational leadership. Unlike leaders with a more control-oriented and hierarchical bent, transformative leaders seek to create a context in which organizational members are motivated by what they consider to be a moral imperative. This imperative is to collaborate with their colleagues and other stakeholders in providing students with the best educational experiences of which they are capable.

part 3

BEYOND TRANSFORMATIONAL LEADERSHIP: BROADENING AND DEEPENING THE APPROACH

seven

THE PROBLEM-SOLVING PROCESSES OF TRANSFORMATIONAL LEADERS

What leaders do depends on what they think. So if we are to understand the sources of those leadership practices that are productive in changing times, as described in earlier chapters of this book, no source could be more fundamental than the thinking and problem-solving processes of leaders engaged in those practices. This chapter uses evidence collected in a comprehensive series of studies on leadership 'expertise' (for example Leithwood and Steinbach 1995) to describe the problem-solving processes of transformational school leaders. We illustrate these processes, as well, by drawing on case-study evidence collected from principals immersed, with teachers and parents, in restructuring schools in response to government policy initiatives in the Canadian province of British Columbia (Leithwood *et al.* 1993b).

The next section of the chapter offers a synopsis of cognitive science orientations to human thinking and problem solving, and summarizes what we have learned specifically about the problem solving of school leaders whose practices conformed to the descriptions of productive leadership outlined in this book. Illustrations of such thinking are provided in the following section.

Before beginning, however, we think it important to explain why considerable space is devoted to describing how the mind works, in general, as well as describing the problem-solving processes of transformational school leaders, in particular. It is because we assume that such explanations are an important contribution, in their own right, to the reflective capacities (or 'metacognition') of our leader-readers. Such capacities are a source of transformational practice. Ours is a relatively 'user-friendly' explanation, however, omitting complexities and nuances not essential to the purposes of this chapter.

Cognitive science perspectives on the problem-solving processes of school leaders for changing times

One of the main products of our studies of school leaders' problem solving was a multi-component model of such processes. This model was shaped by the interaction of cognitive science perspectives on how the mind works and detailed data from principals and superintendents about their thinking. In this section, we outline key features of such a cognitive science orientation and summarize what we have learned specifically about the problem solving of transformational school leaders.

Cognitive science orientations to problem solving are embedded in a broader conception of mental structures and functions. This broader conception explains why people attend to some aspects of the information available to them in their environments, how their knowledge is stored, retrieved and further developed, and how it is used in solving problems (see, for example, Gagné 1985; Newell *et al.* 1990; Rumelhart 1990). From this perspective, problems are defined as circumstances in which a gap is perceived between a current state and a more desirable state (Hayes 1981; Gagné 1985). When both states are clearly known and the procedures to follow (or operators) to get from one to the other are also known, a problem is considered routine or well structured. Lack of knowledge about any of these three elements in the 'problem space' (Newell and Simon 1972) makes a problem more ill structured. Hence both the objective complexity of the problem and the relevant knowledge possessed by the solver combine to determine the degree of novelty or structure of a problem.

Cognitive science orientations to problem solving devote considerable attention to the concept of 'expertise' and the patterns of thought that distinguish between those who possess expertise and those who do not. Expertise is associated with both effective and efficient problem solving within a particular domain of activity, like exercising leadership in school. Research across many domains suggests, for example, that experts: excel mainly in their own domains; perceive large meaningful patterns in their domains; solve problems quickly with few errors; and have superior short- and long-term memories about matters within their own domains. Experts also represent problems at deeper, more principled levels than novices; they spend more time than novices interpreting (as distinct from solving) problems. And experts are much more able to monitor their own thinking than are novices (Glaser and Chi 1988). The amount of domain-specific knowledge possessed by experts and the way it is organized is offered as the primary explanation for these attributes (Van Lehn 1990). General problem-solving processes or heuristics, in the absence of such knowledge, are not considered powerful tools for problem solving. Rather, such processes help people to gain access to useful knowledge and beliefs that they otherwise may overlook.

Well structured problems, usually those repeatedly encountered by expert leaders, are solved with little conscious thought. The problem is recognized as an instance of a category of problems about which the leader already knows a great deal. As Simon argues, 'any expert can recognize the symptoms, the clues, to the bulk of the situations that are encountered in his or her everyday experience. The day would simply not be long enough to accomplish anything if cues didn't do a large part of the work for the expert' (1993: 403). Such recognition permits the leader to access all of the knowledge he or she has stored in long-term memory about how to solve that category of problem. But because no comparable store of knowledge is available for ill structured problems, the leader needs to respond in a more deliberate, thoughtful manner. As those providing leadership face a greater proportion of ill structured problems, better understanding of these deliberate, thoughtful processes becomes increasingly important (Schwenk 1988; Day and Lord 1992), as does enhancing the expertise with which they are carried out. Furthermore, the degree of discretion and the cognitive demands placed on leaders appear to increase the higher their position in the organization (Mumford and Connelly 1991), in part because of the extended time horizons over which solutions to their problems must be planned and the accompanying abstractness of the thinking that may necessitate (Jaques 1986).

The theory and practice of school leaders' problem-solving processes

The two general categories of processes involved in problem solving are understanding and solving (Hayes 1981; Voss and Post 1988; Van Lehn 1990). Understanding processes serve the purpose of generating a leader's internal representation of the problem – what she or he believes the problem to be. Solving processes aim to reduce the gap between current and desired states – how the leader will transform the current state into the more desirable goal state. Understanding and solving often interact during the course of problem solving as feedback from initial steps taken towards a solution builds a richer understanding of the problem. Both sets of processes require searching the contents of memory for existing knowledge helpful in either understanding or solving the problem.

The multi-component model of school leader problem solving emerging from our research includes two components that primarily address understanding – interpretation and goal setting. Two other components are primarily concerned with solving – constraints and solution processes. Components of the model labelled principles/values and mood seem equally relevant to both understanding and solving. This section provides an explanation of the cognitive processes encompassed by each component. In addition, characteristics of expertise in relation to each component are described, based on our own research with school leaders.

Processes designed primarily for understanding problems: interpretation and goals

Interpretation

School leaders are bombarded with much more information from their environments than they can possibly think about (Simon 1993). Furthermore, because this information frequently presents itself as an untidy 'mess', rather than a clearly labelled set of possibilities, there may be a host of potential problem formulations. Problem interpretation is an instance of giving meaning to and evaluating such information (Kelsey 1993). Meaning is created as newly encountered information is compared with those 'schemata' – organized contents of long-term memory – that the problem solver thinks might be relevant (Van Lehn 1990). Such schemata have two parts: one for describing the problem and the other for describing the solution. Non-routine or ill structured problems may be difficult to understand for several reasons. For example, more than one schemata could apply to the problem, sometimes giving rise to the need for a 'trial and error' search for the most workable schemata; two or more schemata may have to be combined in order to adequately cover the whole problem.

The complex process of understanding ill structured problems is aided by the use of problem categories that are learned from experience. As Chi *et al.* explain, 'categorization of a problem as a type cue[s] associated information in [one's] knowledge base' (1981: 22). The search for and combining of schemata can be limited to stored schemata considered relevant to the problem category. A series of studies by Cowan (1986, 1988, 1990, 1991) suggests, for example, that executives normally distinguish between strategic and operational problems, and between technical and human problems. Different processes seem to be used to solve each of these categories of problems.

Problem interpretation involves not only making sense of information by comparing it to existing schemata. It also requires evaluation: the perception of a discrepancy between the leader's understanding of current reality and a more desirable reality. Our evidence suggests that, as compared with their less productive peers, transformational leaders:

- develop a relatively clearer understanding of the problem before attempting to solve it;
- devote more time and effort to the initial formulation of ill structured problems;
- are more inclined to view the immediate problem in its relation to the broader mission and problems of the organization.

Goals

Understanding an ill-structured problem sufficiently well to solve it usually requires decomposing it into pieces that are more manageable (Newell 1975; Hayes 1980). This begins to transform the often abstract, general interpretation of an ill structured problem into a set of more precise goals, which can serve as targets for problem-solving activity (Voss and Post 1988). Given these more precise goals, the leader is better able to compare the current state with the goal at each stage of the process, as is normally possible with well structured problems (Greeno 1978). Similar to what is accomplished through problem classification, such goals also provide relatively direct access to stored knowledge relevant to solving the problem without the need for more elaborate, time-consuming and possibly inaccurate search processes necessitated by vague goals (Greeno 1980).

Regarding goal setting, we have found that, in contrast with less expert leaders, transformational leaders:

- adopt a broader range of goals for problem solving;
- when solving problems in groups, have less personal stake in any preconceived solution because their aim is to arrive at the best solution the group can produce;
- more often establish staff development as one explicit goal, among others, for solving problems in groups.

Processes designed primarily for solving problems: constraints and solution processes

Constraints

The distinction between well structured and ill structured problems is a matter of degree. How much a leader already knows that is relevant to solving a problem is one factor in determining the extent to which a problem is well structured. Another equally important factor is the number of constraints that must be addressed in solving the problem (Reitman 1965; Voss and Post 1988). Once goals are set, much of problem solving involves recognizing and dealing with constraints to accomplishing those goals. Often constraints arise, or are encountered, only in the midst of solving a problem. These may be obstacles (absence of something required in order to continue) or errors (an action taken had an inappropriate result). They may also be distractions (Shank and Abelson 1977); for example, some other problem requiring immediate action comes to the leader's attention. And in the case of multi-step problem-solving processes, the actions taken at a prior step become constraints on possible actions at later steps. For example, in order to cope with the problem of a deficit budget, a superintendent may request all central-office unit heads to cut back 5 per cent on their projected spending for the current year. One unit head refuses to do so – a constraint facing the superintendent in solving the deficit problem. Threatening to fire the unit head unless he or she complies makes 'voluntary restraint' among units an unlikely strategy for coping with the deficit problem in subsequent years.

As compared with less productive leaders, our prior research suggested that transformational school leaders:

- more adequately anticipate many of the constraints likely to arise during problem solving;
- show a greater tendency to plan, in advance, for how to address anticipated constraints;
- respond more adaptively and flexibly to constraints that arise unexpectedly;
- do not view constraints as major impediments to problem solving.

Solution processes

The overt or covert steps or actions taken in order to achieve goals for problem solving is our meaning of 'solution processes'. Such actions or steps result from a deliberate search through memory for relevant procedural schemata. These are structures in the mind about how to perform certain actions; a set of instructions for action – for example, how to develop a budget, how to resolve a conflict with a trustee, how to ensure one's position is made clear in a two-minute radio interview.

Procedural schemata take several forms, each more or less appropriate to different problem conditions. One set of conditions occurs in the face of problems or sub-problems that are relatively well structured. Under this set of conditions, procedural schemata of most use take the form of 'scripts' (Shank and Abelson 1977). These are well rehearsed sequences of actions leading to a desired goal. They may be quite elaborate, including long causal chains of actions and an anticipated role for many other people. But because they are so well rehearsed, they are also fairly rigid. Unanticipated deviations from the script (for example, errors, distractions) require novel responses to be grafted on to the script. Such responses may be thought of as micro-scripts, a type of script that seems relevant, also, when solution processes are developed more spontaneously, during action. Reflection-in-action, to use Schön's (1983) term, involves intuitive and rapid search processes through memory for guides to short sequences of action or micro-scripts.

A second set of conditions occurs when the leader is faced with more ill structured problems or sub-problems. Under such conditions, searches through memory are unlikely to locate a script that will solve the problem. The more likely outcome of such a search will be a 'plan' (Shank and Abelson 1977). A plan describes the choices available to the leader as he or she attempts to accomplish a goal. A plan may include a number of different scripts connected in novel ways (Van Lehn 1990).

For a plan to be developed as a guide to solving an ill structured problem, the leader must still possess considerable, problem-relevant knowledge, although that knowledge initially is not organized as efficiently as is a script for solving the problem. Under a third set of problem-solving conditions, leaders may not possess even this initially inefficiently organized knowledge. When existing stores of problem-relevant procedural knowledge are not available, leaders must rely on a third type of structure called general 'heuristics'. These include such content-free procedures as brainstorming, means–end analysis, use of analogies and metaphors, collecting more information about possible steps and trial and error (Rubinstein 1975; Brightman 1988).

Our studies of school leaders solving problems individually found that, as compared with less productive leaders, transformational school leaders:

- thought through their solution process in considerable detail;
- developed an explicit plan for solving the problem, which often included many steps;
- collected comprehensive amounts of relevant information from reliable sources as part of developing and implementing their solution plan;
- monitored progress with the plan and refined it when outcomes were not satisfactory;
- consulted, often extensively, with others in developing and implementing their solution plan;
- planned for follow-up.

Processes for understanding as well as solving: values and mood

Values

A value is an enduring belief about the desirability of some means or action. Once internalized, a value also becomes a standard for guiding one's actions and thoughts, for influencing the actions and thoughts of others, and for morally judging oneself and others. Conceptualized in this way, values have a pervasive role in problem solving. They shape one's view of the current and desired goal state and figure centrally in the choice of actions to reduce the perceived gap.

To explain how values play such a role, it is necessary to situate them within two structures in the mind. One structure acts as a repository of one's goals and aspirations, as well as at least some of one's values. The purpose of this structure is to evaluate perceived information from the senses, deciding which to ignore and which to process further because of its potential relevance to one's goals, aspirations and values. Such a structure is sometimes referred to as the 'executive'; in Anderson's (1983) Act* theory, the function is performed by a 'working memory'. Situating values in an executive or working memory structure helps explain the pervasive but indirect effects that school leaders' values have on their actions. They provide perceptual screens which, as Hambrick and Brandon (1988) explain, allow the school leader to 'see what he wants to see' and 'hear what he wants to hear'. The leader who values efficiency and frugality in the running of schools may not 'hear' the community's expressions of willingness to spend more money on better education for their children.

Values also seem likely to exist, in two forms, in long-term memory. In one form, they are embedded as integral parts of leaders' organized knowledge structures (schemata) about their organizational worlds, including procedures for how to solve known problems in those worlds. This is their implicit form. While values in this form are an important part of leaders' domain-specific knowledge, leaders often may not be consciously aware of such values and the strength of influence of their implicit values on their actions.

Values may also be stored as independent structures in the mind; their explicit form. School leaders are likely to be consciously aware of their values in this form and, hence, have more control over the influence of such values. Whether in their implicit or explicit forms, values stored in long-term memory have direct effects on school leaders' thoughts about what actions to take – a 'behaviour channelling' effect (Hambrick and Brandon 1988). Nevertheless, even when values are in explicit form, their effects on actions are mediated by the amount of discretion the leader possesses. Leaders' actions are formed from thoughts about many matters in addition to their explicit values. But it is difficult for school leaders to escape from the influence of their implicit values and the values that act as perceptual screens.

Our own research concerning the nature and role of values in school leaders' problem solving suggests that transformational school leaders, as compared with leaders engaged in less productive forms of practice:

- are more aware of their values;
- use their values more regularly in solving problems;
- use values as substitutes for knowledge in solving ill-structured problems.

Mood

Knowledge is stored in the mind in several forms – words and pictures, for example. Furthermore, what is meant by 'knowledge' goes considerably beyond the purely cognitive content implied by the term. In addition to values, as discussed above, other affective states or feelings will also be integrated as part of knowledge structures. A school leader not only has stored in mind a procedure for facilitating the decision making of the school/parent council, he or she also has associated (and therefore unavoidable) feelings about carrying out the procedure – despair, elation, fear, boredom and the like. Both the nature and strength of these feelings shape the mood experienced by leaders during problem solving. Additional feelings, for example, pressure and uncertainty coming from the context in which problem solving occurs, also contribute to the leaders' mood. Research on social cognition suggests that, along with personal goals and the knowledge one possesses, mood has an important influence on the degree of cognitive flexibility the leader is able to exercise during problem solving. Showers and Cantor explain flexibility as '(a) adjusting interpretations in response to situational features; (b) taking control of [one's] thoughts and plans; (c) seeing multiple alternatives for interpreting the same event or outcome; and (d) changing [one's] own knowledge repertoire by adding new experiences and by reworking cherished beliefs, values, and goals' (1985: 277).

Intense moods reduce such flexibility, thereby limiting problem-solving effectiveness. Consistent with this explanation, our research with school leaders has demonstrated that, transformational school leaders, as compared with those exercising less productive forms of leadership:

- are better able to control intense moods and remain calm during problem solving;
- are more self-confident about their ability to solve ill-structured problems;
- treat staff with consistent and genuine respect and courtesy during their interactions.

Transformational school leaders' problem solving illustrated

Background

To bring to life the characteristics of problem solving underlying transformational school leaders' practices, we briefly describe one such leader's thinking. Our data about this principal, his practices and problem-solving processes, were collected as part of a larger study of school change in the context of a major school restructuring initiative in the Canadian province of British Columbia (for example Leithwood *et al.* 1993b,c). This initiative took the form of new programme policies and guidelines for each of the three divisions in a school system: a primary programme; an intermediate programme; and a senior programme.

All schools in the province were expected to implement whichever of these programmes were relevant to their student populations. Such implementation could entail, for example, changes to a school's curriculum, changes in the means of assessing and reporting student progress and alterations in the grouping of students within and across classrooms. Depending on the status of the school at the outset, greater attention might need to be given, as well, to formerly neglected segments of the student population and to the development of closer relationships with the immediate communities, relationships which were to be partner-like in nature.

Not surprisingly, our evidence suggested that schools approached implementation from quite different starting points and developed quite different responses. A considerable proportion of the variation in schools' responses seemed to depend on the nature of leadership exercised in the school. Behind these differences in leadership, of course, were differences in thinking and problem-solving processes. We use the case of Constantine High and its principal Don Fontaine (both pseudonyms) to illustrate the problem solving of transformational leaders. Of all the principals we studied, Don's practices matched most closely the transformational leadership practices described in Chapters 3–6.

Constantine High School

This was a small school, with about 30 teachers and 400 students in grades 8 through 12, located in a well established community with a long history of lumbering and tourism. The community was generally supportive of its school, which was reflected in a significant amount of fund-raising done on a regular basis to support various school projects. A number of years ago the community was successful in restoring Constantine High as a secondary school after it had been made a junior secondary school. The school was situated in a medium sized district at considerable distance from the district office. Several years prior to our study the district had made creative problem solving and critical thinking its priority for professional development within the district. Staff at Constantine had participated in these activities, and considered them compatible with objectives of the province's intermediate programme.

Coincidentally with the arrival of the new principal, Don, at the school three years before our study, the school began a provincial accreditation process, fortuitous in the view of staff, as a help in establishing a climate supportive of teacher initiatives related to the intermediate programme. The accreditation process in British Columbia requires a school staff to describe and assess the adequacy of its own programmes, policies, facilities, community relations and the like. A ministry-appointed external team then reviews the school's assessment of itself, visits the school (sometimes collecting new data), and offers recommendations for school improvement. Problems of a sufficiently critical nature may trigger follow-up auditing of progress.

The school was also successful in its applications for grants from various projects, receiving 'developmental site grants' from the Ministry of Education and Training, as well as a grant to fund the accreditation process. These funds were used to support professional development activities for staff members.

Teachers appeared to be engaging in experimentation with innovative practices and were breaking down some of the traditional isolation among departments and divisions with more cross-grade and cross-subject interaction. They were also investigating the establishment of a teacher advisor system to better serve the students.

The principal's leadership practices

Don Fontaine was in his late 40s and had been principal in this school for three years at the time of the study. He had taught, been a counsellor, and an elementary school vice-principal and principal before becoming a secondary school principal. Evidence collected from a variety of sources in our research suggested that Don's leadership conformed closely to transformational leadership as we have described it in earlier chapters. For example, Don was able to articulate, to his staff, the relationship between the intermediate programme and a set of broad and compelling social needs (for example, preparing students for a rapidly changing future). In this way, he demonstrated the potential for adding moral and ideological value to otherwise less compelling school goals; this, as Shamir (1991) argues, is likely to produce much higher levels of commitment on the part of staff by increasing the intrinsic value of their efforts.

As a further demonstration of transformational practices, Don tried, in a number of different ways, to help staff develop a much broader perspective on their work, a perspective capable of bringing into question taken-for-granted assumptions, and stimulating high-level or double-loop (Argyris and Schön 1978) organizational learning. His efforts conform exactly to Avolio and Bass' definition of 'intellectual stimulation' provided by transformational leaders: 'providing ideas that result in a rethinking of old ways, and enabl[ing] followers to look at problems from many angles' (1988: 34).

Don also devoted considerable energy to building the self-esteem and self-confidence of staff concerning programme implementation. This focus for his leadership is consistent with the claims made for the transforming effects of enhanced self-efficacy on the part of staff (Bandura 1986; Shamir 1991). Don's practices illustrate how strong pressure for change from a leader can be accompanied, nevertheless, by a respectful and supportive attitude towards staff and their capacities to transform their own practices.

The principal's approach to solving the problem of intermediate programme implementation

From earlier sections of this chapter, you will recall our six-component model of problem-solving processes. In this section we describe Don's approach to each of these components.

Interpreting the problem

> When you move people from their [predictable routines] . . . and ask
> them to do something completely different, that is a complex issue
> involving individuals with different degrees of self-confidence in tack-
> ling the issue within the school.

Don interpreted implementing the intermediate programme as *unclear*
because the draft policy documents describing the programme continued to
change. But more importantly, the problem was *complex*, from his point of
view, because teachers had different levels of self-confidence about mastering the change. Building self-esteem was a central feature of this problem,
in Don's view. In particular, he believed that the implementation of new
classroom practices was especially difficult for teachers who taught both
intermediate and graduation level students (grades 11 and 12), for this
reason.

Don also interpreted implementing the intermediate programme as an
opportunity to revisit (and this time actually to make happen) some peda-
gogically exciting ideas from earlier decades. The concepts embodied in the
intermediate programme were familiar to him from his past experiences. He
understood the programme to be a response to changing needs of business
and industry. Business and industry, he believed, were demanding employees
with more broadly based skills. Furthermore, business and industry were
ready to be involved in education as partners in helping schools change to
better meet the demands of today's world. Don understood the philosophy
underlying the intermediate programme to be responsive to such demands,
as well as to the broader social need for people to respect each other's differences.

Don compared the change effort he and his staff were involved in to a
wave. 'We can either get ready, get our surf boards out and ride the wave
and enjoy all the wonder of it, or we can just stand there and let the wave
wash over.' He also interpreted implementing the intermediate programme
as an opportunity to do what he liked to do – get out of his office and talk
to teachers and students about programme improvement.

Setting goals for problem solving

> [I want to] develop [teachers'] self confidence; to give them the impres-
> sion that what they are doing is good – never to give them the opinion
> that what they are doing is somehow wrong or bad or that they have
> been hurting kids by doing it.

The most obvious goal that Don believed needed to be accomplished, if the
intermediate programme was to be implemented well in Constantine, was
to develop the self-confidence of his staff. To do this he focused staff's

attention on why their traditional ways of teaching, appropriate and effective for the educational mission of the past, no longer sufficed for the changed mission the world had come to expect of schools. Teachers' traditional practices were not unequivocally bad – quite the contrary – some of them were just not well matched to the new set of demands faced by today's schools.

As a second goal for solving the intermediate programme implementation problem, Don wanted to empower teachers by encouraging them to think beyond their daily routines, 'to get them on district committees, to get them going out to in-service, to get them out of the situation that they have been operating in order to get the bigger picture'. Yet a third goal Don held for his problem solving was to encourage collaboration among teachers.

Many of the problem-solving goals identified by Don, in one way or another, related to empowering teachers. But when asked specifically, Don explained his overriding goal as making teaching and learning meaningful to students in today's world, a world very different from that of even the recent past.

Nature and use of values in problem solving

> I felt I had to broaden their [staff] horizons and I had to validate the things that they were doing. I had to get their lights from under the bushel and shine so that they could see them.

Values strongly influenced Don's problem solving and most of the values he referred to concerned the staff. He had considerable respect for the school's teachers and believed them to be very caring and supportive people. He viewed one part of his role, as we have noted, as building their self-esteem and self-confidence by validating the things they were doing. Fairness was important. 'We have not tried to put more on their plate than they can handle. Neither have we said, "It is not going to happen".' Don was particularly sensitive to the needs of those who were less confident about change. 'I did not want to, in any way, allow them to get the impression that they were not worthy or that they were being neglected or that people were getting frustrated with them or whatever.' He helped them by offering support and encouragement and invitations to attend conferences. He believed in encouraging staff to take leadership roles and fostering ownership of initiatives. But he tried to assure teachers that he took ultimate responsibility for student progress so that they would feel more inclined to take risks.

His strong focus on staff did not distract Don from an equally strong concern about the consequences of the school's initiatives for students. He believed that students needed the opportunity to think and reflect on their behaviour; they needed to see the consequences of their actions because that helps people accept responsibility for what happens to them. He also wanted his staff to perceive him 'as a person really on the side of the best environment that we can create for kids'.

Don valued the conferences offered by the ministry because they demonstrated the ministry's commitment to the intermediate programme. He also applauded the fact that teachers were well represented in the process because it let teachers see that the programme was not being dictated from the top down. Also valued by Don was the support of senior administration, the enthusiasm of his staff, and the support of parents who said they wanted their children to be treated as individuals deserving of respect.

Respect for each other was a crucial value for Don and respect for the right to be different was, in his view, vital in today's society. In part because the intermediate programme seemed to be based on this notion of respect, Don believed the programme to be worthwhile.

Constraints to problem solving

there are some people whose process of thinking [about] change is logical and sequential. They want to see the outcome. They want the 'i's dotted and the 't's crossed. To make those people feel comfortable has, perhaps, been the greatest challenge.

The main constraint perceived by Don in solving the intermediate programme implementation problem was teachers' reluctance to explore new ideas, although he believed there were few such teachers in his school. His greatest challenge was to help those most opposed to change feel more comfortable with the prospect. He did not denigrate the motives or behaviours of those staff members. Instead, he viewed the problem as a lack of self-confidence, which he could improve by helping to change the focus of the individuals in the system – teachers, community and students. Don believed he could accomplish this by 'unshackling old ties and making people feel comfortable with exploring new ideas'. In Don's view, district-level in-service programmes had encouraged people who were reluctant to change by demonstrating to them how many people were already supportive of the intermediate programme and attempting to implement it.

Don attributed teachers' lack of self-confidence to the fact that they felt unrecognized – not as good as the bigger school in the district. When he came to the school he felt the staff had an inferiority complex. There was, as well, a particular difficulty for teachers who had both intermediate and graduation level students because of conflicting programme requirements.

Strategies for problem solving

> What I did was try to get people excited about getting involved in some other things such as creative problem solving . . . I got them going out so that they could see what was going on out there – steal the good ideas, but also validate what they are doing.

Our data concerning Don's problem solving did not result in the identification of many specific *steps* for problem solving. Several of the steps that were mentioned had to do with overcoming teachers' lack of self-confidence to change. Sending teachers to training sessions was one way he helped people see beyond their daily routines to a broader perspective. He also mentioned a district-level in-service programme with representatives from the teachers' federation, parents, students, teachers and the ministry. Don also took steps to ensure, as we have noted, that teachers interpreted the demands for changed practices not as an indictment of their skill but as an inevitable consequence of a changed school mission. Don believed that, in order for teachers to feel good about change, they had to feel good about themselves.

Don also made 'second-order' organizational changes to support the intermediate programme. He purchased new computers for the science department and reorganized timetables. The school was to begin a new practical arts programme combining industrial education and home economics. 'By collaborating and talking, just making people feel comfortable, they have come up with this.' To encourage collaboration, he scheduled grade eight and ten science classes back-to-back.

This principal's preferred method for monitoring activities in the school was a version of 'managing by wandering about', in the process having conversations with teachers and students. 'I am enthusiastic about what kids do so I try to pass on a little bit of my enthusiasm. I like to talk to teachers and be with teachers and find out what they are thinking and what they are talking about and exchange ideas with them.' This was, in Don's opinion, also a way for staff to get to know him and what he valued. Don also consulted extensively with parents about their expectations and aspirations for the school and their children.

Mood

> Not only does it seem right intellectually, but it really feels right. It really feels good; it feels important.

Don's initial reaction to the intermediate programme was great excitement because the programme represented a 'revisiting' of ideas that were really important for working with students and which somehow were not happening then. He felt confident that his approach to implementation would work.

Summary and conclusion

We began this chapter with the premise that what school leaders do depends on what they think. To appreciate fully the genesis of productive leadership for changing times as it has been portrayed in this book, it is crucial to know how those exercising such leadership think. More specifically, it is important to understand how they go about solving significant problems facing their schools.

The first section of the chapter offered a simple and general cognitive science account of how the human mind functions. This was followed by a more detailed framework for identifying and describing the problem-solving processes of school leaders consistent with this account. A synthesis of evidence from a series of studies about the problem solving of transformational as compared with more typical school leaders was provided, using six elements of such problem solving as the basis of the description.

We then described how one transformational school leader thought through the problem of implementing an externally developed initiative with significant implications for many aspects of the school.

The expert problem-solving processes summarized and illustrated in this chapter serve as guidance for others wishing to move their own practices closer to those described in this book. But it is not uncommon these days to encounter arguments to the effect that models of exemplary practice do not serve this purpose very well. And there is merit to this argument largely because of the circumstances most people find themselves facing when they encounter such models.

The research programme on expert problem-solving processes that provided much of the data for this chapter included an evaluation of the effects of a carefully designed programme for teaching such processes to practicing school administrators (see Leithwood and Steinbach 1995: chapter 12). Evidence from this evaluation supports the contribution to problem-solving expertise of experiences that include, for example: guided practice in solving authentic problems with colleagues; encounters with progressively complex problems; opportunities to acquire crucial knowledge in domains relevant to common categories of problems (for example, school improvement problems, staff conflict problems); and guided opportunities for reflection on one's own and one's colleagues' problem-solving processes.

Clearly, school leaders can be helped to think more expertly about the problems they face with their staffs and communities. And this seems to offer the greatest promise for encouraging those leadership practices for changing times that are described in other chapters of this book.

eight

FOSTERING TEACHER LEADERSHIP

When leadership is viewed as a nonlearnable set of character traits or as equivalent to an exalted position, a self-fulfilling prophecy is created that dooms societies to having only a few good leaders. It is far healthier and more productive for us to start with the assumption that it is possible for everyone to lead. If we assume that leadership is learnable, we can discover how many good leaders there really are.

(Kouze and Posner 1996: 109)

Shared decision making and teacher professionalization are key elements of many school restructuring plans. Both elements require teachers routinely to exercise more leadership outside the classroom than traditionally has been expected of them. So facilitating the development of teacher leadership has become an important part of the role of those in formal school leadership positions. Summed up by Conley (1993: 246), the motivations for advocating such leadership include: the possibilities for reflecting democratic principles of participation in the workplace; enhancing teachers' satisfaction with their work; increasing teachers' sense of professionalism; stimulating organizational change; providing a route to increased organizational efficiency; and revitalizing teachers through increased interaction with their colleagues.

Like many others, we believe that developing teacher leadership is an important part of what those in formal school leadership roles should be doing in these changing times. But specific practices helpful in facilitating such development will need to be crafted on the basis of a better understanding of two key matters: the relationship between formal and informal (or teacher) school leadership, and the nature of teacher leadership and factors influencing the perception of such leadership on the part of teacher leaders' colleagues. Based on a study fully described in Leithwood *et al.* (1997b), the bulk of this chapter addresses these two issues. Implications of the study for the development of teacher leaders by those in formal school leadership positions are discussed in the final section of the chapter.

Conceptual orientation to the study

Four areas of relevant theory and research shaped our collection and interpretation of data collected in this study. These included prior research on teacher leadership, transformational orientations to school leadership, variables influencing teachers' perceptions of teacher leaders, and variables mediating the effects that leaders have on teaching and learning in their schools. This section briefly describes each of these lines of theory and research and indicates the ways in which we considered them to be relevant to our study.

Teacher leadership

Leadership, suggest Sirotnik and Kimball (1996), does not take on new meaning when qualified by the term 'teacher'. It entails the exercise of influence over the beliefs, actions and values of others (Hart 1995a), as is the case with leadership from any source. What may be different is how that influence is exercised and to what end, as we discussed in Chapter 1. In a traditional school, for example, those in formal administrative roles have greater access than teachers to positional power in their attempts to influence classroom practice, whereas teachers may have greater access to the power that flows from technical expertise. Traditionally, too, teachers and administrators often attempt to exercise leadership in relation to quite different aspects of the school's functioning, although teachers often report a strong interest in expanding their spheres of influence (Reavis and Griffith 1993; Taylor and Bogotch 1994). And teachers who are active as leaders through their union work often find themselves in direct conflict with administrative mandates (Bascia 1997).

Teacher leadership may be either formal or informal in nature. Lead teacher, master teacher, department head, union representative, member of the school's governance council, mentor – these are among the many designations associated with formal teacher leadership roles. Teachers assuming these roles are expected to carry out a wide range of functions. These functions include, for example: representing the school in district-level decision making (Fullan 1993); stimulating the professional growth of colleagues

(Wasley 1991); being an advocate for teachers' work (Bascia 1997); and improving the school's decision-making processes (Malen *et al.* 1990). Those appointed to formal teacher leadership roles are also sometimes expected to induct new teachers into the school, and to influence positively the willingness and capacity of other teachers to implement change in the school (Fullan and Hargreaves 1991; Whitaker 1995).

Teachers exercise informal leadership in their schools by sharing their expertise, volunteering for new projects and bringing new ideas to the school. They also offer leadership by helping their colleagues to carry out their classroom duties, and by assisting in the improvement of classroom practice through the engagement of their colleagues in experimentation and the examination of more powerful instructional techniques. Teachers attribute leadership qualities, as well, to colleagues who accept responsibility for their own professional growth, promote the school's mission, and work for the improvement of the school or the school system (Smylie and Denny 1990; Wasley 1991; Harrison and Lembeck 1996).

Empirical evidence concerning the actual effects of either formal or informal teacher leadership is limited in quantity and mixed results are reported. For example, many of the more ambitious initiatives to establish formal teacher leadership roles through the creation of career ladders have been abandoned (Hart 1995a). And Hannay and Denby (1994) found that department heads were not very effective as facilitators of change, largely due to their lack of knowledge and skill in effective change strategies. On the other hand, Duke *et al.* (1980) found that increased participation of teachers in school decision making resulted in a more democratic school. Increased professional learning for the teacher leader has also been reported as an effect of assuming such a role (Lieberman *et al.* 1988; Wasley 1991).

The exercise of teacher leadership is inhibited by a number of conditions. Time taken for work outside the classroom probably interferes with time needed for students (Smylie and Denny 1990). When extra time is provided for leadership functions, it is usually not enough (Wasley 1991). Furthermore, the lack of time, training and funding for leadership roles (Cooper 1988; White 1992) interferes with teachers' personal lives, as well as their classroom work. Cultures of isolationism, common in schools, inhibit the work of teacher leaders with their teaching colleagues, as do the associated norms of egalitarianism, privacy, politeness and contrived collegiality (Sirotnik 1994; Griffin 1995). The effectiveness of teacher leaders is constrained by lack of role definition (Smylie and Denny 1990) and by requiring them to take on responsibilities outside their areas of expertise (Little 1995).

Functions reported for teacher leaders in this literature created expectations about what we might find the functions of teacher leaders to be in our study.

Transformational leadership

As we discussed in Chapter 2, uncertainties about the specific purposes and practices associated with many restructuring initiatives and the importance attached to fundamental organizational change call for commitment-building forms of school leadership with a systemic focus. We have used this line of reasoning in our own efforts to clarify the nature, causes and consequences of a transformational model of leadership adapted for use in schools and described in previous chapters. What is most salient for this chapter about transformational leadership is the claim that it leads to higher levels of personal commitment to organizational goals and greater capacities for accomplishing those goals. This, in turn, is assumed to result in extra effort and greater productivity. Authority and influence are not necessarily allocated to those occupying formal administrative positions, although much of the transformational leadership literature adopts their perspective. Rather, power is attributed by organization members to whoever is able to inspire their commitments to collective aspirations, and the desire for personal and collective mastery over the capacities that are needed to accomplish such aspirations.

The model of transformational leadership developed from our own research in schools conceptualizes transformational leadership along eight dimensions: building school vision; establishing school goals; providing intellectual stimulation; offering individualized support; modelling best practices and important organizational values; demonstrating high performance expectations; creating a productive school culture; and developing structures to foster participation in school decisions. Further descriptions of these dimensions can be found in Chapters 2–6.

Most models of transformational leadership are flawed by their underrepresentation of transactional practices, which we interpret to be 'managerial' in nature, because such practices are fundamental to organizational stability. For this reason, we have added four management dimensions to our own model, based on a review of relevant literature (Duke and Leithwood 1994). These dimensions include staffing, instructional support, monitoring school activities and community focus.

Because this conception of leadership seemed especially productive in school contexts like the ones in which the study described in this chapter was carried out, we were curious about the extent to which teacher leadership reflected key managerial and transformational leadership practices typically associated with formal administrative leaders.

Leadership perceptions

A central premise for the design of this study is derived quite directly from the definition of leadership as an influence process. As Lord and Maher

(1993) argue, such influence depends on a person's behaviour being recognized as, and at least tacitly acknowledged to be, 'leadership' by others who thereby cast themselves into the role of followers. In Greenfield's (1995) terms, followers 'consent' to be led.

Lord and Maher (1993) offer a cognitive explanation for the judgements people make about whether or not someone is a leader. According to their account, salient information about people is processed in two possible ways. One way is to match that information to categories, or leadership prototypes (knowledge structures) already stored in long-term memory. This 'recognition' process on the part of the follower is triggered by observed or otherwise encountered information about the traits and behaviours of another person, who has the potential to be perceived as a leader. These observed traits and behaviours are compared with the traits and behaviours included in the relevant knowledge structure stored in the follower's long-term memory; his or her implicit or explicit leadership theory. Relatively high levels of correspondence between observed and stored traits and behaviours leads to the follower's perception of the other person as a leader.

Followers' assessments of correspondence may occur in a highly automatic fashion. This is likely in cognitively demanding, face-to-face encounters between followers and leaders, when speed and efficiency of processing are demanded by the complexity or sheer amount of information to be understood. Under cognitively less-demanding circumstances, such as prolonged opportunities to work with and observe someone, followers' assessments of correspondence may be more controlled, reflective and self-conscious.

Followers may also develop perceptions of leaders through 'inferential' processes. Such processes depend on the opportunity for followers to observe events in which the potential leader is involved, to assess the outcomes of those events and to draw conclusions about the contribution of the potential leader to those outcomes. Perceptions of persons as leaders result from followers' judgements that those events were somehow salient, that they had desirable results and that the potential leader was instrumental in bringing about those results. As with recognition processes, inferential processes may occur relatively automatically or through more controlled processes.

Recognition and inferential processes are not mutually exclusive and may occur in cycles. For example, one's initial leadership knowledge structures or prototypes are probably the result of inference processes applied through considerable social interaction in both a broad cultural context (outside schools) and the more specific contexts of those organizations in which one participates; schools in this case. Even relatively primitive leadership prototypes, once developed, are then available for use through recognition processes. And the leadership perceptions, formed initially through recognition, may be modified inferentially with opportunities to observe the leader's work.

Two recent studies using an adaptation of the Lord and Maher model (Jantzi and Leithwood 1996; Leithwood and Jantzi 1997) provide evidence concerning the factors that account for teachers' perceptions of transformational leadership among principals. These studies suggest that school conditions were the most powerful variables explaining teachers' leader perceptions. Described more fully below, these conditions encompass the school's mission, vision and goals; culture; programmes and instruction; policies and organization; decision-making structures; and resources. Visibly contributing to each of these categories of school conditions in ways that teachers find helpful is likely to be interpreted by teachers as a sign of transformational leadership. This interpretation seems likely whether the principal is: male or female; young or old; long or short serving in the school; and whether the school is small or large, elementary or secondary.

These results led us to enquire, in the study on which this chapter is based, about the extent to which perceptions of teacher leadership were influenced by factors similar to those that influence perceptions of transformational principal leadership.

School conditions or characteristics mediating leader effects on students

Most of the effects of school leadership on students are mediated by other characteristics of the school (Hallinger and Heck 1996). A significant challenge for both leadership practice and research is to identify those characteristics known to have direct effects on students and to inquire about the nature and strength of the relationship between them and leadership. This challenge had to be addressed in the quantitative portion of the present study because its purposes included estimating the effects of teacher leadership on the school and determining which aspects of the school were most influenced by such leadership.

The seven school-level (non-classroom) characteristics selected as mediating variables were identified through a previously conducted, far-ranging, review of literature concerning school and district effects (Leithwood and Aitken 1995). These features or sets of conditions emerged from the review as having important consequences for school effectiveness. They included: the school's mission and vision; school improvement planning processes; culture; structures for decision making; information collection and decision-making processes; policies and procedures; and school–community relations.

The relationship between formal and informal school leadership

There are likely to be significant differences between formal leaders and teacher leaders both on the issues each are in the best position to address and the strategies available to each for addressing these issues. In this section we describe the relationship between the leadership provided by teacher leaders and those in formal leadership roles, typically principals and vice-principals. We also describe characteristics of the school organization most likely to be influenced by those in formal leadership roles and by teacher leaders. More specifically, we ask which aspects of the school are influenced most by the leadership of teachers, and what is the relative influence on the school of principal leadership compared with teacher leadership.

To address both of these questions, data were provided through a survey conducted with all elementary and secondary teachers in one large school district (4456 teachers) in Ontario. Teachers were asked to rate school characteristics as well as the extent of influence from different sources of leadership in the school, for example, the principal, administrative team and informal teacher leaders. Responses were provided by about 60 per cent of the total teaching population in the district. Procedures used to analyse the data are described in detail in the original study (see Leithwood *et al.* 1997b).

Analysis of the survey responses indicated that teachers had a significant and at least moderately strong influence on all aspects of the school organization. Schools in which teachers were seen to provide more influential leadership were also schools perceived by teachers to be more effective and innovative. Teacher influence was most strongly related to school planning and school structure and organization (characteristics teachers perceived to be least well developed in their schools). A finding that may be somewhat surprising was the relatively weaker relationship between teacher influence and *school culture*; although the influence of teacher leaders was significantly related to a stronger culture, this relationship was weaker than the relationship of teacher influence with five other school characteristics, and only stronger than the relationship with two other characteristics.

Survey responses were also analysed to determine how much of the variation in teachers' perceptions of characteristics of effective and innovative schools was accounted for by the influence of teacher leaders compared with the influence of principals. The pattern for principals' influence is quite different from that for teachers' influence. Although for several characteristics teachers' influence and principals' influence account for similar proportions of the variance, for most characteristics the proportions are quite different, with more variance explained by the influence of principals.

The characteristics for which teacher influence accounted for the most variance were *school planning* and *structure and organization*. Not only were the variances most affected by the influence of teacher leaders, they were also two of the three characteristics for which the influence of principals had less effect than did that of teacher leaders. The explanatory patterns for school mission and school culture were almost identical: principal influence explained just over 20 per cent of the variation, and teacher influence explained about an additional 10 per cent.

Principals' influence was more strongly associated than teachers' influence with teachers' perceptions of the extent to which the leadership they experienced from all sources in the school was transformational in nature. Perceptions of transformational leadership practices explained 42 per cent of the variation in principals' leadership influence, compared with 33 per cent of the influence of teacher leaders. Similarly, principals' leadership influence was more strongly associated with perceptions of effective school management than was teacher leadership influence. These results suggest that school staffs tend to hold modestly different expectations for principal, as compared with teacher, leadership.

To summarize, the principal's leadership was more influential than the leadership exercised by teachers overall. But the leadership of teachers had a significant, independent influence on the school. Furthermore, these two sources of leadership had their greatest influence on partly overlapping aspects of the school. In the case of principals, the independent influence of their leadership was greatest on school improvement planning, school structure and organization, school mission and school culture. The independent effects of teacher leadership were felt most in respect to school improvement planning, and to school structure and organization. School staffs, according to these results, expect different forms of leadership to be exercised by principals and teachers and see such leadership affecting the school in different ways.

The nature of teacher leadership

Although a great deal is known about the types of leadership exercised by administrators, much less is known about the types of leadership likely to be productive for teachers. This section of the chapter describes the forms of teacher leadership valued by teachers. Also described in this section are the factors that account for teachers' perceptions of the leadership of their colleagues.

Data used to address these two matters were provided through a two-stage research process. In the first stage, teachers in six secondary schools undergoing major change initiatives were asked to name those people within their schools, exclusive of the principal and vice-principals, who provided leadership. One hundred and thirty-eight usable questionnaires were returned. Nominees were ranked by the number of nominations received, with those receiving the most nominations at the top of the list.

The second stage involved 40–60 minute interviews with a selection of 57 teachers, approximately ten from each of the six schools. These were teachers who had included among their own nominees at least one of the most frequently nominated leaders in their school. The interview asked each of these 57 teachers about the colleagues whom they had nominated as leaders: why they were viewed as leaders; what they did to provide leadership; and what it was about them that made them leaders. Although the focus for the interview was the three leaders nominated most frequently in each school, teachers were asked an identical set of questions about all of their own nominees. The interviews were audiotaped, transcribed and coded in relation to three categories of leadership qualities:

- Traits: unchanging, internalized characteristics;
- Practices: overt behaviours, functions, tasks and activities;
- Capacities: knowledge, skills and abilities.

Also coded were teachers' perceptions of the outcomes they associated with the exercise of leadership by their teacher colleagues.

Traits

Our data identified six categories of traits: mood, values, orientation to people, physical characteristics, responsibility and personality. Table 8.1 indicates the frequency with which each of these categories was mentioned.

The most frequently mentioned category, values, encompassed ten specific items mentioned from 5 to 73 times. Three of these ten qualities were the most frequently mentioned across all categories of traits. Being committed to one's school and profession was mentioned most frequently, followed closely by the holding of strong beliefs and being committed to the welfare of students. Other values included in this category were: commitment to the community; fairness; concern for the morality of decisions made in the school; commitment to family; being a 'good' person; being humane; and ignoring personal biases. There were virtually no differences among the six schools in the emphasis placed on values and the relative frequency of mention of specific values within this category.

The frequency with which personality characteristics were mentioned was second only to the frequency with which values were mentioned. Most mentioned in this category were openness, honesty and genuineness. Other personality traits identified were outspokenness, a pleasant but commanding presence and energy. Among the less frequently mentioned traits were creativity, humility, enthusiasm and confidence.

Orientation to people was the third most frequently mentioned category

Table 8.1 Leadership categories: dimensions ranked in order of frequency*

Traits		Practices		Capacities		Outcomes	
Values	240	Performs administrative tasks	239	Procedural knowledge	110	Gains respect of staff and students	121
Personality	225	Models valued practices	187	Declarative knowledge	101	Things are implemented well	75
Orientation to people	202	Formal leadership responsibilities	150	Relationships with staff	57	Staff looks to him/her for leadership	65
Mood	135	Supports the work of other staff	147	Problem solver	56	Enhances staff comfort level	52
Responsibility	98	Teaching responsibilities	114	Communication skills	53	Contributes to the culture of the school	45
Physical characteristics	10	Visible in the school	83	Relationships with students	47	Makes us want to emulate him/her	37
		Confronts issues directly/makes hard decisions	64	Visionary	27	Has good effect on students	36
		Shares leadership with others	46	Organized	26	Staff will listen	33
		Personal relationships	28	Self-knowledge	16	Meets high expectations	14
		Takes initiative	27	Global thinker	13		
		Leader	22	Competent	12		
				Focused	10		
				Sets limits on self	8		
				Efficient	7		
Total	910	Total	1107	Total	543	Total	478

* Numbers indicate the number of times each leadership dimension was mentioned by all 57 interviewees

of traits that teachers associated with leadership. This category included being non-confrontational, being caring, having sensitivity to others and having good interpersonal and communication skills. This category also included being supportive, approachable, a good listener and easy to work with, having understanding of others and being appreciative and discreet. Four people mentioned not being defensive as an important orientation to people in those considered to be leaders.

The fourth most frequently mentioned category of traits was mood. Included in this category were quietness, positiveness, having a sense of humour, and being even tempered. Less frequently mentioned were gentleness, not taking oneself too seriously and being serious.

Some aspect of being responsible was mentioned next in frequency. Among the six facets of responsibility mentioned by teachers, being a hard worker dominated in frequency of mention. Also mentioned were being steady and conscientious, having a sense of responsibility and being dependable. Being indispensable was mentioned twice.

Peoples' physical features, the final set of traits, were mentioned a total of ten times as relevant to their perceptions of leadership; in particular being tall, and dressing like a leader.

Practices

What teachers perceive leaders actually to be doing is our meaning of the term 'practices'. The functions, tasks and activities mentioned in the interviews were organized into 11 sub-categories. The most frequently mentioned of these was the performance of administrative tasks, such as working administrative periods in the office, being on committees and organizing specific events (for example running the commencement and spearheading the implementation of special courses).

Modelling valued practices was the next most frequently mentioned subcategory of practice. This included leading by example, interacting with students, being a motivator for staff and students and never missing a day of work. One teacher said, 'He sets the example that there are many teachers who have taught for a long time and who are excellent teachers'. Another said, 'He reminds us of our objectives'.

Formal leadership responsibilities were mentioned next in frequency. This set of practices reflects the number of times teachers were nominated as leaders because of their position; being a department head or being head of a particular committee. Supporting the work of other staff was mentioned almost as often as formal leadership; this referred to the help the teacher provided to his or her colleagues (for example, helps young teachers, helps with course outlines, helps with a difficult class) or the support given to staff (for example, 'kind of stroking people and saying you can do it', 'speaks out on our behalf whether we agree or disagree', 'allows people to vent').

The sub-category 'teaching responsibilities' was the fourth most frequently associated with leadership practices. Specific teaching practices (such as having lessons well prepared and being a good teacher) were mentioned often. Teachers felt that being visible in the school was an important dimension of leadership. Examples of this practice include presenting information at staff meetings, and being a leader in the school and not just in the department. Confronting issues directly, sharing leadership with others, personal relationships, taking initiative and simply 'leadership' were the last five sets of practices mentioned by the interviewees.

As with the values category, the frequency with which teachers mentioned these leadership practices were very similar across schools, except for teaching responsibilities: interviewees in one school mentioned this much more frequently than interviewees in the other five schools.

Capacities

Qualities in the category 'capacities', encompassing a leader's knowledge, skills and/or abilities, were mentioned much less frequently than qualities coded as either traits or practices. This category includes 14 sub-categories.

The most frequently mentioned capacities or skills were associated with 'procedural' and 'declarative' knowledge. Procedural knowledge refers to knowledge teachers have about how to carry out leadership tasks, for example, making tough decisions, knowing how to run a meeting and dealing with administration. As several teachers said, '[She] can put out fires without too much trouble'; '[He] knows how to handle a situation without implicating anyone else'; or '[She] knows how to evaluate our students, modify programmes, develop report cards'.

Declarative knowledge refers to knowledge about specific aspects of the profession; for example, knowledge about government education policy, knowledge about education in general; knowledge about the school, students and the community; knowledge about specific subjects; and knowledge about union issues.

Teachers' ability to work well with their colleagues, a valued category of leadership capacities, included statements about how a particular teacher can motivate staff, work effectively with others and be willing to moderate disagreements.

Being a good problem solver was also seen as an important leadership capacity. For example, one teacher said, '[She] can listen to a discussion and, in the end, filter it all down to what the real problems are'. Getting to the heart of the matter or being able to synthesize information was part of this sub-category. Dealing with difficulties well and being able to think things through are other examples of statements coded as problem-solving skills.

Having good communication skills was mentioned almost as frequently as problem solving. This dimension included being articulate and persuasive and having the capacity to relate well with students, in particular being able to motivate them and being able to understand them.

Other capacities identified by interviewees less frequently included being organized, being visionary, having self-knowledge, being a global thinker, being focused, being able to set limits on self and being efficient.

Perceived outcomes of teacher leadership

The outcomes perceived to be associated with leadership provide important clues about the basis for leader attributions under circumstances in which leadership is experienced long enough to draw inferences from leader effects on the organization. Outcomes of leadership identified by 'followers' tell us something about the needs people have that they hope leadership can meet.

Four hundred and seventy-eight statements were coded as nine different types of outcomes. Most frequently mentioned among different types of outcomes was gaining the respect of staff and students. Next most frequently identified as a leadership outcome was that activities involving the leader were invariably implemented well ('it went off very well', or 'things always work out in the end', or 'he and [T] have taken the track team to extreme heights'). The fact that staff look to a person for leadership was also a frequently mentioned outcome of leadership. Said one teacher, 'I think he's someone they would turn to if they were looking for avenues to proceed'. Also mentioned frequently as leadership outcomes were enhancing staff comfort level, and contributing to the culture of the school.

An additional set of outcomes was mentioned less often in the interviews. That people 'listen' to the leader was mentioned: 'when she speaks up, people listen'. A desire to emulate the leader was also mentioned: 'You're just saying, "hey, if I could be like that" '. Having a good effect on students and meeting high expectations are other types of outcomes mentioned.

Summary

Two purposes were served by this chapter. One purpose was to clarify the relationship between the formal leadership offered by those in school administrative positions and the leadership exercised by teachers. Evidence from a large-scale survey indicated that both principals and teachers had a significant influence on most aspects of the school organization but some aspects were typically influenced more by those in one role rather than another. The independent influence of teacher leaders was strongest (and stronger than the principals' influence) with respect to school improvement planning, and school structure and organization. Principal leadership exercised its strongest independent influence on school improvement planning and school structure and organization, as well as on school mission and school culture. Furthermore, teachers were more likely to associate their principals than their teacher-leader colleagues with effective management and transformational leadership.

The second purpose for the chapter was to clarify the nature of leadership exercised by those teachers perceived to be leaders by their teaching colleagues. Interview data painted a portrait of teacher leaders in terms of their traits, capacities and practices. Composite teacher leaders are strongly committed to their schools, the profession and the welfare of students. They have a positive orientation to their work, a sense of humour, and are warm, dependable and self-effacing. Teacher leaders are open and honest with their colleagues and students, and have well honed interpersonal and communication skills. In addition, they possess the technical and organizational skills required for programme improvement and use them in concert with a broad knowledge base about education policy, subject matter, the local community and the school's students. Armed with a realistic sense of what is possible, these people actively participate in the administrative and leadership work of the school. They are viewed as supportive of others' work and model those practices valued by the school.

Evidence summarized in the chapter reinforces some results of previous teacher leadership research. For example, teacher leaders were reported to stimulate the professional growth of their colleagues (Wasley 1991), and to contribute to an improvement in the school's decision-making processes (Malen *et al.* 1990). They were also perceived to share their expertise, volunteer for new projects, promote the school's mission and work towards school improvement (Smylie and Denny 1990; Harrison and Lembeck 1996).

Although less evidently than among principals, according to our interview data, teacher leaders' practices were perceived to reflect many aspects of transformational school leadership. Most often mentioned were practices encompassed by the dimension of transformational leadership labelled 'individualized support', a set of practices also included in many other leadership models (for example, situational leadership; see Fernandez and Vecchio 1997). In addition, teacher leaders provided their colleagues with 'intellectual stimulation', 'modelled best practices', and helped 'develop structures to foster participation in school decisions'. Some teachers noted that their leader colleagues were visionary, a dimension of most models of tranformational leadership. They also fostered extra effort on their part, a key goal of transformational leadership.

Perceptions of teacher leadership seem to be influenced primarily by the same variables that we found to be the most powerful influences on teachers' perceptions of principals' transformational leadership. For the most part, these variables were not demographic in nature. Neither gender, nor age, nor years of experience on the part of either the leader or teacher, for example, influenced teachers' leader perceptions. What was of most influence was the opportunity to work with the leader on projects of significance to the school and to see evidence of the value of this work to the school. Such direct experience of one's teacher colleagues' contribution to the school also appears to have shaped teachers' choices of colleagues to nominate as leaders.

Evidence from the study described in this chapter also suggests that colleagues' traits are important in forming teachers' perceptions of their leadership. Because our previous studies of teachers' perceptions of principal leadership did not collect data about traits, we cannot comment on whether principals' traits also influence teachers' perceptions of their leadership. But it seems plausible.

Implications for developing teacher leadership

In this concluding section of the chapter, we consider what those in administrative leader roles might do to further develop teacher leadership in their schools. Our primary focus is on informal teacher leadership, although much of what we suggest is also appropriate for the development of those assuming such formal teacher-leader roles as department head and lead teacher. The six implications identified in this section are based on the literature about teacher leadership reviewed at the beginning of the chapter, as well as on the results on the study described in this chapter.

Just enough clarification of roles (and no more)

One of the conditions (identified in the literature reviewed earlier) inhibiting the development and exercise of teacher leadership was lack of role definition (Smylie and Denny 1990). While this condition applies most obviously to formal teacher-leader roles, informal or temporary leadership roles (chairing a taskforce or leading a curriculum development committee, for example) may also be inhibited by this condition. So the implication for formal school leaders, in relation to both types of roles, is to work towards a level of clarity about duties and responsibilities that is suitable for the person assuming the role. Significant variation among teacher leaders in how much role definition is enough ought to be expected, however. Among other things, this variation is a product of teachers' earlier school leadership experiences, tolerance for ambiguity, professional goals and perceptions of colleagues' expectations. So clarifying the role is something that should be done in collaboration with the person assuming the role, in most cases.

In no case, however, should the role definition be so specific as to constrain the exercise of discretion in the role. Although teachers with little experience, for example, may benefit from relatively high degrees of clarity about their leadership duties and responsibilities at the outset, part of their development will entail the assumption of increased autonomy and discretion, and the provision of less external role specification. In a quite fundamental way, a 'well defined leadership role' is an oxymoron.

Gaining a realistic perspective on time

Also identified as a condition inhibiting the development and exercise of teacher leadership, in our summary of the teacher leadership literature, were inadequate overall amounts of time allocated to teacher leadership functions (Wasley 1991), and the use, for teacher leadership, of time that teachers felt they should be devoting to their students (Smylie and Denny 1990). The implications of this obstacle to developing teacher leaders are complex. Clearly it is important that formal school leaders be realistic about the time required for the job and attempt to allocate sufficient amounts. But it is probably just as important to help those new to leadership roles to appreciate the demands of these roles, and the inevitable infringement on what they may consider to be personal time. Formal school leaders, for example, work long hours, typically 50–55 hours a week, including many evenings and weekends.

It is probably also important to help teacher leaders learn how to manage their time outside the classroom, including limiting the number of leadership initiatives in which they become involved. Realistically, one significant leadership initiative at a time, in addition to a substantial teaching load, will place sufficient demands on a teacher's time to preclude comfortably assuming other initiatives. But as with role clarity, there is considerable individual variation among teachers in what they are able to manage. So formal school leaders should act as consultants to teachers as they work out a realistic leadership load for themselves, stressing the importance of having time to reflect on and learn from each of their leadership initiatives.

Creating training opportunities out of leadership tasks

Reflection about on-the-job leadership experiences is one of the most powerful strategies for overcoming lack of training for teacher leaders, an obstacle to their development that was identified in the literature reviewed earlier in this chapter. This claim receives strong support from a series of studies enquiring about the value of a variety of socialization activities experienced by aspiring school administrators (Leithwood *et al.* 1992a; Hamilton *et al.* 1996). Those in formal school-leaders' roles can assist in the training of teacher leaders most directly by providing such leadership opportunities and by participating with teacher leaders in guided reflection on the experiences these opportunities afford. Guided reflection may develop into more intensive coaching and mentoring relationships with teacher leaders, relationships that are themselves powerful tools for leadership development (Hart 1993).

Providing support for challenging leadership assignments

Each of these leadership development strategies begins to address another training-related obstacle identified in the literature concerning teacher leadership: assigning teacher leaders responsibilities outside their area of expertise (Little 1995). Without significant support, such assignments can have a debilitating effect on teacher leaders, undermining their sense of efficacy, reducing the likelihood of gaining satisfaction from their leadership experiences and eroding their motivation to further develop their leadership capacities. But it is precisely the effort required to meet the challenges of new leadership assignments that produces the greatest growth in leadership capacities. The implication is that the responsibilities of teacher leaders should not be restricted to challenges they have already mastered; they should be provided with novel leadership challenges, with support. Those in formal school-leader roles are often in the best position to provide such support.

Building a culture of collaboration

A frequently identified obstacle to the development of teacher leadership is the isolated professional culture common in schools, along with associated norms of egalitarianism, privacy, politeness and contrived collegiality (Sirotnik 1994; Griffin 1995). In the context of such cultures, teachers are unlikely to make use of the leadership capacities of their teacher colleagues to increase the individual and collective impact of their work on students. This means fewer opportunities for teachers to provide leadership to their colleagues, and little motivation for teachers to further develop their own leadership capacities. Such cultures present a significant challenge to formal school leaders in making the case with their staffs that teacher leadership would be a valuable addition to the school and ought to be further developed.

Truly collaborative cultures, in contrast, encourage the exchange of ideas and endorse mutual problem solving, thereby providing rich opportunities for the exercise of teacher leadership, and suitable motivation for potential teacher leaders to develop their capacities. Formal school leaders, then, are likely to develop teacher leadership as they develop more collaborative professional cultures in their schools. Furthermore, as we learned in this chapter, formal school leaders appear to be well positioned to exercise influence on the school's culture, at least from the perspective of teachers.

Research-based guidance about how to do this (for example Firestone and Wilson 1985; Rosenholtz 1989; Deal and Peterson 1990; Leithwood and Jantzi 1990) identifies at least five useful strategies:

1 Strengthen the typically 'weak' culture of the school. This is a culture in which there is little agreement with, or adherence to, common professional norms, values, beliefs and assumptions. This can be done by developing a sense of shared purpose (as discussed, for example, in Chapter 4). As we learned in this chapter, at least from the perspective of teachers, formal school leaders are in the best position to facilitate a sense of shared mission or purpose.

2 Use 'bureaucratic mechanisms'. For example, embed norms of sharing and mutual problem solving in the criteria used for teacher selection and evaluation procedures, and allocate teacher planning time to provide opportunities for mutual problem solving.

3 Create staff development opportunities that acknowledge what can be learned from one's immediate colleagues by engaging members of the school staff in the design and conduct of some of that staff development.

4 Use the many direct formal and informal communication opportunities available to formal school leaders to reinforce key cultural norms, values and expectations. This means that formal school leaders should talk a great deal to staff about the virtues of collaborative work and model such work in their approach to school administration.

5 Use symbols and rituals to support collaborative cultural values; for example by recognizing at staff meetings the collaborative work of groups of teachers and the positive outcomes of that work, and by providing positive feedback to individual teachers, thereby increasing their sense of professional self-efficacy, and along with it, their inclination to share their work with other teachers.

Selecting teachers who already have leadership qualities that are hard to develop

The primary purpose served by the interview data reported in this chapter was to clarify the nature of leadership exercised by those teachers viewed as leaders by their teaching colleagues. Results of these interviews were classified in terms of teacher-leader traits, capacities and practices. Some of the qualities emerging from these data are much easier to develop than others. As a general rule, it is safe to assume a higher probability of developing the practices and capacities identified by our interviewees, than the traits. And while all three categories of leadership attributes are important, our study suggests that teachers' perceptions of the leadership provided by their teacher colleagues is very strongly influenced by these traits.

This has important implications for expanding the teacher leadership available within a school. Formal school leaders are by no means the only influence on who is selected for teacher-leader roles in the school. This is especially the case when those roles are of an informal nature, or when self-selection is possible. But when formal school leaders are able to participate in determining the choice of people for teacher-leader roles, our study recommends a preference for teachers who already display the traits associated with teacher leaders from among those who display comparable levels of development with respect to practices and capacities.

nine

BUILDING TEACHERS' COMMITMENT TO CHANGE

I have found the last couple of years so many things have been going on and so many punches taken at teachers in the education system that people's morale has gone down. So we are not as interconnected as we used to be and I think it is because people are tired. Everybody is getting into the battle. Myself, I have often thought about leaving and going to a different school, a different environment again, but still as long as the government backs off a little bit I guess you can get back to your job.

(High School Teacher)

This chapter clarifies the meaning of 'teachers' commitment to change' and argues for its importance as a focus of attention for leadership in changing times. The roots of teachers' commitment to change are examined and the leadership practices that help to foster such commitment are identified. The chapter summarizes a series of four studies of school leadership and teachers' commitment to change carried out by ourselves and our students (Leithwood *et al.* 1994; Menzies 1995; Wolbers and Woudenberg 1995; Dannetta 1996). This chapter both broadens and deepens the meanings of 'individualized support' and 'modelling', two of the dimensions of transformational leadership discussed in Chapter 5. Our discussion in this chapter also demonstrates the interdependence of transformational practices – they are a 'whole cloth', even though, up to now, we have considered them one at a time.

Teacher commitment to change as a focus for school leaders

A focus on teacher commitment is consistent with the evolution of the change literature over the past twenty years. As Fullan describes it, this evolution began with a relatively narrow preoccupation with the implementation of single innovations, moved through a brief period of concern for how multiple innovations could be managed and on to questions about how 'the basic capacity to deal with change' (1992: 113) can be developed. This contemporary interest in capacity building acknowledges the continuous nature of demands for school change. It also reflects an appreciation for increases in the rates of change now expected of our educational institutions (for example Schlecty 1990).

Teacher commitment has been identified as a key aspect of a school's capacity for change through insights hard-wrung from the experience of innovation failure dating back to the 1960s. As MacDonald concludes, 'It is the quality of the teachers themselves and the nature of their commitment to change that determines the quality of teaching and the quality of school improvement' (1991: 3). Teacher commitment is a function, in part, of factors that are hard (if not impossible) to change – for example, teachers' age, gender and length of teaching experience (Kushman 1992). This is the bad news for those who would intervene to foster increased commitment. The good news is that other, more alterable factors also seem to influence significantly teachers' commitment including, for example, teachers' decision-making power in the school, parental involvement in the school and the school's climate (Smylie 1990).

Of particular interest in the series of studies summarized in this chapter was the influence of school leadership on teacher commitment to change – more specifically, the extent to which transformational forms of leadership contribute to such commitment. Empirical evidence, most of it collected in non-school organizations, has demonstrated the impact of such leadership on organizational members' willingness to exert extra effort (for example Crookall 1989; Seltzer and Bass 1990; Deluga 1991) and, most probably, on their sense of self-efficacy, as well (Shamir 1991). Both of these psychological states are closely related to commitment.

The meaning of teachers' commitment to change

Kushman (1992) contends that, although teacher commitment is central to school reform, it remains an inherently ambiguous concept about which we know very little. Commitment and the closely related concept of engagement are often viewed as different psychological states and several forms of each have been identified. Teachers, it is claimed, may demonstrate commitment to their schools (organizational commitment) as well as commitment to student learning. These are forms of commitment that may have different causes and consequences (Kushman 1992). Organizational commitment is typically thought to include a strong belief in the organization's goals and values, willingness to exert effort for the organization and a strong desire to remain a part of the organization (for example Reyes 1990). Definitions of commitment to student learning, on the other hand, typically encompass feelings of self-efficacy on the part of a teacher, expectations that students will learn and a willingness to devote needed effort to ensure such learning (Kushman 1992). Teacher engagement, Louis and Smith (1991) claim, encompasses engagement with the school as a social unit, with the academic goals of the school, with students and with the discipline or teaching assignment. These forms of engagement appear to fall within the two broader categories of organizational commitment and commitment to student learning.

Sources of teachers' commitment to change

Commitment and engagement may be conceptualized as elements of motivation, a more fundamental psychological state. Comprehensive theories of motivation, in particular those of Bandura (1986) and Ford (1992), predict most of the causes and consequences of teacher commitment and engagement identified in recent empirical research – and more. Motivational processes, according to Ford (1992), are qualities of a person oriented toward the future and aimed at helping the person to evaluate the need for change or action. These processes are a function of one's personal goals, beliefs about one's capacities, beliefs about one's context and emotional arousal processes. In the remainder of this section, we will consider each of these elements of motivation in more depth along with associated conditions likely to help foster teachers' commitment to change. Examples of how leaders might help provide teachers with these conditions are also briefly described.

Personal goals

Personal goals represent desired future states (aspirations, needs, wants) that have been internalized by an individual, for example, a teacher's desire for a manageable class. The term 'personal' is significant. School staffs set goals for their improvement efforts, for example. But such goals do not influence the actions of individual teachers and administrators until they make them their own. But goal-setting activities in schools often fail to accomplish this internalization. In such cases, the resulting goals have little meaning to teachers and often cannot be remembered even though they might appear prominently in written material about the school.

While personal goals are an important launching pad for motivation, they must be perceived by teachers to possess four qualities in order to actually energize action. First, goals energize action only when a person's evaluation of present circumstances indicates that it is different from the desired state. For example, a teacher who judges his class already to be well managed perceives no need to act or to change with respect to this goal. Clearly, the easiest way to avoid change is to set goals that are being accomplished already, an action (co-opting the change) not unheard of in the school improvement business (Berman and McLaughlin 1977). Second, personal goals are more likely to energize action if they are perceived to be hard but achievable. 'A more manageable class' would qualify on this count if the teacher's current class was regularly out of control for reasons the teacher believed she or he at least partly understood. Louis and Miles (1990) have reported increased likelihood of change in schools where the innovation is perceived to be challenging but 'do-able'.

Third, to energize action it also helps if goals are perceived to be clear and concrete: 'developing a more manageable class' is probably not as motivating as 'reducing the time wasted in making transitions from one activity to another'. This is the case because what teachers need to do is much more evident to them. The goal almost specifies the action to be taken. Finally, goals are more likely to be energizing when they are short term, but understood within the context of longer term and, perhaps more important, more obviously valuable goals ('this week I will try to keep the transition from reading to maths to under three minutes as a start toward a more manageable class'). As Ford points out, highly motivating goals often result from 'goal setting techniques that emphasize ... constant improvement toward explicitly defined goals that are more challenging than current levels of achievement or productivity, but also well within reach if effort and commitment are maintained' (1992: iii).

These energizing qualities of personal goals are independent of the specific content of those goals. And the number and nature of personal goals, in terms of content, is enormous (Ford identifies 24 categories of such goals). Such acknowledgement casts a different light on the two types of teacher commitment studied by Kushman (1992) and the four forms of teacher engagement described by Louis and Smith (1991). These types and forms of commitment and engagement can be viewed as different content goals. Construed in this way, it seems likely that teachers have many more types and forms of professional commitment and engagement than the empirical literature has so far enquired about. As a consequence, teachers may be committed to or engaged by many more aspects of their work environment than have been considered by relevant research to this point.

To sum up, motivational theory redefines the objects of teacher commitment and engagement (for example, to the school, to student learning, to one's discipline) as personal goals. It also identifies conditions that must prevail if such goals, or different forms of commitment and engagement, are to energize action toward school change. These conditions, an important focus of attention for school leaders, include:

1 Adoption, as personal goals, of at least a significant proportion of the goals adopted by the school's change initiatives. Commitment to such initiatives will depend, in part, on the teacher's perception of compatibility between personal goals and the school's goals for change. Louis and Smith (1991) identify such congruence as an indicator of the quality of work life influencing levels of teacher engagement with their work.
2 An appreciation by teachers of a significant gap between their current practices and those implied by the changes being proposed within their schools.
3 A perception, on the part of teachers, that participating in the school's change initiative is a significant but achievable challenge. Shedd and Bacharach (1991) argue that teaching provides intrinsic motivation under the restructuring initiatives that conceptualize teaching as a highly complex act and help teachers significantly expand their technical repertoires and their capacities to apply them reflectively and constructively. Contributing to the perception of a goal's achievability are opportunities to learn more about how the goal can be accomplished (Rosenholtz 1989; Reyes 1990; Kushman 1992).
4 A perception by teachers that they know, specifically and concretely, what they will need to do (or that such specificity can be developed) eventually, to implement changes being proposed for their school and classes. Rosenholtz (1989) and Shedd and Bacharach (1991) identify the importance of positive, constructive feedback to teachers as one means of meeting this condition.
5 A belief by teachers that they know the next manageable steps that need to be taken in their schools and classes eventually to accomplish the overall goals for change that their schools have set.

Related research has suggested that for organizational goals to become internalized by individual teachers, the following conditions also should be met:

1 Goal-setting processes should be highly participatory. Heald-Taylor (1991) found that when school goal-setting processes met this condition, teachers developed greater understanding of and commitment to school goals.
2 Goal-setting processes should be ongoing, with continuous efforts to

refine and clarify the goals yet to be accomplished. Leithwood *et al.* (1992b) found that such ongoing efforts kept school goals 'alive' in teachers' minds and contributed to a gradual increase in the meaningfulness of these goals for teachers.

We return to those conditions leading to harmonization of teachers' personal goals and the goals of the school, as a whole, later in the chapter. At that point, we will also describe leadership practices likely to be helpful for this purpose.

Capacity beliefs

Two sets of 'personal agency' beliefs (beliefs about one's own capacities) interact with teachers' personal goals to help determine the strength of motivation to achieve such goals. The first set, capacity beliefs, includes such psychological states as self-efficacy, self-confidence, academic self-concept and aspects of self-esteem. It is not enough that people have energizing goals in mind. They must also believe themselves capable of accomplishing these goals. Evidence reviewed by Bandura suggests that:

> People who see themselves as [capable or] efficacious set themselves challenges that enlist their interest and involvement in activities; they intensify their efforts when their performances fall short of their goals, make causal ascriptions for failures that support a success orientation, approach potentially threatening tasks non-anxiously, and experience little in the way of stress reactions in taxing situations. Such self-assured endeavor produces accomplishments.
>
> (Bandura 1986: 395)

Perceived capacity or self-efficacy increases the intrinsic value of effort and contributes to the possibilities for a sense of collective capability or efficacy on the part of a group, as well.

Teachers' beliefs about their own professional capacities are often eroded by taken-for-granted conditions of their work. These conditions include infrequent opportunities for teachers to receive feedback from credible colleagues about the quality of their practices as a consequence of isolated school cultures and ineffective supervisory practices (Rosenholtz 1989). Smylie's (1990) review of research on the consequences of teachers' beliefs about their own professional efficacy described significant relationships between such capacity beliefs and the effectiveness of classroom practices, student learning and the likelihood of engaging in classroom and school improvement initiatives.

Increased perceptions of capacity or self-efficacy may result from teachers considering information from three sources. The most influential source is their actual performance: specifically, perceptions of success perhaps formed through feedback from others. Success raises one's appraisal of one's efficacy, although such appraisals are shaped by the difficulty of the challenges one is facing, effort expended, amount of help received, and other circumstances. Teachers who actually try out new practices in their classrooms, with sufficient on-site assistance to ensure success, will possess this kind of information.

Vicarious experience, a second source, is often provided by role models. However, to have a positive effect on self-efficacy, models who are similar to or only slightly higher in ability provide the most informative, comparative information for judging one's own abilities. Further, observers benefit most from seeing models 'overcome their difficulties by determined effort rather than from observing facile performances by adept models' (Bandura 1986: 404). It is also likely to be more helpful, for example, for two teachers to work as a team on implementing cooperative learning strategies, than only to have an 'expert' demonstrate such strategies (such demonstrations might be especially helpful for the team part way through their struggles, however).

Finally, verbal persuasion – the expressed opinions of others about one's abilities – may enhance perceived self-efficacy. But for this to occur, persuaders must be viewed as relatively expert or at least credible judges of such expertise. A principal, vice-principal or department head can perform this role effectively when teachers believe them to be knowledgeable about the changes being proposed in their school. Such persuasion will often take the form of evaluative feedback.

Conditions likely to give rise to positive capacity beliefs on the part of teachers concerning change being initiated in their schools include:

- feelings of success in their initial efforts to implement those restructuring initiatives; these feelings may be enhanced by supportive feedback from administrators, peers and students (Smylie 1990);
- appropriate models for the new practices to be implemented;
- strong encouragement from credible colleagues about their ability to master the change initiatives; this is a part of one of the quality of work life indicators that Louis and Smith (1991) found to be associated with teacher engagement – frequent and stimulating interaction among one's teaching peers in the school.

An important influence on the level of a teacher's commitment to a goal for change, then, is the teacher's perception of whether they are capable of accomplishing the goal. Those in school leadership roles contribute to such feelings or beliefs, for example, to the extent that they provide credible feedback about efforts to accomplish such goals and create opportunities for other respected colleagues to do the same.

Context beliefs

A second set of personal agency beliefs are context beliefs. These are beliefs about whether, for example, 'the school administration or the central office will actually provide the money and professional development that I will need, as a teacher, to "destream" my grade 9 classes'. Many experienced teachers have developed negative or sceptical beliefs about aspects of the context in which they work over their careers. These beliefs arise as a consequence of being associated with mismanaged, ill conceived or short-lived initiatives for change (Huberman 1988; Fullan 1991).

A classic example of a short-lived policy initiative guaranteed to stimulate such negative beliefs occurred in the province of Ontario between 1993 and 1997. In 1993, persuaded by the substantial evidence that heterogeneous grouping of students generally carries advantages for most students, the government of the day legislated 'destreaming' of grade 9 classes from what, at the time, was a set of basic, general and advanced streams. Four years and one new government later – after often reluctant, but considerable efforts by teachers throughout the province to comply with this legislation – the policy was reversed.

Negative context beliefs arising from teachers' experiences with previously mismanaged, ill conceived, or short-term change initiatives, such as this one, may easily graft themselves on to teachers' perceptions of current change initiatives in their schools. When this happens, teachers' motivation to implement those initiatives is significantly reduced ('this too shall pass').

Conditions giving rise to positive context beliefs include:

1 Teachers' perceptions of an overall school culture and direction that is compatible with their personal goals and not overly controlling of what they do and when they do it (feelings of discretion). The contribution of autonomy and discretion to teachers' commitment is evident in studies by Louis and Smith (1991) and by Shedd and Bacharach (1991). Participatory forms of decision making are particularly powerful ways of exercising this discretion (Imber and Neidt 1990; Louis and Smith 1991; Shedd and Bacharach 1991; Chase 1992).

2 Teachers' perceptions that their working conditions permit them to accomplish their school's change initiative and that information is available to them about the expectations of relevant others (principals, superintendents), constraints on what is possible, policies or regulations that must be considered and the like. Rosenholtz's (1989) evidence points to 'teacher certainty' as an important contributor to commitment.

3 Teachers' perceptions that the human and material resources that they will need to achieve their goals for change are available (Louis and Smith 1991; Leithwood *et al.* 1992b).

4 Teachers' perceptions that the interpersonal climate of the school,

provided by leaders and teaching colleagues, is a supportive, caring and trusting one. Chase (1992), for example, found that teacher engagement was positively associated with staff collegiality and solidarity, as well as perceptions of administrators as caring and concerned for staff welfare.

To sum up, it is not enough for teachers to have goals compatible with their schools' change initiatives. Teachers must also believe that they are personally able to achieve those goals and that their school environments will provide the support that they require. School leaders have many opportunities to contribute to such beliefs. They can do this, for example, by encouraging teachers to participate in school decision making, allowing reasonable degrees of autonomy in implementing school decisions, ensuring that the material resources needed by teachers to implement such decisions are available and fostering a supportive interpersonal climate in the school.

Emotional arousal process

Emotions are relatively strong feelings that are often accompanied by some physical reaction (like a faster pulse rate) – satisfaction, happiness, love and fear, for example. These feelings have motivational value when they are associated with a personal goal that is currently influencing a person's actions. Positive emotions arise when an event promises to help meet a personal goal; negative emotions when chances of achieving one's goal are harmed or threatened.

Whereas capability and context beliefs are especially useful in making big decisions (for example, 'Should I actually try to use these new "benchmarks" in reporting my students' progress to their parents?'), emotions are better suited for the short term. Their main function is to create a state of 'action readiness', to stimulate immediate or vigorous action by reducing the salience of other competing issues or concerns; 'I'm so excited by the reaction of the students to journal keeping, which I just saw in the classroom next door, that I'm going to try it tomorrow'.

Emotions may also serve to maintain patterns of action. Indeed, this may be their most important function in relation to restructuring initiatives. As teachers engage from day to day in efforts to restructure, those efforts will be sustained by a positive emotional climate. Conditions supporting such a climate are likely to include:

- frequent positive feedback from parents and students about their experiences with the school's change initiatives;
- frequent positive feedback from one's teaching colleagues and other school leaders about one's success in achieving short-term goals associated with change initiatives; this might take the form of celebrations of success and contributions to the school's efforts, and it might also be a

function of frequent collaboration with other staff members on matters of curriculum and instruction;

- a dynamic and changing job.

In short, emotional arousal processes help teachers persist in attempting to accomplish long-range goals when evidence of progress is meagre. These processes also help maintain effective practices under less than favourable conditions. Those in school leadership roles can contribute to positive emotional arousal, for example, by passing on to teachers compliments overheard about their work, and by drawing teachers' attention to the value of practices in which they are engaged but may not consider to be anything special. School leaders can also create opportunities for teachers to work on new school or district curriculum and instructional projects in which they are likely to have a strong interest.

School leadership practices and teachers' commitment to change

In this section, evidence from our studies is summarized about the influence of school leadership practices on teachers' commitment to change, and the nature of the practices that account for such influence.

Framework and methods for the studies

Each of the four studies was guided more or less explicitly (more in the case of the quantitative studies, less in the qualitative studies), by a transformational approach to school leadership which assumed most of the dimensions of such leadership identified in Chapter 2, and explained more fully in Chapters 3–6. Prior theory and research suggested that each dimension of this form of leadership would contribute to the conditions fostering teacher commitment as follows:

Identifying and articulating a vision and fostering the acceptance of group goals

These first two dimensions of transformational leadership theoretically foster teachers' commitment, primarily through their influence on personal goals: for example, encouraging the personal adoption of organizational goals and increasing goal clarity and the perception of such goals as challenging but achievable. The inspirational nature of a vision for the school may also foster emotional arousal processes, whereas the promotion of cooperative goals may positively influence teachers' context beliefs.

Providing individualized support

This dimension seems likely to influence context beliefs, assuring teachers that the problems they are likely to encounter while changing their practices will be taken seriously by those in leadership roles and efforts will be made to help them through those problems.

Intellectual stimulation

Such stimulation seems likely to draw teachers' attention to discrepancies between current and desired practices and to understand the truly challenging nature of school restructuring goals. To the extent that such stimulation creates perceptions of a dynamic and changing job for teachers, it should also enhance emotional arousal processes.

Providing an appropriate model

This leadership dimension is aimed at enhancing teachers' beliefs about their own capacities; their sense of self-efficacy. Secondarily, such modelling may contribute to emotional arousal processes by creating perceptions of a dynamic and changing job.

High performance expectations

Expectations of this sort help teachers see the challenging nature of the goals being pursued in their school. They may also sharpen teachers' perceptions of the gap between what the school aspires to and what is presently being accomplished. Done well, expressions of high expectations should also result in perceptions among teachers that what is being expected is also feasible.

Contingent reward

Traditional conceptions of transformational leadership (for example Burns 1978) consider this dimension to be 'transactional' in nature. But the possibility of providing informative feedback about performance in order to enhance teachers' capacity beliefs, as well as emotional arousal processes, makes this set of practices potentially transforming too. Furthermore, some studies have found contingent reward to be just as strongly associated with enhanced commitment, effort, and job satisfaction as are other dimensions of transformational leadership (Singer 1985; Spangler and Braiotta 1990).

Two of the five studies summarized in this chapter (Leithwood *et al.* 1994; Wolbers and Woudenberg 1995) explicitly viewed the effects of leadership on teachers' commitment to be mediated by, or interact with, conditions found within the school and the wider environment in which the school is located. Some of these conditions and the wide ranging review of literature that was their source have been mentioned in earlier chapters (see, for example, Chapter 8).

At the school level, these conditions included school goals, school culture, school programmes and instruction, school policy and organization and school resources. Beyond the school, we incorporated into our studies initiatives by ministries of education, school districts and local school communities.

Those interested in the details of the research methods used in the four studies will want to read our original reports. Only a brief summary is provided here.

Two studies were quantitative in nature, involving samples of teachers in two Canadian provinces: 534 primary-grade teachers from 77 schools in British Columbia, in the case of Wolbers and Woudenberg (1995), and 168 secondary school teachers in nine secondary schools in one large district in Ontario, in the case of Leithwood *et al.* (1994). The remaining two studies used qualitative methods. Menzies (1995) collected interview data from a total of 18 teachers in three community colleges in Ontario. Dannetta's (1996) data were provided through interviews with 15 'career' secondary school teachers (20 or more years teaching experience with no intention of moving to administrative roles) from three schools in one school district in Ontario. Survey results from the quantitative studies were analysed using simple descriptive statistics as well as path analysis. Interview data were transcribed and content analysed. Taken together, these four studies provided answers to three questions.

Question 1: How much variation in teachers' commitment to change is explained by the effects of in-school and out-of-school conditions and school leadership?

The simplest answer to this question, provided by our two quantitative studies, is about 40 per cent. Alterable variables not included in the studies (for example, school size), unalterable variables (for example, gender, age) and measurement error probably account for the remaining 60 per cent. Menzies's (1995) finding that the commitment of community college teachers varied by age, gender and length of experience helps to identify what some of those unalterable variables might be.

The studies provided a more complex version of this answer, however. When sources of teacher commitment (personal goals, capacity and context beliefs, and emotional arousal processes) are examined separately, it appears that the alterable variables in our framework (leadership, in-school, and out-of-school conditions) still account for about 40 per cent of the variation in teachers' personal goals. But personal goals have very strong direct effects on context beliefs and weaker but significant effects on capacity beliefs. This more complex answer to the first question recommends that school leaders give primary attention to teachers' personal goals and their harmonization with school goals in efforts to foster teachers' commitment to changes in the school necessary to the accomplishment of those goals.

Question 2: What is the relative influence of transformational school leadership on the sources of teachers' commitment to change, as compared with other potential influences?

Evidence from our two quantitative studies provided the simplest answer to this question. The total effects of transformational leadership are marginally but consistently greater than the total effects of in-school and out-of-school conditions. This is the case when sources of commitment are treated as a composite (or single) variable, as well as when the four sources are considered separately.

Our two qualitative studies also provide relevant evidence in response to this question. Dannetta (1996) found that among the 15 influences on their commitment identified by teachers, seven were directly or indirectly impacted by the actions of those in formal leadership roles (for example, workplace conditions, struggles with priorities, opportunities for professional growth, participation in decision making). With his findings as a whole in mind, Dannetta concluded that 'there were as many factors that influenced teacher commitment over which the principal had control, as there were ones over which the teacher had control' (1996: 91). Department heads were also an important influence on teachers' commitment in this study. Community college teachers interviewed by Menzies (1995) identified those in immediate leadership roles as having sometimes positive and sometime negative influences on their commitment. But in either case the influence was a strong one.

It seems reasonable to conclude from this evidence that what those in leadership roles do may well be the single greatest influence on the sources of teachers' commitment to change. Furthermore, transformational leadership practices have an important positive influence on those sources of commitment. This conclusion is consistent with evidence reported by Tarter *et al.* (1989), who found that the leadership of the principal (not conceptualized as transformational) explained a third of the variance in teachers' organizational commitment.

So among those influences on the sources of teachers' commitment to change measured in our studies, school leadership, in general, and transformational school leadership, in particular, is 'the winner by a neck'. An important additional finding is that the effects of school leadership are both indirect and direct, the direct effects acting primarily through teachers' personal goals.

Question 3: What is the relative contribution to teachers' commitment of different types of leadership practices?

From the perspective of transformational leadership practices, 'providing models' and 'individualized support' were the only two categories of practice apparently making no contribution to teachers' commitment in our two quantitative studies. Three dimensions of transformational leadership did have significant total effects on teachers' commitment. These were the three direction-setting dimensions, building a vision for the school, developing consensus about school goals, and demonstrating high performance expectations. These results add support to the importance we attached earlier to personal goals.

Summary and conclusion

Teachers' commitment to change was conceptualized in this chapter as a function of teachers' personal goals, their context and capacity beliefs and emotional arousal processes. This motivation-based conception of commitment overlaps with, but is importantly different from, the meanings typically associated with organizational commitment, commitment to student learning, teacher engagement and teacher job satisfaction. These distinctions are not trivial. For example, there is some evidence of an inverse relationship between organizational commitment and commitment to change on the part of private-sector managers (Stevens *et al.* 1978). At least conceptually, then, commitment to change ought to be a more powerful predictor of teachers' responses to school change initiatives than these other psychological states, which, although intuitively and semantically similar, give rise to quite different behaviours.

Our studies of influences on teachers' commitment to change took into account not only leadership but also conditions inside and outside the school that might affect teachers' commitment. Each of these categories of conditions appeared to exercise a significant influence on teachers' commitment. But especially strong as influences were the direction-setting dimensions of leadership: building shared vision; creating consensus about school goals; and demonstrating high performance expectations. These dimensions of leadership made their greatest contribution to the motivational conditions associated with teachers' personal goals; such goal-related conditions, in turn, were significantly related to teachers' context and capacity beliefs.

This pattern of results seems to be consistent with self-concept based explanations of transformational leadership. Shamir argues that 'such leaders increase the intrinsic value of effort and goals by linking them to valued aspects of the followers' self-concept, thus harnessing the motivational forces of self-expression, self-consistency, specific mission-related self-efficacy, generalized self-esteem and self-worth' (1991: 92).

While the implications of these results are most obvious for school-level leaders, there are significant implications for district-level leaders, as well. Teachers' commitment to change is subtly but significantly influenced by district-level conditions. Given such effects, it seems important for those outside the school, primarily district staff, to consider, as an important part of their work, directly fostering those conditions in the school associated with teachers' commitment. An inspiring district mission, developed with the advice of all district stakeholder groups, for example, is likely to provide a useful point of departure for staffs in clarifying goals for themselves and their schools. A collaborative district culture is likely to make it much easier for school staffs to move toward a more collaborative school culture, creating, in turn, context beliefs supportive of school restructuring initiatives. Firestone and Rosenblum (1988) identified the provision of adequate buildings, curriculum materials and curriculum alignment as district conditions also likely to foster what the present study viewed as positive, teacher context beliefs.

It seems evident, as well, that district staff have an important contribution to make towards the development of those aspects of transformational school leadership that are commitment building for teachers; for example, providing opportunities for principals to learn about how to create compelling school visions with their staffs and how to develop staff consensus around specific goals for school restructuring. Less obviously, district staffs might also allow themselves to be more visibly influenced in their directions and actions by school leaders; the data of Tarter *et al.* (1989) demonstrated that principals foster teacher commitment only when their influence with superordinates is perceived by teachers to be high.

ten

CREATING THE CONDITIONS FOR GROWTH IN TEACHERS' PROFESSIONAL KNOWLEDGE AND SKILL

Almost all school reform and restructuring initiatives assume the need for significant changes in classroom practice. Some of these initiatives are quite explicit about what the nature of such changes ought to be; teaching for understanding, heterogeneous student grouping and authentic assessment are common examples. Other initiatives, site-based management principal among them, are explicit about the changes to be made in the organization surrounding the classroom. Within the context of such changes, it is assumed that improvements (unspecified at the outset) in classroom practices will be stimulated, although in unpredictable ways. Whether implicit or explicit, these changes in classroom practices invariably require additional knowledge and skill on the part of teachers.

The nature of such knowledge and skill is easier to identify and typically more restricted in nature when the classroom changes associated with school restructuring are explicit. New practices specified in a curriculum framework, or as a set of curriculum standards, for example, will usually require primarily 'how to' or procedural knowledge on the part of teachers. This is so whether the detailed nature of the change has been well specified or, as is more often the case, considerable additional specification remains to be worked out by those implementing the change. It is still the 'how to' that is being further developed. And the development of procedural knowledge focuses attention on the individual teacher's mastery of new practices in school contexts. How formal school leaders can create conditions that facilitate such mastery is the theme of this chapter. It deepens, beyond what has been reported to date, the meaning of 'intellectual stimulation', in particular, a dimension of transformational leadership discussed in Chapter 5, and shows how this dimension intersects with other important leadership practices.

When classroom changes to be made are discretionary at the outset, and determined through group or whole-school decision making, the knowledge and skill required of teachers is much broader in scope. Eventually, teachers need to develop the kind of procedural knowledge already alluded to in relation to the classroom practice they choose to implement. But the route to such knowledge is through significant deliberations with others about 'what' needs to be done and 'why' it is important. Deliberations about what and why focus attention not only on individual mastery but also on the group or the team and how collective learning among teachers occurs and can be supported. This is the focus of Chapter 11.

Development of individual teachers' capacities in a school context

Clarifying the problem

The jobs of formal school leaders with significant administrative responsibilities are typically described as hectic, fast paced and unpredictable. It is probably unrealistic, as a consequence, to expect them to create carefully planned and independent, 'formal' conditions for teacher development in their schools. None the less, the most meaningful forms of teacher development are fostered most directly and powerfully by conditions unlikely to be found outside the school (Louis and Kruse 1995). Few schools, however, seem able to provide such conditions in the absence of leadership initiative (Rosenholtz 1989). Teacher development, it would seem, is between the proverbial rock and a hard place.

How can formal school leaders realistically support individual teachers as they attempt to further develop their professional knowledge and skill? In this section we argue that one powerful answer to this question is to encourage teacher participation in well conceived school-improvement processes. Such processes not only create conditions for teacher development, they also distribute those conditions broadly throughout the school's social organization. In particular, it is this broad distribution of teacher-development conditions that makes such development a manageable challenge for formal school leaders; it is also what makes their contributions highly significant. Evidence used in support of this argument is from research reported in more detail in Leithwood *et al.* (1991b).

Conditions for teacher development

Learning and acting are interestingly indistinct, learning being a continuous, life-long process resulting from acting in situations.

(Brown *et al.* 1989: 33)

Why is the context created by participation in a well conceived school-improvement process likely to contribute significantly to teacher development? Our argument, in brief, is this. The work of teachers is accomplished through 'practical thinking', a type of thinking embedded in activity. The learning required for teachers to further develop their practical thinking is usefully conceptualized as 'situated cognition' (Lave and Wenger 1994). Situated cognition requires teachers to be immersed in authentic, non-routine professional activity embedded in a supportive school culture. Participation in well conceived school-improvement processes provides such authentic, non-routine activity and a supportive culture.

Among the most promising efforts to understand and improve teaching are those that conceptualize it as problem solving within a specialized field of practice (for example Berliner 1988; Kagan 1988; Scardamalia and Bereiter 1989). For experienced, expert practitioners, such problem solving draws on a large repertoire of previously acquired knowledge. This knowledge is applied automatically to routine problems and, through reflection, in unique patterns, which appropriately acknowledge the demands of more complex, novel and/or unstructured problems. In contrast to the emphasis devoted to problem-solving *processes* in Chapter 7, with respect to administrators, this chapter focuses on the domain-specific knowledge critical to problem-solving expertise, in this case with respect to teachers.

Everyday thinking or practical thinking are terms used to portray the mental processes engaged in by experienced expert practitioners in any real-life context, such as teaching, as they apply their knowledge in the solving of problems. Such processes are 'embedded in the larger, purposive activities and functions to achieve the goals of those activities' (Scribner 1986). Those goals, which may be short term or long term in nature, are achieved given the actual facts of the situation as the practitioner discovers them (Wagner and Sternberg 1986). People's past knowledge is of considerable use to them when they are engaged in practical thinking in order to solve real-life problems.

Scribner (1984) has identified five components of expert practical thinking. Expert practical thinkers, for example, demonstrate a capacity to:

- formulate problems within a 'situation' that can be handled using well developed, reliable solutions;
- respond flexibly to similar problems, using different patterns of their existing repertoire in order to fine-tune a solution to the occasion;
- exploit (positively) the social, symbolic and/or physical environment as a way of reducing the cognitive demands placed on the individual for solving the problem;
- find the most economical solutions (those requiring least effort) that are, nevertheless, effective;

- make extensive use of their existing task- and situation-specific knowledge for problem solving.

Expert, practical problem solving depends on ready access to an extensive repertoire of problem-relevant knowledge. Such knowledge is about what actions to take to solve the problem as well as the social and physical context in which the problem is embedded; it is also about the larger set of activities – procedures and processes – enveloping efforts to address individual problems (Mehan 1984). As Bransford (1993) notes, then, this knowledge required for practical problem solving is conditionalized; it includes information about the conditions and constraints of its use, much of which is tacit (Sternberg and Caruso 1985). This is what is meant when the cognitions of expert, practical problem solvers are referred to as 'situated'. Useful, robust knowledge for practical problem solving does not consist of self-sufficient, abstract concepts. Rather such knowledge is partly constructed from 'the culture and the activities in which the concept has been developed' (Brown *et al.* 1989: 33). Furthermore, such knowledge is accessed and used in ways that take advantage of the environment to help solve the problem. So, teachers' situated knowledge, for example, 'connects teaching events with particular environmental features such as classrooms, time of year, individual people, physical surroundings, specific pages of text and more abstract subject matter knowledge' (Leinhardt 1988: 147).

If the knowledge required for expert, practical problem solving is situated, as we have described, what general conditions give rise to its acquisition? These conditions include participation with others in authentic, non-routine activities. The contribution of active participation in developing robust, useful knowledge is evident in the analogy of concepts as tools (Brown *et al.* 1989). Concepts, like tools, can only be fully understood through experience with their use and the refined appreciations (including tacit knowledge) that occur as a result of feedback from such use.

Participation with others, especially members of the field of practice, teaching in this case, who are more expert in some areas, substantially extends the potential for individual development. Explanations for this effect began, most notably with Vygotsky's (1978) conception of a zone of proximal development. He argued that processes involved in social interaction are eventually taken over and internalized by a person to form individual cognitive processes. Hence, participation with others in addressing a problem that demonstrates processes more sophisticated than those possessed by the individual potentially stimulates growth in the individual's problem-solving capacity. This is likely, at least:

- when group processes are at a challenging but comfortable level of sophistication beyond the individual;
- when the group process adjusts the difficulty of tasks for individual

members so that they are manageable for those members (Mehan 1984; Rogoff and Lave 1984; Wertsch *et al.* 1984);

• when there are opportunities for individuals to reflect on differences between their own processes and those used by the group.

For useful, robust, situated knowledge to develop most readily, participation with others must also be an activity that is authentic – circumstances that involve the ordinary activities of whatever the culture is within which the practitioner works (for example, classroom teaching). Authentic activities are embedded in the social and physical context that must be accounted for in problem solving and so must be represented in the knowledge structures stored by the practitioner. Knowledge for problem solving will be readily accessible, as Sternberg and Caruso (1985) argue, to the extent that the cues needed at the time of access were encoded (or acquired or learned) when the knowledge was originally being stored.

Finally, the authentic activities in which teachers participate must also be non-routine if they are to contribute to further development; furthermore, teachers must be assisted in reflecting critically on these activities. As Greene explains, 'The cycles of routine that the rhythms of institutional life seem to require lead practitioners to reconstruct each day in its own image, making it difficult to step back, and to look, even briefly, with the eyes of a stranger' (cited in Rudduck 1988: 206). Non-routine, in this sense, does not necessarily mean novel, although it may. It means looking at one's usual practices through fresh eyes; developing a capacity, as Rudduck (1988) argues, for the kind of 'constructive discontent' with one's existing practices that will fuel the motivation for professional learning.

Studies of leadership and teacher development

To accomplish the main purposes of the chapter, data were extracted from two, more comprehensive, studies of policy implementation and school improvement: one conducted in Ontario (Leithwood and Jantzi 1990), and the other in British Columbia (Leithwood *et al.* 1993b).

The Ontario study was initially carried out in 12 schools (nine elementary and three secondary) selected as exemplary with respect to their school-improvement processes through a two-stage process that we will not detail here. Each of these schools was then visited by two researchers for two days. The principals and all staff involved in the improvement effort (on average, 11 people) were interviewed during this time. Based on findings from the interviews, a survey was prepared and distributed to the staffs of an additional 37 schools associated with a school-improvement project sponsored by the Ministry of Education; but we will not report these data here.

Whereas the Ontario study involved schools, each of which had identified its own focus for school improvement, all schools in the BC study were attempting to implement a portion of the province's *Year 2000* (British Columbia Ministry of Education 1989) policy called the Primary Program. Among other things, this programme attempted to restructure the first four years of schooling by instituting means for continuous student progress and a constructivist view of learning with its attendant implications for instruction. More authentic forms of student monitoring, parents as partners in instruction and a bundle of other innovations consistent with the same philosophical thrust are also part of the Primary Program.

Twelve schools (four in each of three districts), which had volunteered to be early implementors of the Primary Program, or 'lead schools' as they were called, were included in the study. Both interview and survey data similar to that collected in Ontario were also collected in these schools.

An illustration of teacher capacity development in a school-improvement context

A case study from the Ontario study is used in this section to illustrate how teacher development can be supported by formal school leaders in a school-improvement context. Southern Ontario Elementary School (SOES) is a kindergarten to grade 6 school with about 400 students and 27 staff members offering programmes in both English and French. The school is located in a small town with a relatively stable population. Many of the teachers, particularly in the English programme, had grown up in the town and returned there to teach. The students were characterized by some teachers as 'top and bottom, very little middle ground with about two-thirds at the lower end'.

The school-improvement effort at SOES was initiated by the principal a few months after being assigned to the school. The principal was an administrator who exhibited many of the qualities we have associated with transformational leadership. A desire to improve student achievement and student self-esteem as well as a belief that planned change was necessary to achieve such goals provided the rationale for the principal's initiation of the change process within the school. She was influenced in this decision by her experience as a member of a district taskforce of nine principals that had been established to review current research on effective schools. This taskforce demonstrated the district's support for school improvement efforts aimed at building more effective schools. The initiative at SOES appears to have been an indirect result of the district's priority in this area, rather than a response to a specific board directive.

The principal was familiar with the school because she had visited it numerous times during her five years as a primary and special-education consultant. After being appointed to the school in February, the principal spent five months talking to parents, staff and trustees to ensure that she was thoroughly informed about the school and its needs. At the conclusion of this needs assessment she 'thought it was really important for us to get together to talk about what we truly believed and valued and why we were all here'.

The principal was able to use her staff development fund to take the entire staff, including support staff, for a two-day retreat late in June to work out a school mission statement. A district consultant was invited to act as the facilitator for the retreat. According to one staff member, 'we broke into four groups and we asked how we would get to life-long learning. Then we pooled our responses and crossed out things that were repetitive or the whole group couldn't support. We got it down to four statements. We almost had it set when one teacher said it didn't do it for him, so we went at it again and now it's good.'

In September there was another meeting at which the statement was reviewed and reaffirmed. Sub-goals for each of the four components of the mission were developed to form the school growth plan. According to the principal, 'any serious decision making comes back to the mission statement'. Because of the process used to develop the mission statement, staff members had a sense of ownership, perceiving the statement to be their own and not something imposed upon them by external policy. As one staff member pointed out, 'before the retreat someone from the district office had come and talked two or three times about effective schools, but the goals for our school were set by our staff'.

Committees were set up within the school to respond to the mission statement and growth plan. The Positive Environment Committee, which was established to develop the code of behaviour in consultation with teachers, students and parents, was one of the most active committees. Also established were social and assembly committees that had ongoing responsibilities for planning events. The Computer Committee was responsible for providing resources and in-service to all staff. There did not appear to be one single committee responsible for coordinating the school-improvement effort; the principal and to some extent the vice-principal coordinated the effort and delegated tasks and responsibilities as appropriate. The mission statement provided the rationale for all activities within the school, including the development of new teaching strategies to complement its goals.

The staff agreed that the principal was the key leader in supporting and guiding staff throughout the process, a good example of the vision-building practices associated with transformational leadership: 'She sets the pace, sees the whole process, sees where we are and keeps us going on it'; 'She's the overall leader, helped if you needed it, got funding . . . you can go talk to her if you're feeling low and think it isn't working'. The principal was successful in obtaining additional funding to provide resources for teachers in the form of professional development activities as well as equipment and supplies for classrooms. According to the principal, 'most of the extra money from the taskforce went into planning time, which was where the teachers wanted to spend the money'. During the first year, before funds were available for supply teachers, she and the vice-principal took students to the gym for activity sessions so the teachers could have more in-school planning time, thereby 'structuring' the school in ways we associated with transformational leadership in Chapter 6. She also booked time to go into the classrooms to monitor what was happening and to be helpful, one means of providing the individualized support associated with transformational leadership in Chapter 5.

The principal was very conscious of encouraging staff members to develop their interests and leadership potential and then to share out-of-school learning experiences with their colleagues; a form of 'intellectual stimulation', as we described it in Chapter 5. She saw herself as 'a people developer, with the role of developing the staff professionally and providing the wherewithal so they can [develop]'. The principal used her own expertise in learning styles to provide workshops in that area for the staff. She was also aware of the need to maintain staff morale by providing recognition for work being done, a form of 'contingent reward'. For example, each staff meeting began with 'good news' about something she'd seen in a classroom or that someone else wanted to share. At the end of the year there was an event at which they would look back at their accomplishments and celebrate what they had achieved that year. Achievements were mentioned in the school newsletter. This kind of recognition was also given to students at assemblies and during all-school announcements.

Staff development was a priority for the school-improvement effort. During the first year there were workshops on learning styles, some of which were provided by the principal, as noted earlier, who had considerable expertise in the area. Over the next two years, workshops were also held on peer coaching, classroom management and use of computers. At the time of the study, cooperative learning strategies were the focus for staff development, with most of the expertise provided by one of the teachers, who had been given release time to participate in a board in-service programme with the expectation that the knowledge gained would be shared. External personnel also came into the school to help with staff development. District consultants came on a number of occasions to work with the teachers around planning and new teaching strategies; 'The language consultant came in once with every grade team, about five or six visits. She was great and took the units we'd planned back to the board office where they were typed up. It gives you a clean copy and they share the units with other schools.' All respondents referred to direct contact with at least one consultant around the change effort, and it is clear that these consultants, in addition to the principal, were viewed as sources of individualized support and intellectual stimulation.

Teachers were also provided with materials to help implement new teaching strategies. Professional readings were shared with staff, often by the principal, to increase their understanding of effective schools research (more intellectual stimulation). Money was spent on providing tape recorders and manipulative materials for hands-on learning. Perhaps the most significant expenditure, at least from the teachers' point of view, was the money allocated for supply teachers to provide release time for team planning; 'We were provided with supply teachers during the day for team planning; we get a half day at the start and it's an incentive to keep going'.

The principal used a staff decision-making model, involving staff in all decisions that affected them directly. Collaboration among staff was promoted through the use of team planning, particularly within grade levels where colleagues assumed responsibility for the planning and preparation of learning packages. According to the principal, teamwork was a focus before the year began; 'the timetable was set up so people can plan together. We meet as teams to look at each child and learning styles and try to set up classrooms to match. We work as a team together.' The staff appeared to provide mutual support throughout implementation of the growth plan as a result of working on these teams. They grew to be comfortable with asking for help, evaluating their own work on an ongoing basis and sharing their experiences: 'My colleagues are really good. When I was on the grade 1 team – teaching grade 1 for the first time – the team took me under their wing, for example, they'd leave work in my mail box. They're not hoarders . . . In our team planning we all took a share; there was no leader except the consultant. We all pulled our weight'; 'it brought the staff together, there was a lot of sharing'. The committee work also fostered collaborative decision making within the school. We see here one avenue through which the 'culture-building' dimension of transformational leadership can be exercised.

Collaborative decision making also included students, particularly when developing the behaviour code. The school had a mascot, 'Little SOES', who was used to develop a sense of community in the school. Assemblies were used to recognize student achievement and to provide them with an opportunity to develop public-speaking skills for the purpose of enhancing their self-esteem. Students of all ages participated in the daily announcements; for example, they could read their favourite 'joke of the day'. Another way of involving students was through the introduction of safety patrols.

The principal made a concerted effort to improve the relationship with the community by involving parents in developing the discipline code and surveying the community about the school growth plan, an aspect of leadership discussed in Chapter 6. A booklet describing school programmes was prepared and distributed after the survey indicated that parents did not know what was being taught. A special meeting had been held to introduce the mission statement and goals to the parents. Opportunities were provided for parent learning, for example, a workshop on learning styles was given to parents and another was planned for April of the research year. Parents were involved in fund-raising for the school and had formed a parent group to support the school programme.

The school-improvement effort was not without problems. There appeared to have been some frustrations in the early stages as they were trying 'to get everyone on board' – 'in getting agreement among all staff there's a fine line between doing this to death and doing an effective job'. Some felt pressured by the number of initiatives and the lack of time to be properly trained. Said one teacher, 'There were so many elements . . . too much . . . you need to stay focussed and not do too many things and become too stretched to be as effective as possible'. Even though there was release time for team planning some staff members still felt lack of planning time was a problem. 'This takes a lot of sheer energy; if you're going to do it well, it takes untold hours,' commented another teacher.

Some respondents identified frustrations related to the number of children in the school with learning problems and the long time it took to get help: 'There's a problem with teaching to learning styles because when we find children with problems it's three or four months before the specific testing is done and this is after parents have signed forms and they get concerned. The paper backlog is a county-wide problem.' It is likely that this would have been a problem even if there were no school-improvement effort. However, the use of new teaching strategies that included focusing more on individual students' needs may have highlighted a problem that did not have a solution at the school level.

The collaborative decision-making and colleague support system that was part of the process appeared to be a factor in reducing anxiety and preventing it from derailing the initiatives. As one teacher noted, 'I feel free to express my point of view if something isn't working, it's a non-threatening administration . . . People in this school really say what they think, it really amazed me at first but it's worthwhile to do that. It helps to go back to the drawing board to check out what's happening and whether we really intended that.' When some teachers felt overwhelmed with the learning styles concepts in the early stages the principal broke implementation into stages, beginning with activity packages one year and multi-sensory kits the next.

The respondents identified a number of outcomes from the improvement effort. The initiative further strengthened staff relationships and put the administration closer to the classroom. Teachers were working together more and students were more positive in their relationship with staff. Teachers were responsible for sharing information about students with each other. 'There's more sharing and communication among teachers about students, their needs, progress and problems. More teachers are aware of student problems and styles that will make a difference.' Through working together teachers were developing consistency around learning styles and the behaviour code, although there were still some concerns expressed about the code not being applied consistently.

There was some recognition of the efforts at SOES from people external to the school. More visits were made to the school by senior administrators, community members and people from other schools. Changes in the school programme were reflected in more positive attitudes of students towards school and greater student involvement in the classroom.

Importantly for this chapter, the teachers felt that their own knowledge increased; they had developed a repertoire of teaching strategies, although a few teachers felt the shift in emphasis had reinforced the way they had been teaching for some time. There was an attempt to meet individual needs of the students by sharing information and trying to identify the learning style of the student to place the student in an appropriate setting. Teachers felt more willing to try new things. 'I now use different groupings and not as much whole group,' observed one staff member. 'I use centres and have more awareness of using all the senses in my teaching.' 'Students can lie on the carpet to read a book; five years ago I would never have done that but now I'm comfortable with that.' 'I always grouped but the manner in which I group now is cooperative . . . We're now focused on both the social and academic goals whereas before we didn't instruct in the social area.'

The school improvement effort allowed for professional growth at all levels according to those interviewed. Individuals learned and applied new strategies to the classroom, providing new experiences for the students. 'Before the change there was support for individual initiatives but now there is stretching, pulling and nudging,' claimed a teacher. Staff generally were more motivated to learn through attending workshops and reading. A few teachers gave workshops and received recognition for their increased expertise.

The process of developing the mission statement and school growth plan resulted in a widely shared sense of purpose with common goals. The mission statement became the basis for school policies and programmes and, through the school growth plan, brought about a range of new instructional practices within the classrooms.

School improvement and teacher development

The case of SOES, one of 24 developed in our Ontario and BC research, was selected for this chapter because it illustrates especially clearly, and also in a representative way, how participation in a well conceived school-improvement process contributes to teacher development, especially in the presence of a transformational principal. Such participation:

1 Provides for *active engagement* of teachers in practical problem solving: in the SOES case, for example, such engagement was a product of involvement in all categories of decisions about the purposes and means for school improvement.

2 Ensures that new practices are introduced at a *challenging but comfortable pace*: comfortable because teachers, not external change agents, controlled the pace in a way that made sense to them (for example, practices related to learning styles were implemented in stages over several years); challenging because decisions about pace belonged to the group. Few individuals could remain immune to the pressure from peers to change at a reasonable pace.

3 Ensures that the activities in which teachers are engaged are *authentic*: in the SOES case, teachers shared with the principal the task of determining the school's mission, identifying priorities for action and developing strategies to address these priorities. Clearly, changes in teacher practices associated with the school-improvement effort stemmed from teachers' views of what was important to do for the school.

4 Engages teachers in *non-routine* problems: for example, the staff retreat in June for the purpose of developing a mission statement for SOES caused teachers to look at their school through fresh eyes.

5 Creates a *supportive school culture* for teacher development: this manifests itself in SOES for example, in the form of grade-level team planning, timetabling to allow teachers to meet, and extensive teacher sharing of experiences and instructional materials.

Leadership and teacher development: looking across the cases

The SOES case illustrates well many conditions that foster teacher development and some of the leadership initiatives that facilitate these conditions. To determine more comprehensively how school leaders foster teacher development we used data about such leadership from all 12 schools involved in our Ontario study, SOES among them. Figure 10.1 was developed from our interview data as a way of helping to explain how both transformational and transactional leadership practices, as they have been described in earlier chapters, stimulate teacher development in a school-improvement context.

There are three indirect paths from transformational leadership practices to teacher development activities. Two of these paths include provision of the monetary or other types of resources (release time, consultants, materials and the like) required to support teacher development activities. The third indirect path reflects the importance of the school leader attending to the development of a supportive school culture. Elements of such a culture include cohesiveness among staff, collegial support and collaborative decision making. In the 12 Ontario cases, these elements emerged directly from the efforts of school-improvement teams, who had been delegated considerable leadership authority and responsibility by the principal. Sometimes principals were part of these teams but they were rarely the chairs.

Teacher commitment was strongly linked both directly and indirectly (through school culture) to teacher development activities. In three of the 12 case schools, one transactional leadership practice, in particular, contributed to this commitment: offering teachers not committed to the schools' improvement efforts the chance to transfer to another school and replacing these teachers with those who were committed.

Summary and conclusion

The evidence reviewed in this chapter suggest that school leadership initiatives can contribute significantly to teacher development. This is the case when school leaders:

- ensure that adequate financial, time, personnel, materials and other resources necessary to support teacher development activities are available;
- provide opportunities for teachers to develop a shared view of the school's overall mission and more specific goals to which they are strongly committed;
- help teachers assess their own needs for growth and gain access to sources of assistance inside or outside the school;
- foster the development of a collaborative school culture within which opportunities exist for authentic participation in decision making about school-improvement efforts and meaningful interaction with colleagues about collective purposes and how to achieve them;
- build feelings of self-efficacy by recognizing teachers' accomplishments and by providing support to help reduce anxiety about tackling new initiatives;
- share or distribute the responsibility for teacher development broadly

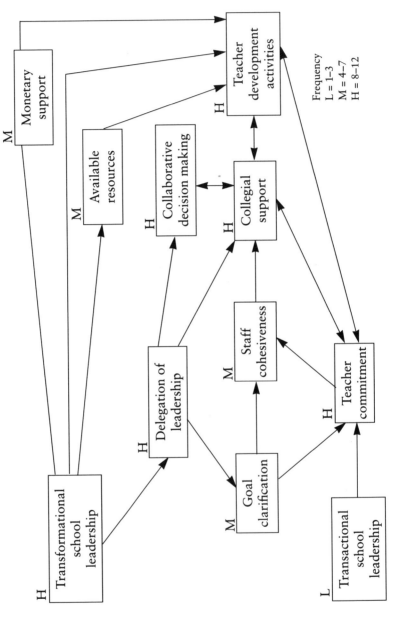

Figure 10.1 The variables and relationships linking administrators' actions and teacher development activities

throughout the school – for example, to teachers' colleagues, to teachers themselves, to external people who may be assisting in the school-improvement effort, and to the school-improvement initiative in which teachers are engaged.

Teachers typically claim that on-the-job learning is the most valuable source of their own professional development (Leithwood *et al.* 1992c; Hamilton *et al.* 1996). We have tried to explain in this chapter why this claim should not be surprising. Teachers, we have argued, accomplish their work through practical thinking and problem solving. The learning required to further develop such practical thinking is usefully conceptualized as situated cognition; this is learning that occurs through active engagement in authentic, non-routine tasks or problems within a supportive school culture. Evidence suggests that such problem-centred learning accounts for the bulk of adult learning (Knowles 1980; Brookfield 1984), not only the learning of teachers.

Participation in well conceived school-improvement processes, we argued further, offers especially fertile opportunities for the development of teachers' situated cognitions. Such processes stimulate more reflection on existing practices than is typical, present more novel problems to be addressed and often create new resources that can be used to support teacher development. Well conceived school-improvement processes also stimulate the creation of increasingly collaborative school cultures thereby making more accessible, to individual teachers, the expertise of their colleagues. Perhaps most importantly, well conceived school-improvement processes clarify school purposes, sharpen the priorities for collaborative action in the school and, in the process, enhance teachers' commitment to a set of shared goals. Case-study data summarized in this chapter illustrated how these conditions for teacher development manifested themselves in one school involved in a sustained improvement effort.

Conditions most likely to foster teacher development in the school do not emerge without substantial effort. While many formal school leaders would argue that the everyday demands of their jobs preclude such effort, we believe the opposite to be the case. Their close participation in the daily routines of school life and ongoing interactions with teachers about changes required for school improvement offer optimum opportunities for contributing to teacher development (Barth 1981; Dwyer 1984; Leithwood 1990). Some school administrators seem unable or unwilling to use these opportunities. Others are not only able and willing but, as Reid's (1991) evidence suggests, view teacher development as their central function. Indeed, the most intriguing result of Reid's study with 16 teachers and four principals who held this view was that 'in every instance of on-the-job learning described by teacher participants, there is principal involvement' (1991: 508).

This will come as a great surprise to many teachers and principals. Evidence summarized in this chapter identifies specific initiatives that school leaders can take to foster teacher development within a school-improvement context. These initiatives, we claimed, are part of a transformational orientation to school leadership. While evidence from our Ontario and BC studies gives weight to the value of some transformational dimensions of leadership for school improvement, transactional leadership practices are probably more important than they appear to be in these studies, largely because of limitations in our data. Like Deal and Peterson (1991), for example, we believe that well conceived school-improvement efforts are well managed; to use their terms, leaders of such efforts attend to both the instrumental (rational, managerial, technical) and symbolic (cultural, expressive) aspects of leadership. In fact, based on some clues in our own evidence we take this proposition a step further, particularly, as it concerns teacher development. Leaders who foster such development through school-improvement processes don't just attend to both transformational (or symbolic) and transactional (or instrumental) tasks; they use instrumental tasks for transformational purposes. This means helping teachers to find meaning in, and learn from, tasks situated in school-improvement processes that might otherwise be viewed as only instrumental, and perhaps mundane or unremarkable. Our own model of transformational school leadership awards less importance than does much current literature to organizational rituals, ceremonies and other events designed specifically for symbolic purposes. Empirical evidence in support of their contribution to organizations is surprisingly shaky. Because they do not directly serve school-improvement functions, these events may be viewed by many teachers not only as nonauthentic but as a trivialization of both school-improvement goals and teachers' professional commitment to working toward those goals. As a minimum, it seems evident that the same leadership practices are interpreted quite differently by their recipients (Yammarino and Bass 1990).

This chapter has deepened, beyond what has been reported to date, the meaning of 'intellectual stimulation', a dimension of transformational leadership discussed in Chapter 5. Also evident in this chapter is the interaction between this and most other dimensions of such leadership.

eleven

LEADERSHIP FOR ORGANIZATIONAL LEARNING

As a species, birds have great potential to learn, but there are important differences among them. Titmice . . . for example, move in flocks and mix freely, while robins live in well-defined parts of the garden and for the most part communicate antagonistically across the borders of their territories. Virtually all the titmice in the UK quickly learned how to pierce the seals of milk bottles left at doorsteps. But robins as a group will never learn to do this (though individual birds may) because their capacity for institutional learning is low; one bird's knowledge does not spread.

(de Gues 1996: 99)

Organizational learning (OL) is a multi-level phenomenon. It takes place in many different organizational 'units'. At one end of this continuum is the individual who learns within the context of the organization, the focus of Chapter 10. At the other end is the collective learning of the whole organization. In the midpoint of these extremes is the small group or team, with variations on these discrete units ranging from dyads of organizational members to multiple groups. Understanding the learning that occurs within these different units of the organization, and how to foster it, is a vital matter if we are to better appreciate what is entailed in successful school restructuring.

Whole-school learning is an especially critical matter as district-level organizations are weakened, eliminated or allocated less central roles in directing the activities of schools. And within schools, groups, committees, teams and taskforces are increasingly allocated the responsibility for thinking on behalf of the organization as a whole (Kasl *et al.* 1997). This heightened significance is due, in part, to the widespread adoption of site-based management, a key element of the restructuring agenda in many juris-dictions (Mohrman *et al.* 1994; Murphy and Beck 1995). Such groups, it is claimed, are more apt to represent the range of interests in a school than is an individual. They may produce more creative solutions than an individual, and their members and associates are more likely to understand and support decisions made through participation in such decisions. Communication is also likely to improve among members when they are meeting together regu-larly. Team participation is believed to be a valuable developmental experi-ence (Brightman 1988; Eisenstat and Cohen 1991).

After an explanation of how collective learning might be understood, this chapter explores, at both the small group and whole organization levels, the conditions that foster or inhibit its development, and how leaders can assist in providing conditions that enhance such learning.

Sources of evidence

Our account of collective learning processes is based on relevant theoretical literature. However, our accounts of leadership and other conditions that foster collective learning draw on evidence from seven studies carried out by ourselves and our students. Four of these studies were about team learning and leadership, and three were about whole-school learning and leadership.

Team learning studies

One of our four studies of team learning (Leithwood *et al.* 1997) was based on group data as well as a survey, and was carried out with six teams in five secondary schools. The three remaining studies of team learning examined the problem-solving processes of both male and female educational leaders while working with staff groups. A variety of data were collected in advance of each study to ensure that those included were exercising transformational forms of leadership. One study was with elementary school principals (Leithwood and Steinbach 1991), one with superintendents (Leithwood *et al.* 1993d) and one with secondary school principals (Steinbach *et al.* 1996).

Whole-school learning studies

Each of our three studies inquiring about organizational learning in schools as a whole (Leithwood *et al.* 1995; Leonard 1996; Sharratt 1996) was guided by the same framework of ideas, used qualitative, multi case-study data, and analysed these data in comparable ways. However, both geo-graphical location and educational context were quite different across the three studies. One of the studies (Leithwood *et al.* 1995) was carried out in the Canadian province of British Columbia in the context of schools responding to the province's comprehensive Year 2000 school restructuring policy (British Columbia Ministry of Education 1989). A second of these studies occurred in the Canadian province of Newfoundland (Leonard 1996), with schools that were part of a pilot project concerned with local school councils. The third study (Sharratt 1996) was in schools located in one large school district in south-central Ontario (also a Canadian province) and was part of an experiment in technology integration. Both interview and survey data were collected, in the three studies as a whole, from a total of 111 teachers in 14 schools.

Collective learning processes

Collective learning is not just the sum of individual learning even though individual learning is a necessary part of collective learning. Nevertheless, most accounts of collective learning assume that it is either literally or meta-phorically very similar to individual learning. In these accounts, cognitive explanations of individual learning are used to represent the nature of collective or organizational learning (OL) processes (for example Hedberg 1981; Gioia 1986; Cohen 1996; Cohen and Bacdayan 1996).

The metaphorical use of individual cognitive process to explain OL has added considerably to our understanding of collective learning. An obvious example of such use is Morgan's (1986) image of organizations as brains; a more subtle use is Cohen and Bacdayan's (1996) analysis of organizational routines as if they were individual procedural memories. Such evidence notwithstanding, it is important to be clear on the limitations of this approach. As Cook and Yanow (1996) enquire, why should two things so different in other ways as individuals and organizations be expected to carry out the same processes in order to learn? Additionally, cognitive conceptions of individual learning are very much under development and, in many respects, contested. Although they have contributed a good deal to an appreciation of how learning occurs among individuals, they cannot be adopted uncritically, even as metaphors, for insights about OL.

For the concept of organizational learning to be viable, it is useful to have a concept of a collective mind that is doing the learning, even if such mind is not the seat of cognitive activity. Wegner suggests that:

[collective] mind may take the form of cognitive interdependence focused around memory processes . . . people in close relationships enact a single transactive memory system, complete with differentiated responsibility for remembering different portions of common experience.

> People know locations rather than the details of common events and rely
> on one another to contribute missing details that cue their own retrieval.
> (cited in Weick and Roberts 1996: 332)

According to this explanation, only individuals can contribute to a collective mind and only the minds of individuals can be conceptualized as a set
of internalized processes controlled by a brain. Collective mind must be an
external representation; mind as activity rather than mind as entity. The collective mind, then, is to be found in patterns of behaviour that range from
'intelligent' to 'stupid'.

Collective learning develops from the actions of individuals as those individuals begin to act in ways heedful of the 'imagined requirements of joint
action' (Weick and Roberts 1996: 338). These requirements might be implied
in the organization's culture (Cook and Yanow 1996). But they could also
include more immediate and explicit demands on joint action. Schoenfeld
(1989), Hutchins (1991) and March (1991) describe the type of learning in
which individual members of groups engage in 'mutual adaptation', an essentially connectionist view of individual learning applied to the collective.

Mutual adaptation can be of two sorts. One sort is largely unreflective.
For example, in the case of Hutchins' (1991) navigation team, when individual team members confronted a change in what they believed was
required of the whole team, each of the members adapted their usual contribution to the team as best they could, hoping that other members would be
able to do whatever else was required. This was implicit negotiation of the
division of labour. When it seemed not to be sufficient as a response to the
team's new challenge, individual members then attempted to recruit others
to take on part of what was assumed to be the individual member's part of
the team's job, a second form of mutual adaptation.

In the case of Schoenfeld's (1989) research team, the task was to construct
a coherent explanation for a set of data about a student's mathematical
learning processes. Individual members or subgroups of the whole team
typically constructed their own explanations of the data set first. Then they
shared these explanations and engaged in some form of interaction, which
often produced a shared explanation significantly different than any of the
individual member's or subgroup's explanations. Schoenfeld describes the
process as follows:

> Let the subgroups be A and B, the idea [original explanation] in its old
> form X1, and in its improved form X2. The schema [process] goes as
> follows:
>
> - A either ignores or rejects X1 (so X1 would remain as it is);
> - B considers X1 important (but is unlikely to produce X2);
> - In group interactions, B convinces A to seriously consider X1;

- A suggests the change from X1 to X2, which the group ratifies;

Hence the group produces the change from X1 to X2, while neither subgroup A [n]or B would have done so by itself.

(Schoenfeld 1989: 74)

In both the Hutchins and Schoenfeld examples, an imagined new challenge for the team serves as the stimulus for individual team members to adapt their contributions to the team's actions. In this way, the individual is contributing to the learning of the team. As other team members adapt their contributions not only in response to their sense of the team's new challenge but also in response to the responses of other members, each team member learns about the adequacy of her initial response and perhaps the need to adapt further. This is the way in which the individual learns from the team. And, as Schoenfeld explains, 'the result of the group interactions extended significantly beyond the "natural" sum of the contributions that could have been made individually by the people involved' (1989: 76).

This theoretical account of OL processes provides background for understanding the main focus of the chapter – leadership and other conditions that foster and inhibit these learning processes.

Conditions influencing small-group learning

In this section, we review a selected body of literature about the conditions influencing small-group learning by way of background, and then describe the results of our own research.

Background

Much of what prior research has contributed to our understanding about conditions fostering group learning is summed up in a framework developed by Neck and Manz (1994). Their efforts to explain effective group learning take, as a point of departure, research concerning a form of dysfunctional group behaviour that Janis (1983) labelled 'groupthink'. According to Neck and Manz, learning on the part of a group is directly influenced by the nature of the group's leadership, as well as by a set of conditions for learning that grow out of the group's collective culture, something that leadership may also influence. The outcome of such learning (as described in the earlier section of this chapter explaining collective learning processes) is a pattern of action. This may be a change from an earlier pattern, or continuation of an existing pattern after, for example, carefully weighing alternatives and finding that current patterns remain a sufficient response to the stimulus prompting the group's thinking.

Defining the outcome of a group's work as a pattern of actions begs the question, however, of how to judge the effectiveness of that action, a critical question for most people concerned about group learning in schools. Hackman (1991) and his colleagues offer one response to this question. They define group effectiveness along three dimensions, each of which can be measured in a variety of ways. These dimensions include: the degree to which the group's products (decisions, actions and the like) meet the standards of quality, quantity and timeliness of group's 'clients'; the degree to which the process of carrying out the work of the group enhances the capacity of the members to work together interdependently in the future; and the degree to which the group experience contributes to the growth and personal well-being of its individual members.

Patterns of action are the direct result of interrelationships among the individual cognitions of group members, characterized earlier as mutual adaptation. Based on their consideration of groupthink, Neck and Manz (1994) suggest that these adaptive processes are most effective when the conditions for group learning include: encouragement of divergent views; open expression of concerns and ideas; awareness of limitations and threats to the work of the team; recognition of members' uniqueness; and discussion of collective doubts.

The extent to which such conditions are manifest depends on three aspects of the group's culture, in the Neck and Manz framework. One aspect is the dominant attitudes held by the group's members towards the team's work; the belief, for example, that problems are opportunities to overcome challenges rather than obstacles that will lead to failure. That these attitudes have an important effect on the group's thinking is also supported by evidence from studies of expert group problem-solving processes (Leithwood and Steinbach 1995).

A second aspect of team culture influencing collective learning is team 'self-talk'. For both individuals and groups, it has been suggested that self-talk can serve as a tool for self-influence, directed at improving the personal effectiveness of members (Weick 1979; Janis 1983; Neck and Manz 1994). Such talk may be aimed at putting social pressure on team members deviating from the group, as is the case in instances of groupthink. However, group self-talk may also focus on the importance of what Senge (1990) refers to as personal mastery – efforts by each team member to continuously improve the individual capacities they contribute to the collective effort. This seems likely to have quite positive effects on team learning.

Group vision is the final aspect of team culture having a bearing on group learning. This vision provides a relatively coherent sense of the group's overall purpose as well as its more immediate goals. When the vision is widely shared and understood it may become a primary resource for the group in determining what it needs to learn. More tacit and deeply imbedded assumptions about purpose and mission appear to be the main source of members' understanding of the group's vision (Leithwood *et al.* 1995).

Conditions within the group that foster learning

Informed by this background, one of our studies inquired about conditions influencing the collective learning of six groups of teachers, variously labelled as committees, taskforces and teams, in five secondary schools (Leithwood *et al.* 1997d). Results of this study support the importance of many of the conditions identified above, are silent on others and add some conditions not mentioned in the background literature.

The six groups sorted themselves into two main categories based on the presence or absence of conditions identified in the background literature as fostering or inhibiting group learning. Groups A, B and C experienced conditions that could eventually lead to groupthink, a type of faulty decision making that could prevent them from meeting their goals. We refer to them as 'low potential' groups. Groups D, E and F, on the other hand, mainly experienced conditions likely to foster their collective learning. They were, in our terms, 'high potential' groups.

Low potential groups A and B each had a shared purpose, whereas group C did not. Group A did not *encourage divergent views*, group B did so but moderately and group C did more so than even 'high potential' groups D and E. However, for groups B and C the only positive instances of divergent points of view being encouraged occurred during the interview for our study, when members were observed openly disagreeing with each other. It was much the same for *open expression of ideas*, with the positive scores of groups B and C mainly reflecting direct observations of members openly expressing their opinions during the interview or else replying to direct questions about how open they were. However, the following comment from one group member is more indicative of how that group typically operated: 'I think we spend more time avoiding hurting the other person or avoiding conflict with the other person, than actually having it'.

The *awareness of limitations* condition for group learning 'involves a realistic appraisal of difficult situations that leads to the necessary preparation and application of skills to overcome existing challenges' (Neck and Manz 1994: 939). Being aware of limitations is a necessary condition of group learning, but only if those limitations are acknowledged by group members and they are not completely debilitating. Too many perceived limitations might also be counterproductive. Group A mentioned very few limitations, whereas groups B and C mentioned many and the interviews conducted for the study appear to have been the first opportunities that group members had to give voice to those limitations.

Members of group A *interacted* a great deal while members of groups B and C did not. One member of group B said, for example, 'I don't think we, as a group, handle conflict that well. I think we take it to the back room all the time . . . we don't sit here and talk it out; we go to our own colleagues . . . instead of sorting it out together.' Similarly, a member of group C noted, 'I think we all want the best for the school, but I don't know whether we have been able to share exactly what our feelings are . . . I've never talked outside of the meeting to anybody about what's going on in our meetings.'

Whereas group A had too much *autonomy*, it was not mentioned by group B and group C felt they had none at all. In spite of only one explicit comment, group A appeared to have very *high morale*. There were no indicators of morale for group B and evidence from group C showed very low morale. All three teams complained about the lack of *time* to meet.

The extent to which the teams experienced *cohesiveness* was manifested by evidence of shared beliefs (for example, 'We're very unselfish about time'), shared culture (for example, 'I guess we're very pragmatic people') and agreement among members during the interview. According to Neck and Manz, 'the primary antecedent condition necessary for groupthink is a moderately or highly cohesive group' (1994: 932). Janis (1983) has argued that 'the more amiability and *esprit de corps* among the members of an in-group . . . the greater the danger that independent critical thinking will be replaced by groupthink' (quoted in Neck and Manz 1994: 932). This was the defining feature of group A. They were friends who saw each other constantly, and were motivated by the same goals.

Some forms of cohesiveness are desirable and necessary for team learning, however, while others are destructive. Group norms that promote constructive thinking are valuable. Group norms that create 'pressure towards consensus' (Neck and Manz 1994: 943) can lead to groupthink. All of the high potential teams exhibited substantial amounts of cohesiveness. While members maintained their separate identities, they shared certain beliefs and values that helped them work together successfully. They were all committed to the task at hand, and they all wanted the best for the school.

Whereas group A was too cohesive, team B was not cohesive enough. As one member noted, 'there's four or five camps officially or unofficially and they swing around on the issues and stuff like that'. These members also contended that their differences had been a source of conflict.

Group C provided an example of shared beliefs that were counterproductive. They were joined by common feelings of distrust, discontent and dissatisfaction, much of which was directed towards the school's administration.

There was no *discussion of collective doubts* by group A, limited evidence of such discussion for B, and ample evidence for C (but only during the data collection interview).

Group structure was relaxed and flexible for group A, which was also notable as being the only team in the school that did not have an administrator as a member. Group B membership included all staff with positions of responsibility, but there was lack of continuity because those positions were temporary. There was lack of continuity for group C as well, and its members met every two or three weeks. Members of group C were not all volunteers.

This study found support for many of the conditions reported in prior research to both foster and inhibit group learning. It also found evidence of a number of additional conditions that seemed important in the context of the work being carried out by the six teams. The three low-potential teams illustrated how the absence of just some of these conditions seriously threatened their effectiveness. In contrast, the high-potential teams reflected all of the conditions fostering group learning.

From this evidence, conditions fostering group learning include:

- shared and clearly understood purposes for the group's work among its members, giving rise to a sense of cohesiveness;
- encouragement of the expression of divergent points of view;
- open expression of ideas by individual members during group meetings;
- awareness and explicit acknowledgement of limitations in the group's knowledge and skill for the purposes it is attempting to accomplish;
- intense and reasonably frequent interaction among members of the group;
- balanced autonomy – enough to enable the group to act in a way that its deliberations suggest is effective, but not so much that the group does not consider the views of those for whom it is working and serving;
- high levels of morale within the group;
- enough time to meet as a group;
- discussion of collective doubts;
- relaxed and flexible group structure.

Evidence about conditions external to the group that foster learning

The same study providing the data reported above also enquired about conditions external to the team that influenced group learning. Relatively few such conditions were reported. Group members felt that the school district, Ministry of Education and Training and the local school community, for example, did not positively influence their learning. Most of the negative influences on learning were attributed to lack of adequate resources, or the turbulent environment created by the ministry. Groups had mixed feelings about the influence of school conditions on their learning. Perceived as positive influences were staff support, school growth and shared beliefs.

Negative influences included staff resentment, apathy, suspicion and isolation. Lack of resources and teacher burnout were other negative influences.

Leadership for small group learning

Our description of how transformational leaders solve problems with staff groups is organized around the six components of a problem-solving model. These components, emerging from our efforts to make conceptual sense of the data we have collected about both individual and group problem solving, were discussed in much more detail in Chapter 7.

Data were collected in all three of our problem-solving studies through 'stimulated recall' interviews, in which the leader audiotaped a committee meeting called to address a school or district change initiative chosen earlier as an issue that was a high priority for the committee. Following the committee meeting, leaders were interviewed about what they were thinking at various points during the meeting, using the tape of the meeting to aid their memory. Both the leaders and the interviewer stopped the tape frequently to ask questions or to offer information about intentions and thought processes.

Problem interpretation

This component of problem solving is about a leader's understanding of specifically what the nature of the problem is, often in situations in which multiple problems may be identified. Transformational leaders differ significantly from their more typical leader colleagues in their approach to problem interpretation. For the most part, these are differences in degree. Conscious reflection on the nature of the problem being faced is one aspect of problem interpretation. Although such reflection is not extensive on the part of expert leaders either, the importance of having a clear interpretation of the problem was addressed. As one elementary school principal said, 'To me, the critical part is identifying what the problem is . . . and the problem is different for different people'.

Transformational leaders working with groups took into account the interpretation others had of the problem they were addressing more frequently than did their typical colleagues. They explicitly checked their own assumptions and actively sought out the interpretations of group members, as well. Less expert leaders tended to assume that group members had the same interpretation of the problems as they had.

Another difference in problem interpretation between expert and typical leaders concerned the context in which problem interpretation took place. Transformational leaders viewed the immediate problem being addressed by the group in the context of the larger mission and problems of their schools.

As one such leader noted, by way of example, 'Discipline is a school thrust [and] the [Professional Activity] PA day [we had on it] was too brief. We need to equip ourselves with more strategies, refine our skills, because of the greater challenges we [now] face in the classroom, for example, the integration of special kids.'

Problems were often interpreted by transformational leaders as opportunities to deal with multiple issues. One secondary-school principal used the problem of integrating arts and technology in the curriculum not only as a way to prepare 'students for a life in the future' but also as a way both to attract more students to the school and to promote racial harmony.

Finally, a particularly striking difference between transformational and typical leaders was the degree of clarity they had about their interpretation of the problem and their ability to both describe their interpretation to other group members and to indicate the reasons they had for such an interpretation. An expert elementary-school principal explained to the group he was working with, for example:

> Earlier in the fall we had a discussion about a house system and some of the ideas were of some concern to one division more than another. I don't think you were really able to come to a decision that it should be school wide and yet there was a feeling that it might very well work out . . . We took it to a lead teacher meeting . . . with some guidelines I had. We've done some revising of those guidelines and what I will give you is an outline of that and some of the ideas behind it. Hopefully, then, the meeting will come to you as a house system that could really work for [this school]. I favour [that happening] – under the whole philosophy we have here of lots of participation and low key amount of competition. This does not really deal with school teams . . . We're talking about in-school activities and its not just sports teams and I think that's part of what [S] is after too. Each of you will get a sheet with a revised set of guidelines and thoughts and [S] will carry forth from here.

Typical leaders were frequently unclear about their interpretations and had difficulty in explaining the reasons for the interpretations they held.

Goals

This aspect of problem solving includes the relatively immediate purposes that the leader is attempting to achieve in response to his or her and the group's interpretation of the problem. Transformational and typical leaders shared many similarities in this component of their problem solving. They had multiple goals for problem solving – usually six or seven goals in relation to any given problem. Furthermore, both transformational and typical leaders made a point of sharing their own goals with other group members involved in problem solving. Most leaders also set goals not only for the problem to be solved but for the meeting in which group problem solving was to occur.

However, in spite of the similarities, our three sets of leaders (elementary-school principals, secondary-school principals and superintendents) differed on two important dimensions of goal setting in small groups. One of these differences concerned the relationship between the leaders' goals for problem solving and the goals that other staff members held. Among elementary-school principals, transformational leaders indicated a strong concern for the development of goals that could be agreed on by all or most members of the group, for example: 'I want this to go, quite frankly I do. But I want it to be something that [the group] have set up [in] the way [in which] they can make it work. It's not something I intend as principal to give out great big awards for . . . I want the teachers to feel comfortable that they are able to build a programme.'

Typical elementary-school principals, in contrast, were concerned only with achieving their own goals and with persuading their staffs to agree with them about what those goals should be. As one such principal said, 'I think I got them [the teachers] to identify the several key areas that are relevant from my point of view'.

A second difference between transformational and typical elementary-school leaders with respect to goals was the stake held by the leader in a preconceived solution. Typical leaders were often strongly committed to a particular solution prior to entering the 'collaborative' problem-solving process and constantly manipulated the process in an effort to gain support for that solution. Transformational leaders, on the other hand, had much less stake in any particular preconceived solution. They wanted the best possible solution the group could produce, and took steps to ensure that such a solution was found. As one said, 'I can either see it happen or let it wash through and say it was a good try, maybe another time. I'm willing to go with it either way.'

In contrast (and much to our surprise), in our study of superintendents' group problem solving (which included only transformational leaders), we found that they brought to their meetings a well worked out solution to whatever was the problem on the agenda. And they were quite explicit (at least to the interviewer) about the fact that they knew exactly what they wanted to accomplish. Transformational secondary-school principals fell somewhere between. They had a preferred solution, but also a lack of certainty about when or how to share it. One principal said, 'I like to let things sort of go and get people talking because I think it's more effective if people come to some agreement rather than always being told'. Yet, a bit later, she added, 'I have confidence in that group that, with discussion, they will come to some realization of where I maybe have in my head, where they want to go'. Transformational secondary-school principals were more conscious than their elementary colleagues of the need to build commitment through staff ownership of the solution. But, at the same time, they grappled with the dilemma of how to share decision making while making sure that their vision was being met.

Superintendents did not appear to face this conflict. The purpose of their meetings was to make sure that everyone at the table understood and agreed with the already well worked out solution. And they were quite skilled at it. As one director said, 'I'm very pleased because it's going exactly where I wanted it to go and it's coming from them. I'm not telling them what we're going to do; they are telling me what I'm going to do, but they are telling me what I want to hear.'

Transformational elementary-school principals set goals related to all stakeholders, but were usually most concerned with programme and student goals. Their secondary-school counterparts were most concerned with staff development goals. One principal, who was not the chair of her meeting, followed the content of the meeting while 'watching the way [the chair] processes the meeting because I want to give her feedback later'. Helping teachers become leaders and fostering shared decision making were two goals that were often in conflict with the transformational leader's desire to see his or her position put into place. One principal expressed the conflict this way: 'I'm very direct in certain situations, but I don't think when I'm trying to do leadership training that I should be direct . . . then it's my idea. Maybe it's my idea anyway.'

Superintendents were also concerned about building the capacity of individuals and groups to solve future problems more expertly. As one said, 'My role is to make them as effective as possible. Therefore I feel that I have to do that in every respect, not only as they conduct their daily work or entertain all their leadership assignments, but also as individuals.' Superintendents did not see any conflict between the role of building staff capacity and accomplishing their own goals.

Values

This component of problem solving refers to the relatively long-term purposes, operating principles, fundamental laws, doctrines, values and assumptions guiding a leader's thinking. All three groups of transformational leaders that we studied had their specific role responsibility as the value they most frequently mentioned. Secondary-school principals, for example, were very aware of what they were trying to do in small-group sessions. Some talked about the awkwardness that can exist when the principal is not the chair. For example, 'it is a difficult [situation] to be in, because you see, I'm the principal of the school and she is the chair of the committee, but I view my role, for the most part . . . as being a committee member. She is in charge, but, yet in other ways, people look at the situation differently, because they still somehow see me as being in charge.' Also like their elementary-school colleagues, respect for others, especially staff, was mentioned next most frequently by both secondary-school principals and superintendents. Knowledge was highly valued by all three groups of transformational leaders.

Constraints

This component of problem solving concerns the barriers or obstacles that must be overcome if an acceptable solution to the problem is to be found. Transformational elementary principals, for example, were able to anticipate many of the obstacles likely to arise during group problem solving. Typical principals either did not anticipate such obstacles or identified relatively superficial obstacles; even when these principals did anticipate obstacles, they rarely considered, in advance, how they might respond to those obstacles should they arise. This is in contrast to transformational leaders, who planned carefully in advance for how they would address anticipated obstacles should they arise. In addition, these leaders adapted and responded in a flexible way to unanticipated obstacles that arose. One principal explained, 'The point he is making which I hadn't taken into account . . . I'm bringing up discipline, so obviously it's interpreted that I'm not happy with discipline in the school'. The principal goes on to say, 'I am glad that point has been raised. By doing this, I'm not saying that things are falling apart. People are on top of things and I appreciate that. At the same time, its something we must continually be at'. He then provided a personal example of a difficulty he had in handling a discipline problem.

Transformational leaders tended not to view obstacles as major impediments to problem solving in the same way that typical leaders do. Furthermore, whereas transformational principals were concerned to learn and build on the perception of their teachers, typical principals viewed differences in their perceptions and those of their teachers as frustrating constraints. Secondary-school principals and superintendents were similar to expert elementary-school principals in their handling of constraints. All three groups of transformational leaders were adept at anticipating constraints and at handling unanticipated ones flexibly.

Solution processes

Everything the leader does to solve a problem in the light of his or her interpretation of the problem, principles and goals to be achieved and constraints to be accommodated, are part of this component of problem solving. Each of the three groups of transformational leaders we studied was able to maintain smoothly functioning group processes. Each group planned well for their meetings, provided clear introductions and outlined to the group the process for problem solving (except when they were not chairing the meeting). These transformational leaders remained open to new information, and summarized, synthesized and clarified information where necessary. They also had strategies for keeping the group focused and allowing for discussion. They checked for consensus, agreement and understanding. Although all sets of leaders were able to indicate their points of view without intimidating others, the transformational secondary-school principals seemed to voice those points of view more often than the others. All sets of transformational leaders also planned for follow-up of group decisions.

Affect

Feelings, moods and a sense of self-confidence are important aspects of the leader's experience when involved in problem solving. All groups of leaders, whether transformational or not, appeared calm and confident during problem solving with their staffs. Some typical principals, however, tended to reveal, during post-meeting interviews, that they had actually experienced anxiety or frustration during the problem-solving meeting.

Other

Our transformational leaders demonstrated strong reflective dispositions, which enabled them to learn from experience, a factor that appears to contribute to their success. One superintendent commented, 'So while [group member] was saying, "Here's the problem as I see it", I've identified another problem that I want to raise with him in terms of how we get secondary-school programmes written, rewritten, refined, and perhaps it's time to reconceptualize'. Transformational leaders reflected on their own performance, and on their role in the meeting. Secondary-school principals also reflected on the conflict they experienced in wanting to give decision-making power to their staff, on the one hand, and having solutions adopted, which they sometimes preferred. One principal described the need to find the right balance while emphasizing the importance of trusting the capabilities of her staff:

> I think there's really an important balance between giving people free reign to do what they want to do and making sure that everything goes well . . . You want them to take risks. I don't think you move very far very fast if you don't have risk takers and I think . . . I have to be a major risk taker. If I'm not willing to trust the capabilities of my staff, I'm not going to get far at all. So there is a balance between, you know, encouraging them, having them use their own ideas and being creative . . . and laying on too much of your own agenda. You have to be careful.

The thoughtfulness with which these leaders dealt with the direction and autonomy dilemma was very apparent.

All transformational leaders made use of humour to diffuse tension in group meetings and to clarify information.

Whole-school learning

Conditions for whole-school learning

Our three studies of whole-school learning examined conditions fostering and inhibiting learning both inside and outside of the school. Although ministries of education and local communities provided some conditions that teachers identified as relevant for their learning, by far the largest number and most influential conditions outside the school were associated with the school district.

District conditions fostering whole-school learning

Teachers in the three studies identified five categories of district features, and a total of three dozen specific features within these categories, associated with their OL processes. Little distinction was evident in the data between district conditions that affected individual learning and conditions that affected collective learning.

The *missions and visions* of school districts were potentially fruitful sources of learning for school staffs. But to realize this potential, such visions had to be clear, well understood and meaningful. To foster organizational learning in schools, district visions and missions also had to engender a sense of commitment on the part of school staffs. When these conditions were met, and when district visions acknowledged the need for continuous professional growth, teachers and administrators used the visions as starting points and frameworks for envisioning more specific futures for their own schools. In the process, staff were also establishing the long-term goals for their own professional learning. Widely shared district missions and visions, furthermore, sometimes provided filters for screening and evaluating the salience of external demands for change. Also, they served as non-prescriptive clues about which initiatives, taken by schools, would be valued and supported by district personnel. As one principal said, in the context of implementing school councils, 'Most of the initiatives, for instance, on the pilot projects that we are involved [with] in our school, they have all been district originated, so for that reason I think they have a vision towards school improvement and accountability for our school'.

'Collaborative and harmonious' captures much of what was considered to be important about district *cultures* when they contributed to OL. Rather than a 'we–they' attitude, perceived to promote hostility and resistance toward district initiatives, learning appears to have been fostered by a shared sense of district community. This sense of community was more likely when there was interaction with other schools (for example, feeder schools), something noticed when it did not happen. As one teacher in our studies complained, 'They don't get together here . . . it wouldn't be hard for two or three schools to get together and have a little science fair and involve everybody. I don't see . . . that kind of thing happening very often.' Sense of community was also more likely when there was clear communication and support for district initiatives (training, professional development), and when disagreements in the district were settled in ways perceived to be 'professional'. District cultures fostered OL when the need for continuous change was accepted, and when new initiatives clearly built on previous work.

District *structures* fostered OL when they provided ample opportunity for school-based staff to participate in shaping both district and school-level decisions. As one teacher in our studies explained, 'The committees get the job done because committees consist of people who are experiencing the difficulties and the questions and the problems, or the goods and the strengths of the programme, and bring it back and that's what gets shared'. Participation in district decisions also taught those involved about the wider issues faced by the district and those influences not readily evident in schools that were, nevertheless, germane to district decisions. Considerable delegation of decision making to schools (possibly through site-based management) enhanced opportunities for improving the collective problem-solving capacities of staff. Such decision making also permitted staff to create solutions that were sensitive to important aspects of the school's context. Multiple forums for participation in district decision making were helpful, as was (in the case of Study Three) the electronic networking of schools.

To foster learning, it was perceived to be useful for districts to use many different *strategies* for reaching out to schools – through newsletters, workshops, informal and electronic forms of communication and the like. Especially influential were workshops and mentoring programmes, and specific change initiatives designed to assist in achieving district goals and priorities. Strategies that buffered schools from excessive turbulence or pressure from the community were also identified as helpful for learning.

District *policies and resources* identified as promoting learning included the provision of release time for common planning and for professional development, especially when these resources could be used in flexible ways. Access to special expertise or 'technical assistance' in the form of consultants, lead teachers and classroom visitations, for example, was also claimed to foster learning, although teachers reported that such resources were, by now, quite scarce ('in the past' they had been quite useful). One means identified for creating a critical mass of expertise about a focus within the school from which others could learn was to ensure that more than one participant from a school attended the same in-service event. In districts that had professional development libraries or central resource centres, teachers cited them as significant aids to their professional learning.

Among district conditions, *policies* and *resources*, especially professional development resources, were most often cited as important by teachers in their learning. As one teacher explained approvingly, 'This summer the school board offered a lot of courses – day courses, week-long courses – open and available to any teacher who chose to take advantage of them'. There was, however, considerable variation among schools within the same district in the conditions which fostered their learning.

Conditions in the school fostering whole-school learning

Across all three of our studies of whole-school learning, conditions parallel to those identified for the district were associated by teachers with their collective learning. But three sets of these conditions were especially important. These were conditions related to culture, structure and policies/resources, and it is only these that we discuss.

Teachers in all three studies frequently identified specific features of their *school culture* that fostered OL processes. Such cultures were described as collaborative and collegial. Norms of mutual support among teachers, respect for colleagues' ideas and a willingness to take risks in attempting new practices were also aspects of culture that teachers associated with their own learning. Some teachers indicated that receiving honest, candid feedback from their colleagues was an important factor in their learning. Teachers' commitments to their own learning appeared to be reinforced by shared celebrations of successes by staff and a strong focus on the needs and achievements of all students. Collaborative and collegial cultures resulted in informal sharing of ideas and materials among teachers, which fostered OL, especially when continuous professional growth was a widely shared norm among staff. One teacher in our studies explained, for example, 'I think at grade levels we keep in very close contact . . . we make sure that . . . we run ideas by each other. We may not be doing exactly the same thing at the same time but it's more or less a team approach.'

For the most part, *school structures* believed to support OL were those that allowed for greater participation in decision making by teachers. Such structures included: brief weekly planning meetings; frequent and often informal problem-solving sessions; flexible and creative timetabling; regularly scheduled professional development time in school; and common preparation periods for teachers who needed to work together. Other structures associated with OL were the cross-department appointment of teachers, integrated curriculum teams and team teaching. When decisions were made by staff through consensus, something easier to do in smaller schools, more learning was believed to occur. The physical space of schools had some bearing on teachers' learning, when it either encouraged or discouraged closer physical proximity of staff.

Policies and resources were a third set of especially important conditions fostering or inhibiting the collective learning of teachers. Teachers reported that current and sufficient resources to support essential professional development in aid of school initiatives were a decided boost to their learning. Within their own schools, teachers used colleagues as professional development resources, along with professional libraries and any professional readings that were circulated among staff. Access to relevant curriculum resources and to computer hardware and software aided teachers' learning, in their view, as did access to technical and programme assistance (for example, consultants, technology site administrators) for implementing new practices. Teachers also noted that access to some community facilities helped them to learn.

Leadership for whole-school learning

Defining our meaning of school leadership in our three studies of whole-school learning were practices of those in formal administrative roles, usually principals, that help determine the direction of improvements in the school and that influence the nature and extent of efforts by school members to learn how to bring about these improvements. Research on such learning in non-school organizations suggests that leadership by those in formal leadership roles is an especially powerful influence on OL both directly and indirectly (Kofman and Senge 1995). Mohrman and Mohrman assert that such leadership 'entails being a continual catalyst for the change process by formulating and updating a compelling change agenda, helping the organization envision the future, unleashing the energy and resources to fuel the change process and helping the organization experience change as success rather than failure' (1995: 101). Senge views such processes as the outcome of leaders acting as stewards, designers and teachers. By enacting such roles, they help build organizations 'where people expand their capabilities to understand complexity, clarify vision, and improve shared mental models' (Senge 1990: 340).

These views resonate closely with the conceptions of transformational school leadership described in earlier chapters of this book, for which there was preliminary evidence of effects on OL as we began our studies of whole-school learning. As a consequence, the starting point for our perspective on leadership in the three studies was the eight dimensions of leadership practice associated with this model. These dimensions include practices aimed at identifying and articulating a vision, fostering the acceptance of group goals and providing individualized support for staff members. Transformational leadership practices also aim to stimulate organizational members to think reflectively and critically about their own practices, and to provide appropriate models of the practices and values considered central to the organization. Holding high performance expectations, building shared norms and

beliefs (culture) and structuring the organization to permit broad participation in decision making can also have important consequences for OL.

With this initial view of transformational school leadership, our studies
asked: What sorts of leadership practices on the part of school administrators contribute significantly to OL and to the conditions that foster OL?
Are these practices consistent with our initial model of transformational
leadership or should this model be revised or abandoned? Evidence from the
three studies, while supporting our expectations concerning the relevance of
the eight dimensions of transformational leadership to whole-school learning, added important detail to those dimensions.

Identifying and articulating a vision

Of the total number of associations made by teachers in our three studies
with the principals' vision building, more than half were associated with
school conditions (which in turn impacted on their collective learning). For
example, although a relatively rare occurrence, some principals' visions
were reported to have a powerful impact on the culture of the school. And
a modest number of teachers described how the principal's vision directly
influenced their collective learning.

Fostering the acceptance of group goals

Although there was at least one teacher comment from most schools affirm-
ing their principals' role in goal development, most of the comments simply
indicated that the principal initiated the process, was a member of the goal
setting committee, or asked for input. For example, the principal of one
school was reported to be actively involved in building a consensus about
goals. That same principal was also the only one who was viewed (by three
teachers) as helping staff develop individual growth plans. During goal setting, the principal in another school was perceived to foster OL by encouraging staff to reflect systematically on the activities of the past year, and the
extent to which these activities had moved them closer to their goals.

Conveying high performance expectations

There was relatively little evidence from our studies that principals in the 14
schools, as a group, held high performance expectations for their staffs, at
least that their staffs could detect. But those few principals who were viewed
as conveying such expectations demanded high 'professionalism', and held
high expectations for professional growth.

Encouraging teachers to be creative and to try new strategies were indicators of high expectations to teachers. For example, one teacher said that
her principal's commitment to fulfilling provincial mandates and keeping the
school on the 'cutting edge' of changes in education encouraged the staff's
commitment to the same vision. Another teacher in the same school said that

her principal's expectation that staff will try new teaching strategies influenced her to learn about them. In another school, professional growth was a 'taken-for-granted' expectation.

Providing appropriate models

Many teachers across the 14 schools included in our three studies believed that their principal was a good role model and that this fostered their collective learning. These principals set an example by working hard, having lots of energy, being genuine in their beliefs, modelling openness, having good people skills and by showing evidence of learning by growing and changing themselves. Being involved in all aspects of the school and showing respect for and interest in students was also considered to be 'walking the walk'. One principal modelled good instructional strategies in the classroom.

Providing individualized support

Most teachers in all case-study schools indicated that their principal supported their professional learning efforts. Typically this meant providing resources to aid professional learning in the form of money, books, furniture or materials. Teachers in several schools considered their principal to be particularly adept at procuring funds to assist with their professional development. Some teachers reported that their principals even used their own administrative professional development funds for things that teachers needed. Other kinds of tangible support for professional learning included providing release time or other scheduling help, sharing information or finding speakers and encouraging participation in decision making by collecting and distributing information.

Providing moral support was mentioned by many teachers in almost all schools. There was a sense that these principals 'are always there for us', did whatever they could to get staff what they needed, and generally supported what teachers did. Sometimes this support was shown by an eagerness to listen and by being accessible, fair, open and sympathetic. Sometimes support was shown by offering positive reinforcement that made staff feel appreciated and encouraged further learning. Support was also shown in the form of encouragement to take risks. And leaders' signs of appreciation were reported to encourage collaboration among teachers.

Providing intellectual stimulation

About a third of all teachers interviewed in our three studies claimed that their principals challenged them intellectually in one way or another. Sometimes this meant passing on information from journals or other sources, bringing new ideas into the school and providing professional development at staff meetings. Yet other forms of intellectual stimulation included organizing and chairing professional development sessions, finding out what staff needed to learn, encouraging staff to put on workshops or to lead staff meetings and discussing individual teachers' progress in achieving personal growth goals.

Building a productive school culture

Although many teachers did not consider their principals to have much influence on school culture, most principals were perceived by at least some of their teaching colleagues as being fundamental to that culture. Inspiring respect, being kind, thoughtful, sincere, honest and hard working were attributes that contributed to this perception. Demonstrating an interest in students and clearly setting their needs as a priority was considered to be an important influence in half of the schools.

A strong belief in the value of honest and open communication, collegiality and a willingness and ability to be flexible were considered to be characteristics conducive to a collaborative culture in which collective learning was fostered. Teachers also valued principals who showed them respect, treated them as professionals, and who were an integral part of the staff. Being seen as working more for the school than for the school district was mentioned by one teacher as being important. Hiring staff who share the same philosophy (for example, a commitment to the use of technology) or who can work well with existing staff was mentioned by some teachers as a way that their principals contributed to a collaborative culture.

Principals also influenced culture by encouraging parental involvement in the school. Teachers in two of the BC schools that we studied credited their principals' philosophy with fostering their child-centred culture. One teacher said her principal set that tone by 'putting student needs above timetable needs', for example. Another teacher claimed that respect among staff for students was engendered by the administrator's actions. A third teacher in the same school believed that the principal's actions demonstrated clearly the importance of being understanding of people from many nationalities and backgrounds. In one school, the principal's strong belief in collaborative decision making fostered a collegial culture, according to some teachers.

Helping structure the school to enhance participation in decisions

More teachers talked about leadership influences on this aspect of school structure than on any other school condition. In spite of the high degree of collaboration exhibited in these schools, several teachers noted that their principals could make unilateral decisions when appropriate or when the need for efficiency was paramount. Principals encouraged participation on committees and supported the committee structure by being actively involved and by organizing or spearheading activities. Many teachers applauded the autonomy their principals gave them to make their own decisions in certain areas. About a third of the principals shared power and responsibility by asking teachers to give workshops, lead staff meetings and help manage the budget, and by delegating many duties to the vice-principals.

To facilitate collaboration, some teachers said their principals altered working conditions by making changes to the physical plant (for example, creating convenient meeting rooms), restructuring the timetable (for example, creating large blocks of time for language arts), and by arranging for leadership positions specifically designed to foster their learning.

Summary and conclusion

Organizational learning is increasingly an expectation and requirement for those people in schools facing significant restructuring. Like other types of organizations, school systems are working toward flatter structures that are intended to distribute the responsibility for thinking about organizational effectiveness broadly among its members, and to release problem-solving capacities seriously constrained by hierarchy. In this chapter we have explored the meaning of 'organizational learning'; a complex and elusive idea, but one of central significance to the authentic reform of school organizations.

Organizational learning, we argued, includes individual learning in organizational contexts – the theme of Chapter 10, although not labelled as such. Organizational learning includes, as well, the learning that occurs within small groups and across whole schools, the focus of this chapter. Specifically, we explored the conditions fostering such learning, and forms of leadership giving rise to such learning. We achieved this using evidence from seven studies carried out by our students and ourselves.

Leadership, our evidence clearly suggests, can make a huge difference in how well small groups and whole schools learn. In the case of small groups, effective leadership entails helping to manage the group processes so that, as purposes are clarified, the best ideas of all members are surfaced and healthy debate is ensured to clarify alternative courses of action, and consensus is created around well explored choices. Such leadership also involves the stimulation of 'group reflection', by which we mean following-up group decisions and refining courses of action on the basis of actual experiences.

Across whole schools, leadership giving rise to learning sometimes involves direct leader–teacher interaction. This is the case with some forms of intellectual stimulation and individualized support provided to teachers by transformational school leaders. But, just as importantly, leadership for whole-school learning requires leaders to become 'organizational designers'.

Much of the contribution that leaders, especially those in formal administrative roles, make to the learning of their colleagues depends on properties of the school organization, over which they have considerable control – missions, cultures, structures and resources for example. Collective capacity development on a broad scale depends on building conditions into each of these organizational properties that not only do not inhibit, but also create the opportunity for learning. These conditions were described at length in the chapter.

twelve

MAINTAINING EMOTIONAL BALANCE

Alienation is produced by workplace arrangements that divide or fragment the individual from the social entity. Alienation results . . . when a person's activity becomes a means to an end, rather than an end in itself.

(Sandelands and St. Clair 1993: 441)

Burnout is a label used to define the stress experienced by those who work in interpersonally intense occupations subject to chronic tension (Cunningham 1983), such as teaching. This form of stress manifests itself as a state of physical, emotional and cognitive exhaustion, which produces feelings of alienation, indifference and low self-regard (Huberman 1993). The most commonly used instrument for assessing burnout, the Maslach Burnout Inventory (MBI) (Maslach and Jackson 1981), defines it in terms of three dimensions: emotional exhaustion, depersonalization and a reduced sense of personal accomplishment.

Symptoms of burnout are both organizational and personal. Organizational symptoms include, for example, increased absenteeism, performance decline and poor interpersonal relations with co-workers and, in the case of teachers, students (Cunningham 1983). At a personal level, teachers who experience burnout: are less sympathetic towards students; are less committed to and involved in their jobs; have a lower tolerance for classroom disruption; are less apt to prepare adequately for class; and are generally less productive (Farber and Miller 1981; Blase and Greenfield 1985). Perhaps even more germane to school restructuring is the evidence, reviewed by Cunningham (1983), that teachers experiencing burnout tend to be dogmatic about their practices, and to rely rigidly on structure and routine, thereby resisting changes to those practices.

Clearly, these symptoms are anathema to these changing times in schools. To be successful, school reform efforts require, for example, increased levels of commitment to school goals (Fullan 1993) and greater sensitivity by teachers to the diverse needs of their students. Many school reform initiatives also demand an expanded, more flexible instructional repertoire on the part of teachers (Murphy 1991) and more collaborative working relationships with fellow teachers (Lieberman *et al.* 1988), students and parents (Connors and Epstein 1994).

Whereas the effects of burnout undermine the success of school reform and restructuring efforts, the conditions in which teachers involved in restructuring often find themselves provide fertile ground for the development of burnout. These are conditions that may further exacerbate the effects of an already stressful job. Estimates place the percentage of the teaching population experiencing such stress at any given time as ranging from about 15 to 45 per cent (for example Leach 1984; Schlansker 1987; Friedman and Farber 1992; Tuettemann and Punch 1992).

Beyond 'business as usual', however, restructuring requires teachers to adopt new and ambiguous roles outside the classroom, roles that often bring them into conflict with the traditional roles of school administrators. Engagement in these roles places considerable demands on their time and often leads to feelings of work overload. Many teachers also experience considerable stress as their expectations for how restructuring will proceed confront a far less than ideal reality (Conley 1993; Louis and King 1993; Prestine 1993). This is the case especially for those exceptionally enthusiastic teachers who are often among the first to implement new practices associated with restructuring (Huberman 1993). These conditions are typically viewed as powerful contributors to teacher burnout (for example Cunningham 1983; Milstein *et al.* 1984; Byrne 1994).

Sustaining and institutionalizing school restructuring initiatives, then, appears to depend, in no small measure, on preventing burnout as a result of teacher participation in such initiatives. This chapter examines how those in school leadership roles may help prevent teacher burnout and contribute to the maintenance of 'emotional balance', in the words of the title. It is based on a study of transformational leadership and teacher burnout reported in greater technical detail in Leithwood *et al.* (1997c).

Explaining teacher stress and burnout

This section of the chapter reviews prior research in response to four questions:

1 What factors other than leadership help explain teacher burnout and its avoidance?
2 What specific leadership practices are significantly related to teacher burnout and its avoidance?
3 What is the relative importance of school leadership as a factor in explanations of variation in teacher burnout?
4 How do leadership and non-leadership factors interact to explain variation in teacher burnout?

Eighteen empirical studies of teacher burnout were identified as germane to these questions. These were studies published between 1984 and 1995, with the exception of one study published in 1983. Each study included leadership among the variables investigated, although it was not always a central focus of the research, and in some studies it was a component of one or several more inclusive variables such as 'social support' or 'participative decision making'. Research methods used in the 18 studies varied in terms of subjects, school level, sample sizes and data collection techniques. This is generally considered to be a good thing, especially when studies using different methods report similar results.

Results of the studies, all of which were concerned with burnout or a close proxy, were analysed by coding the causes of burnout in relation to one of three major categories described below. A voting method (total number of positive, negative or not significant relations reported among variables) was used to assess the strength of the evidence supporting a positive or negative relationship between each cause of teacher burnout. We now turn to a summary of what these studies have to say about each of the four questions identified above.

Factors other than leadership explaining teacher burnout

Two categories of non-leadership factors, *personal* and *organizational*, were identified as influencing burnout in the 18 studies. Also used as conceptual organizers in many of the studies reviewed, those categories encompass all of the specific, non-leadership factors influencing burnout identified in those studies.

Personal factors
A total of 17 different such factors were identified in the studies reviewed. Nine of these exacerbate and eight reduce burnout. Each of these specific factors appears to fit within one of four sub-categories: demographic characteristics, general personality factors, psychological traits and motivational disposition. The first two of these sub-categories are largely unalterable, and the remaining two alterable. The number of studies providing evidence

about the contribution of each personal factor to teacher burnout never exceeded three. For ten of the 17 factors, support was provided by only one study.

With respect to *demographic characteristics*, burnout is marginally less likely with younger, female teachers. It is also less likely for teachers with very little and quite extensive (more than 24 years) experience. Length of teacher experience alone has not been shown to influence burnout. Demographic characteristics typically explain little of the variation in teacher burnout.

With respect to *general personality* factors, burnout is less likely for teachers with personalities that avoid the extremes of competitiveness, impatience and striving for achievement. In reference to *psychological traits*, teachers with an internal locus of control and a strong sense of purpose in their professional and personal lives (the opposite of 'anomie') are less likely to experience burnout. Finally, the *capacity beliefs* of teachers, part of a larger set of motivational conditions discussed below (and in Chapter 9), influence the likelihood of burnout. Teachers with high levels of self-esteem, positive self-concept and professional self-efficacy are likely to be more resistant to burnout.

Organizational factors

Thirteen organizational factors were identified as increasing, and 12 factors reducing the likelihood of teacher burnout. Each of these specific factors can be grouped together into one of three clusters: job demand (or pressure), social support and organizational support. Of the 25 organizational factors, evidence of a significant relationship with teacher burnout was limited to only one study for 17 of these factors. Student misbehaviour received support from the largest number of studies for contributing to burnout (six studies). Support of friends, family and colleagues, and having an influence on decision making in the school were identified most frequently as reducing burnout (seven and five studies respectively).

In relation to *job demand*, burnout is less likely for teachers who are without excessive demands on their time and/or energy, do not have to deal with constant and severe student misbehaviour and do not experience serious role conflict and ambiguity. Burnout is also less likely for teachers who do not experience significant pressure from others to change their practices, and who do not perceive excessive societal pressure for change.

With respect to *social support*, burnout is less likely for teachers who receive such support from friends, family and colleagues, have opportunities to share professional experiences and do not experience feelings of professional isolation. Burnout is also less likely for teachers who receive recognition for their efforts and achievements.

Organizational support conditions reducing the likelihood of burnout include opportunities to change assignments or types of work, and to work within flexible, non-hierarchical, administrative structures. Access to adequate physical facilities that can be used in flexible ways, and access to support personnel (also a form of social support) reduce the likelihood of burnout, as does having an influence on decisions, and job security.

Leadership practices explaining variation in teacher burnout

Leadership practices identified in the 18 studies, as significantly associated with teacher burnout, were almost always treated 'piecemeal'. None the less, these factors clearly reflect behaviours associated with six of the eight dimensions of transformational leadership, as we have discussed it in earlier chapters (none of the factors contributing to burnout were related to vision building or the development of shared goals). By 'associated' we usually mean that transformational practices are well suited to preventing the burnout factors from arising in the first place. The results of our review of such factors are summed up as follows:

- *Modelling*: practices associated with this dimension that contribute to burnout include inconsistent behaviour, lack of follow through, favouritism, and harassment on the part of leaders.
- *Providing individualized support*: addressed by this dimension of trans-formational leadership are burnout factors including low levels of struc-ture and consideration by leaders, failure to provide essential resources, lack of administrative support, lack of trust in teachers' professional ade-quacy and lack of several different types of 'support'. In these studies sup-port was defined by the House and Wells (1978) taxonomy to include emotional, appraisal, instrumental and informational support.
- *Providing intellectual stimulation*: the one burnout factor addressed by this dimension of transformational leadership was lack of knowledge on the leader's part.
- *Building a productive school culture*: leaders valuing integration of staff, and staff assisting one another were practices ameliorating burnout associated with this dimension of leadership.
- *Structuring*: non-participative, authoritarian leadership styles, and low levels of structure and consideration, are factors contributing to burnout explicitly eschewed by those engaged in the structuring dimension of transformational leadership.

By far the most support from the 18 studies was available for factors associated with providing individualized support (11 studies), whereas hold-ing high performance expectations (four studies) received the next largest amount of support. These results may be interpreted as helping to clarify the particular nature of the contribution that some dimensions of transformational leadership make to its overall effects.

In most cases, however, burnout factors do not capture the full range of intentions and practices for the leadership dimension to which they relate. Furthermore, there is no reflection in the burnout factors of the first two dimensions of transformational leadership concerned with direction setting. One may argue that this is hard evidence of their impotence in relation to burnout. Results from the qualitative studies that directly asked teachers to identify leadership practices that reduced or promoted stress (Blase 1984, 1986; Blase *et al.* 1986; Cherniss 1988) would seem to support this interpretation. In the case of the quantitative studies, however, their piecemeal approach to leadership may have resulted in these dimensions of leadership simply having been overlooked.

The relative importance of leadership factors

Our review of the literature suggested that leadership factors may have been underestimated in explanations of teacher burnout. First, many of the specific organizational factors (for example, organizational rigidity, hierarchical administrative structure), along with some of the alterable personal variables (self-efficacy) are either as easily conceptualized as leadership factors or are unarguably influenced by leadership factors. In particular, distinctions made between organizational and leadership variables often appear to be arbitrary. All but three of the 13 organizational variables contributing to burnout (student misbehaviour, pressure for change, and excessive societal expectations) could be considered as direct or indirect products of leadership and administrative practice. Indeed, some aspects of student misbehaviour (those influenced by the development and systematic application of discipline policy, for example) and change (for example, the initiation of various 'improvement' efforts by a principal) might also be viewed in this way. Similarly, among the 12 variables reducing the likelihood of burnout, only support of friends, family and colleagues, and sharing professional experience seem independent of administrative practice.

A second reason for suspecting that leadership factors may have been underestimated is that a very high proportion of the 18 studies that included leadership factors in their design reported significant associations between such factors and teacher burnout. Only Benson and Malone (1987) and Byrne (1994) failed to report such results.

These reasons notwithstanding, the associations reported between leadership and burnout are more variable and often weaker than associations reported between burnout and both organizational and personal factors. Aside from inevitable variation in results due to differences in research methods, these uneven and weak associations may be a function of confounding leadership and (especially) organizational variables in some studies (for example Mazur and Lynch 1989) and, in others, by redistributing leadership effects across factors not conceptualized as leadership (for example Russell *et al.* 1987).

Putting it all together: a model for explaining variation in teacher burnout

Figure 12.1 summarizes the factors and relationships making up a model for explaining variation in teacher burnout growing out of our review of research. The three major categories of factors associated with burnout and discussed above are incorporated in this model. In reality, these factors undoubtedly are related in much more interactive ways than could be captured in a simple figure such as Figure 12.1.

Personal factors are conceptualized as 'mediating' – standing between and modifying – the effects of both leadership and organizational factors. This is consistent with the conclusion that Byrne (1994) drew from her data about both self-esteem and locus of control variables. In our model, 'unalterable' personal factors have been eliminated, primarily because we were interested in factors subject to change especially by school leaders. In addition, however, one of these sub-categories (demographic) explained little variation in burnout in the 18 studies.

Not included among alterable personal factors in Figure 12.1 is the sub-category 'psychological traits', defined in the studies reviewed as anomie and locus of control. In Figure 12.1, anomie, usually defined as a sense of meaninglessness and feelings of alienation, was considered to be an aspect of burnout rather than a factor contributing to burnout. Locus of control was reconceptualized, after Bandura (1986), as an aspect of self-efficacy.

With these changes, all personal factors in our model are subsumed by a comprehensive, social cognitive theory of human motivation (Bandura 1986; Ford 1992), a theory described in some detail in Chapter 9. According to this theory, self-concept, self-esteem and self-efficacy give rise to 'capacity beliefs'. These are beliefs about one's personal ability to cope with the challenges one is facing. A second 'context' belief concerns the support one will receive from the environment in which one is working. Our model reconceptualizes the sub-categories 'job demand' and 'social support' from the organizational category of variables in Figure 12.1 as beliefs about the relative supportiveness of one's context for successfully meeting the demands of one's job; a personal rather than organizational set of factors.

In addition to these two sets of beliefs, a person's motivation, according to this theory, is influenced by personal goals, especially judgements about

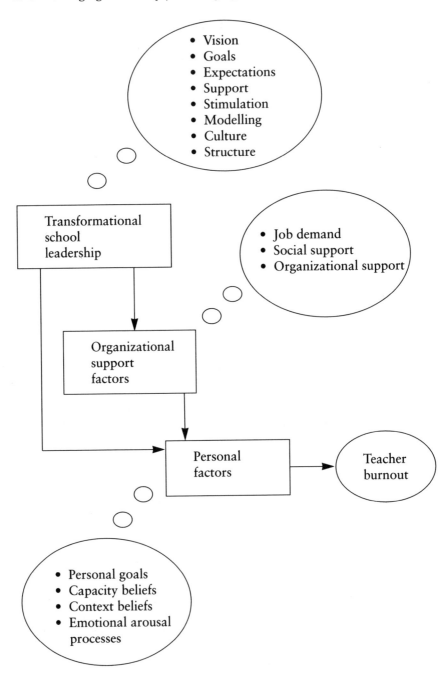

Figure 12.1 A model for explaining variation in teacher burnout

their achievability, and the amount of change their achievement would entail. Finally, this theory also identifies as motivating, especially in the short run, positive rewards, sources of satisfaction and excitement experienced from day to day. These are 'emotional arousal processes'.

Figure 12.1 not only predicts that the effects of both leadership and organizational factors will be mediated by personal factors but also that the effects of leadership on personal factors will be both direct and indirect, through organizational support factors.

Testing and refining the explanation of teacher burnout

The studies we reviewed told us a good deal about the causes of teacher burnout, the importance of school leadership in explanations of such burnout, and the types of leadership practices most likely to help prevent burnout. This section outlines an empirical study we conducted to further the knowledge provided by the 18 studies, especially knowledge about the nature and effects of school leadership.

Data used for this purpose was provided by 331 of the 555 teachers (60 per cent) in the business, technology and health faculties of three community colleges selected to be within a three-hour driving radius of Toronto. Data were summarized using basic descriptive statistics and path analysis outlined in more detail in our original report (Leithwood *et al.* 1997c). Path analysis provided estimates of the independent strength of relationships among the set of variables in our model (as depicted in Figure 12.1), and also indicated the proportion of variation in teacher burnout explained by the whole model and by each of its individual sets of variables.

Results

Figure 12.2 provides a non-technical summary of the results of testing a general as well as more detailed version of our model of teacher burnout using a form of path analysis. These refinements of the model described in Figure 12.1 resulted from a preliminary analysis of the survey responses.

The three sets of variables (or causes of burnout) included in Figure 12.2 (leadership, organizational factors and personal factors) combine to explain a total of 30 per cent of the variation in teacher burnout. Although all relationships between variables in the model are statistically significant, some are stronger than others. The asterisks on the lines joining variables indicate this (* = weak relationship; *** = strong). So, as Figure 12.2 indicates, there is a weak relationship between personal factors and burnout, and a moderately strong relationship between leadership and personal factors. Strong relationships exist between leadership and organizational

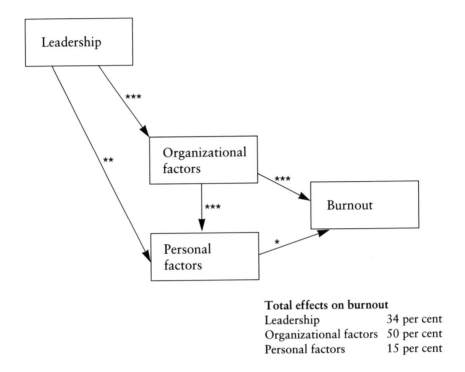

Total effects on burnout
Leadership   34 per cent
Organizational factors 50 per cent
Personal factors   15 per cent

Figure 12.2 First empirical exploration of model for explaining variation in teacher burnout

factors, organizational factors and personal factors and between organizational factors and burnout.

In this model, the direct and indirect effects of leadership explain about a third of the variation in burnout accounted for by the model; organizational factors explain about half and personal factors, about a sixth.

The model developed to this point explains almost a third of the variation in burnout among community college teachers included in the sample. Although the largest proportion of the variation remains to be explained, the power of this model compares favourably with the small number of other models for which comparable information is available. Surprisingly, only two of the 18 studies reviewed in the first stage of our research (Byrne 1994; Brissie *et al.* 1988) provided this critical information. Byrne's model explained up to 29 per cent of the variation in teacher burnout, and that of Brissie *et al.* about 44 per cent. Unlike most other models, furthermore, ours is limited to potentially alterable factors. It seems reasonable to conclude, then, that teacher burnout is significantly *created by* and *ameliorated through* factors over which those in the school organization have some, or considerable, control. Furthermore, this seems largely to be the case whatever personal predispositions teachers bring to their work.

We also tested a more detailed version of the model in order to assess the independent effects of each of the four personal factors on burnout, and to examine the effects of leadership and organizational factors separately on each of these factors. Of the four personal factors, results suggested that teachers' context and capacity beliefs are weakly but significantly and positively related to burnout. Personal goals was related weakly but negatively to burnout. Capacity beliefs had the largest total effect on burnout followed by context beliefs and, indirectly through capacity beliefs, emotional arousal processes.

Both leadership and organizational factors have moderate to strong effects on teachers' context beliefs and personal goals. Organizational factors also have moderate effects on capacity beliefs, and the largest total effects on burnout.

This evidence is in distinct contrast with that of Byrne. In summing up the most consequential aspects of her study, she argued for the prominence of personal factors, in particular self-esteem, which acts as 'a critical and controlling factor in the predisposition of teachers to burnout' and which 'functions as an essential mediator variable through which the effects of environment-based organizational factors filter' (1994: 567). Our results indicate, however, that personal factors lag behind both leadership and organizational factors in their total effects on teacher burnout.

It is tempting to explain away these differences as, for example, a function of the two samples, Kindergarten to grade 12 teachers in Byrne's study and community college teachers in ours, and while there is some justification for this explanation, it ignores an important conceptual issue largely unaddressed by models of burnout other than our own and Byrne's. This is the 'constructed' nature of both leadership and organizational factors. It is not the 'objective' condition of such factors that influences burnout: it is the teacher's personal evaluation of those conditions. So the same 'objective' school structures, for example, may be interpreted by one teacher as overly rigid, thereby reducing choices for action and contributing to stress. Another colleague will view the same structures as providing the clarity and discretion needed to respond comfortably to the challenges of the job.

If teacher burnout depends on such a constructed reality, as surely it must, then models of burnout ought always to locate personal factors as mediators of the external environment, however that environment is construed. This means that, in the case of our own work, the model arising from our review of the literature (Figure 12.1) is correct in its assertion about the place of personal factors. Our path model (Figure 12.2) may be telling us that the specific factors that we conceptualized as organizational factors in this study might better be conceptualized as an extended set of context beliefs.

The underestimated effect of leadership on teacher burnout

The total effects of leadership on burnout were significant and moderate in our study, considerably more than personal factors and substantially less than organizational factors. These are effects of leadership, largely realized indirectly through their effects on organizational factors. In direct opposition to claims arising from Byrne's (1994) study, for example, this evidence further fuels our suspicion that prior research has underestimated leadership as a factor in the creation and amelioration of teacher burnout, probably because of inadequate conceptualization and measurement. Our results, however, are the outcome not just of measuring aspects of leadership derived from any coherent view, but of using a transformational conception demonstrated, through previous enquiry, to have influence on most of the personal and organizational factors included in the model explaining burnout.

The significant effects on teacher burnout suggested by our data still seem likely to underestimate the power of leadership, however, because of our inability to construct, from the available data set, adequate measures of each of the dimensions of transformational leadership. Instead, a single scale was constructed to represent such leadership, one largely composed of individual survey items reflecting each of the dimensions of transformational leadership. This means, for example, that the one dimension most frequently identified in prior research (for example Blase and his colleagues 1984, 1986a, b; Blase and Greenfield 1985; Blase *et al.* 1986) as strongly related to burnout, 'individualized support', had little influence on the explanatory power of the leadership construct in our burnout model.

Summary and conclusion

This chapter began with concern over the fate of significant and potentially useful efforts at school improvement, efforts often given the label 're-structuring'. While initiatives travelling under this label are quite diverse, they typically share an implicit expectation that teacher-implementors are prepared to develop new capacities and will be committed to making the often poorly specified restructuring initiatives work in real schools and classrooms. Clearly, already overly stressed or burned out teachers are unlikely candidates for such a challenge. And the conditions created by restructuring initiatives can exacerbate tendencies towards becoming overly stressed or burned out.

In response to this concern the chapter aimed to clarify the conditions giving rise to teacher burnout and to identify what can be done, especially by school leaders, to prevent burnout. This was done by reviewing recent empirical studies in which leadership was explicitly included as a possible influence on burnout and its avoidance. From the results of this review a tentative model for explaining variation in teacher burnout was developed. Included in the model were personal factors, leadership and organizational factors. Results were also reported of our testing and refinement of the model using survey data collected from community college teachers in Ontario.

What are the implications of these results for school leaders? As a way of organizing our response to this question, we adopt Maslach and Jackson's (1981) three dimensions of burnout: depersonalization, emotional exhaustion and a reduced sense of personal accomplishment. In relation to each of these dimensions, we consider what school leaders might do to prevent teacher burnout, in light of the evidence reported in the chapter.

Preventing a sense of depersonalization

According to evidence reviewed in this chapter, a sense of depersonalization is likely when teachers assess the goals of the school to be incompatible with their own professional goals. Depersonalization is also a consequence of organizational decision-making processes that do not allow teachers to shape the means of accomplishing such goals, for example the policies and procedures guiding their work, the distribution of resources in support of their work and the structures that surround it.

School leaders can prevent or reduce teachers' sense of depersonalization by:

- developing with staff goals for the school that most staff believe meaningfully and authentically address the needs of their students;
- assisting individual teachers to develop meaningful and challenging individual professional goals that are compatible with the school's goals;
- creating shared decision-making structures and processes that encourage personal investment by teachers in the work and success of the school.

Fostering a sense of personal accomplishment

Teachers, we have learned in this chapter, are likely to experience a reduced sense of personal accomplishment when they judge as inadequate their own capacities to respond to the challenges they face; challenges presented by their schools' restructuring efforts, for example. A reduced sense of personal accomplishment among teachers also arises from a belief that support available to them from other members of their school is less than they need. Lack of clarity about their own professional goals and the school's goals contributes to a reduced sense of personal satisfaction among teachers, as well, because it makes difficult the self-evaluation of one's progress.

School leaders are likely to maintain or enhance teachers' sense of personal accomplishment when they:

- Assist teachers in 'setting directions', clarifying their individual professional goals, as well as the goals of the school. Personal accomplishment is enhanced especially when a small number of clear manageable priorities is the result of such direction setting.
- Ensure that teachers believe they have adequate amounts of 'individualized support': strong moral and instrumental support from school leaders and other colleagues in the school should they choose to undertake significant changes in their classroom practices. Perhaps the most powerful means of ensuring an adequate amount of support is to build a school culture that includes norms of mutual support among teachers, including the provision of honest, candid feedback among colleagues.
- Provide feedback to teachers with respect to their work, rewarding them for successful practices and for the risks associated with efforts to improve their practices. Such 'contingent reward' may prevent a reduced sense of personal accomplishment by reducing the uncertainties teachers frequently have about the relative merit of their work due, in part, to the typical isolation of that work from the scrutiny of other adults (Hargreaves and Macmillan 1992).
- Provide teachers with the 'intellectual stimulation' necessary to increase their professional knowledge and skill, in particular the knowledge and skill required for them to successfully implement those changes in classroom practices included in whatever restructuring and reform initiatives the school may be engaged. Collaborative and collegial cultures typically lead to the informal sharing of ideas and materials among teachers, an important means of fostering growth in professional capacities.

Preventing emotional exhaustion

Among teachers, as we have learned in this chapter, emotional exhaustion is likely to be a consequence of finding little in their day-to-day work to stimulate their excitement and enthusiasm. Emotional exhaustion is more likely, as well, in work environments that make it difficult for teachers to achieve their primary source of satisfaction; observing students learning from their instruction and enjoying the process. Such exhaustion may also result from feelings that the whole organization, or key leaders within the organization, are holding unrealistically high performance expectations. While this dimension of leadership practice may exacerbate teachers' sense of emotional exhaustion, this is likely to be contingent upon, for example, the situation in which those practices are experienced and the state of teachers' existing expectations for themselves.

When teachers are already committed to significant restructuring, for example, and working hard to understand what it means for their own classroom practices, overly high performance expectations are likely to produce debilitating levels of anxiety and stress. Under such conditions, individualized support seems more likely to be helpful.

On the other hand, high performance expectations may be useful as a means of initiating change in circumstances characterized by teacher complacency, a widely shared belief among staff members in the superior quality of the instruction already being offered to students, or blindness to the special needs of a particular group of students in the school.

School leaders can minimize or prevent emotional exhaustion by:

- helping individual teachers identify short-term signposts of progress in meeting their own and the school's improvement goals;
- rotating teachers' classroom assignments so as to ensure that the same teachers do not always have, year after year, especially difficult students to work with – students who present exceptional discipline and instructional challenges, for example;
- providing, as much as possible, adequate financial and material resources in support of teachers' work;
- personalizing performance expectations in light of teachers' individual progress and needs for extrinsic motivation (many teachers will find such motivation to be irrelevant).

Hargreaves and Fullan, in arguing that teachers are engaged in a moral mission, suggest that in complex times pursuing such a mission can be 'an emotional roller coaster': 'Choosing demanding purposes and sticking with them in difficult times draws on every ounce of emotion teachers have. The pleasures and rewards to be gained from this kind of emotional engagement as a teacher are immense, but the risks of exhaustion and disillusionment . . . are equally great' (1998: 59). To know that there are ways in which those exercising school leadership can help their teaching colleagues to cope with these risks is an important source of hope in the face of what often seem like overwhelming challenges.

thirteen

CONCLUSION: FUTURE SCHOOLS AND LEADERS' VALUES

Observers and participants in organizational life ought to be more cognizant of the power of images and expectations. What we need therefore are good images, or as Morgan (1993) would put it 'imaginization' . . . The focus is on affirmation of [the positives], and this is deliberate, because it frequently produces positive outcomes.

(Gephart *et al.* 1996: 360)

Changing times demand different leadership. With that premise as a point of departure, previous chapters of this book have described the results of our research over the past half dozen years concerning transformational approaches to leadership in schools engaged in 'restructuring'. Our understandings of such leadership have evolved considerably over the course of our studies and this is reflected in the variations in dimensions and specific practices that have been described as transformational in many of the chapters.

Research described in previous chapters has demonstrated that transformational approaches to leadership can make significant contributions to a number of important outcomes for which schools are responsible. In addition, this research has produced relatively detailed, illustrated descriptions of leadership practices that are transformational, specifically in school settings. We have uncovered the cognitive processes giving rise to transformational practices in restructuring contexts. And, finally, we have broadened and deepened understandings of the nature and effects of transformational leadership by examining the contributions of such leadership to a number of those school conditions and teacher qualities that explain school success.

But the term restructuring describes a present focus for school reform. As many teachers will be quick to predict, 'this too shall pass'. So the purpose of this final chapter is to raise our sights above the present horizon, to imagine what schools might be like in their 'post-restructuring' phase and to consider what the consequences of this future might be for leaders.

Of course, this is no easy chore, especially with respect to tomorrow's schools. But developing defensible visions or images of what those schools should be is an important step in their creation, as the quotation opening this chapter suggests. So the purpose of this chapter is to examine some of the more salient aspects of schools and their wider social contexts and to begin to consider some of their implications for those who would exercise leadership in the development of future schools. The chapter examines, as well, some important assumptions about how schools change, since the task of those providing leadership entails not only helping to formulate an image of future schools but also assisting in the transformation of present schools. We think these are appropriate considerations with which to conclude the extended treatment of transformational leadership provided by the book.

Attempting detailed predictions about either the change processes or the nature of future schools clearly would be foolish, however. There are simply too many variables of which to take account. So the picture of each painted in this chapter is done in broad strokes. Inferring the detailed implications for leadership practice of approaches to change and images of future schools would also be foolish. What does seem within reach, however, is the identification of values to which those exercising leadership will need to adhere in order to help transform schools.

Broad trends stimulating the evolution of schools

The social, economic, technological and political contexts within which schools find, and anticipate finding, themselves are obviously crucial considerations in the design of future schools. Such considerations, however, are seriously complicated by the conflicting implications for schools of many such contexts. None the less, the implications of context, including conflicts in the directions they suggest for future schools, provide much of the basis for future school design.

While there are many contextual forces impinging on the direction of future school designs, the six to be examined here illustrate (perhaps even represent) the problems for which designers of future schools must seek solutions. Many dimensions of schooling are touched by these forces. But the focus of this analysis will largely be restricted to their influence on the allocation of power and decision-making authority, and more generally to school structure. Two of these forces press schools towards greater centralization, and two towards greater organizational decentralization. The final two forces fundamentally challenge the institutionalization of schooling as it has been conceived traditionally.

Centralizing forces

End of the 'borrow now: pay later' school of public finance

In the 1990s, developed countries around the world have found themselves seriously challenged by debt. Furthermore, there is enough public concern for the long-term consequences of ignoring public debt to make both deficit and debt reduction politically attractive goals. In addition, these debt-reduction programmes arrive as many countries are beginning to experience noticeable increases in the proportions of their populations that are aging. These populations have no direct need for public educational services so are less disposed towards willingly allocating their taxes to schools; they also are in greater need of medical and other social services than they were earlier in their lives (Ng 1992).

The combined effects of government debt-reduction programmes and increased competition for public funding by other social services is significantly eroding the resources allocated to public schooling. This is creating pressure on schools toward greater centralization. Such centralization, it is argued, will allow more efficient use of available resources through so-called economies of scale. Greater centralization of functions such as transportation and purchasing, the combining of programmes and institutions and the amalgamation of central office structures are all manifestations of responses to this pressure for centralization as a means of becoming more efficient.

End of the belief that all non-traditional family structures are rare enough to be safely ignored by schools

There was a time, not very long ago, when a good many teachers resented the 'intrusion' of their students' unmet social, emotional and even basic physical needs into the school's primarily intellectual curriculum. With some justification, these teachers complained that responding to such needs was the proper role of parents and social workers; it was not the role of teachers.

Teachers with this complaint often assumed that most of their students came from the kind of functional, two-parent nuclear families that, in western cultures, were widely believed to be both typical and ideal. Indeed, this was the kind of family around which schools were originally designed; families which were (and still are) thought to reliably provide the 'social capital' that Coleman (1987) has demonstrated is an essential foundation for children to acquire if they are to cope productively with the intellectual challenges for which schools have historically been considered responsible.

Few teachers still feel confident in assuming that their students come from such families and possess the psychological robustness that is at the core of Coleman's meaning of social capital. While many children still do, of course, evidence concerning the widespread existence of alternative family structures has become too pervasive to ignore (Oderkirk 1994). At the heart of the problem for children of the widespread emergence of what Elkind (in an interview with Marge Scherer) has called 'postmodern permeable family' (Scherer 1996: 6), is the erosion of the kinds of familial educational cultures directly responsible for social capital development. These cultures are built on an unqualified acceptance of the child's worth and include, for example, high value awarded to education in the home, encouragement and direct help available from adults in the home for children with their schoolwork and physical space available for study and homework. Walberg (1984) has referred to these features, together, as the alterable curriculum of the home.

To be more precise, however, it is not alternative family structures themselves that are responsible for an erosion of family educational cultures and, as a result, social capital. Rather, the erosion is due, in part, to the enormous amount of time that many parents now have to devote to work and to further developing work-related skills in order to make certain that their children are provided for (Scherer 1996). The erosion is also a product of the economic disadvantages that often accompany some forms of the postmodern family structure. For example, although single-parent families are quite capable of providing stimulating educational cultures in the home when they are not also suffering undue financial hardship, a very large proportion of single-parent families do suffer such hardship (Oderkirk and Lochhead 1992).

What a great many teachers and other educators now believe, that they did not believe before, is that development of social capital is something for which they must take some responsibility. There is also a belief that schools by themselves are not very well equipped to do this job. So this has become a force for engaging, for example, in partnerships with other social agencies to better position their students for success at school. Full service schools and other forms of service coordination in which schools play a role (Smylie and Crowson 1996) indicate how this has become a centralizing force for schools.

Decentralizing forces

End of society's willingness to assign major decision-making authority to professional expertise

This is a force or a trend being experienced widely throughout the professions. Most professions acquired their status through a willingness on the part of large segments of society to cede them considerable responsibility and authority for decision making. Such willingness was based on the assumption that members of the professional group possessed privileged technical knowledge and skill unavailable to non professionals about a set of problems of critical importance to a large proportion of the public.

While the status and autonomy in decision making awarded to school professionals never matched that of medicine or law, for example, professionals of all types have been experiencing a rapid decline in the public's willingness to continue ceding such power. As Bryk explains, there is 'a renewed belief in the power of democratic activity to pull societal institutions from the quagmire of professional control' (1988: 232). This belief is a consequence of, for example, generally higher levels of public education, greater access by the public to information previously possessed largely by members of the professions, and a growing perception that many professionals have betrayed the public trust.

Widespread initiatives by governments around the world to award parents more direct control over schools by establishing either advisory or decision-making roles for parents on school councils (Murphy and Beck 1995) are the most obvious manifestations of this decentralizing force on schools.

End of the public school's technological naïvety

A second decentralizing force is evident in the recent trend among schools to more rapidly adopt current electronic technology and to more fully integrate it into the educational and administrative work of the school. While availability and integrated use are not the same thing, it is telling that between 1983 and 1994 the number of US schools with at least one computer rose from 18 per cent to 98 per cent (Mehlinger 1996). Serious use of electronic technology has been a long time coming and until quite recently seemed anything but inevitable. Even now, many mature technologies (televisions, video recorders) have achieved only marginal status in schools in spite of what was perceived, by their advocates at least, to have 'revolutionary' potential.

The computer, however, has become ubiquitous in our society and such widespread use has brought pressures and incentives for schools to adopt it in a meaningful way from many sources. For example, the Education Summit held by the US president and state governors in April 1996 resulted in a resolution to ensure all US schools access to the internet within half a dozen years. When AT&T recently introduced its internet access service, it offered a discount to schools, presumably with the aim of capturing a large share of what the company believes will be a huge market (Gurley 1996). Increasingly, schools report on their own work to make use of microcomputer technology to achieve existing and new educational goals (Weiss 1996).

While providing access to information is by no means all that schools (or computers, of course) do, it is a significant part of their current function. And mostly they bring 25 or 30 students together at the same time and in the same place to do it. The reasons for such an arrangement are no longer compelling, however. At least part of the time, students now can access information, discuss it with teachers, fellow students and others without being in the same physical location. As video conferencing technology becomes more available and of higher quality, the reasons for students always to be in the same place at the same time will erode even further. This is one of the reasons that conventional classroom structures should not be an assumed feature of future schools.

De-institutionalizing trends

Contemporary understandings of how learning occurs

Constructivism is the label most often used to describe understandings of learning that have emerged from the work of contemporary cognitive scientists (McLaughlin and Talbert 1993). A good many curriculum and instructional initiatives are based on constructivist theory. Lampert's (1990) work on the teaching of mathematics and Scardamalia and Bereiter's (1986) work on the teaching of writing composition are examples of instructional applications, and California's curriculum frameworks are examples of curriculum applications.

As long as constructivist theory is applied to the teaching of literacy and numeracy, as they are in elementary schools, its implications are largely restricted to increasing the size and changing the nature of teachers' instructional repertoires. But the implications are much more profound as such theory is brought to bear on the teaching of domain-specific knowledge especially in secondary schools confronted with the task of preparing students for transition to work or to tertiary education. Such schools are frequently criticized because they provide their students with 'inert knowledge', to use Bransford's (1993) term.

Inert knowledge is acquired in contexts separate from those in which it is expected to be applied (schools, for example). As a consequence, those who possess it have considerable difficulty even recognizing instances in which it would be relevant to use, never mind having the capacity to use it to guide their actions. To be of actual use, cognitive scientists suggest that knowledge needs to be both 'situated' and 'proceduralized' (for example Rogoff 1984; Wagner 1987; Brown *et al.* 1989).

When people learn in the context in which their knowledge is subsequently to be used, they acquire much more than the explicit knowledge that is part of the planned curriculum. They also acquire the 'tacit' (Polanyi 1967) or everyday knowledge that, in combination with the explicit knowledge, provides the depth of understanding and the skill required for practical problem solving. Authentic learning of useful knowledge, then, depends on involvement in solving real problems within some domain of practice.

Schools, however, were created with the express purpose of separating students from such 'messy' involvement in order to pour a pristine form of knowledge into their heads; historically, this has been a form of knowledge largely useless for all but the playing of Trivial Pursuit, using a form of instruction that did not recognize the need for students to personally construct their own meaning. Most efforts to solve the inert problem in secondary schools involve, already, modest forms of de-institutionalization; cooperative education is perhaps the best known North American example. Many of the school-to-work transition initiatives associated with the 'new vocationalism' (Goldberger and Kazis 1996) also entail the provision of significantly more workplace contexts for formal education.

Widespread recognition of the need for lifelong learning

In her proposed new agenda for education, Chapman refers to 'the learning society and knowledge economy' (1996: 1) as the broad policy context within which future schools must be designed. This is a context that acknowledges lifelong learning as instrumental to a rapidly changing job market as well as to opportunities for individuals to choose from 'a rich range of options, from which they may construct a satisfying and enriching pattern of activities and life enhancing choices for themselves' (Chapman 1996: 3). According to Chapman, future schools also must be designed in recognition of a context that privileges those with the capacities to access, make sense of and use both sources and quantities of information unimagined until quite recently.

Widespread commitment to lifelong learning is a de-institutionalization force on schools since it clearly implicates people in systematic education at all stages in their lives. Present school designs, in contrast, respond to a set of requirements that were relevant (and to some extent remain so) for those at pre-adult stages in their lives. These requirements include, for example, custodial care, physical security, limited life experiences, uncertain motivation for learning the formal curriculum and immature levels of cognitive development. To the extent that meeting such requirements is irrelevant in the education of adults, the traditional design of schools cannot be justified. Furthermore, many adults do not depend on formal institutions of any kind for their learning, relying instead on personal reading, practical experience, deliberation with other colleagues and the like. So just redesigning existing school organizations is not obviously a solution.

Images of future schools

Taken together, these conflicting forces for change suggest at least three criteria that future school designs ought to meet; inclusiveness, efficiency and effectiveness, and adaptability. First, future schools will need to be more inclusive in their decision making and more comprehensive in the dimensions of student growth (social and emotional as well as intellectual) for which they consider themselves at least partly responsible. This criterion responds to the diversity of student needs arising from alternative family structures, and the desire for greater non-professional control of schools. An image of future *schools as communities* begins to address this criterion.

A second design criterion for future schools is that they will need to become more efficient and effective in accomplishing the outcomes for which schools traditionally have been held accountable. This criterion emerges most obviously from the sometimes dramatic reductions in public funding allocated to schools, reductions likely to continue for some time into the future, along with persistent calls for greater public accountability. Imagining *schools as high reliability organizations* is a response to this criterion.

As a third criterion, future schools will need to be increasingly capable of adapting productively to changing expectations about what they are to accomplish and changing knowledge about best practices. Not only are expectations changing, but they are becoming more ambitious, as is evident in the pressures on schools to develop students who will be able to function well in a technologically sophisticated world. These changing expectations are being accompanied by new instructional practices (those arising from new understandings of how learning occurs, such as cooperative learning strategies, for example), which teachers must master and which school organizations need to determine how to support both structurally and culturally. This predictable, and unending stream of changes in expectations and practices recommends the design of *schools as learning organizations*.

School as community

A school modelled as community, according to Bryk and Driscoll, 'is a social organization consisting of cooperative relations among adults who share common purposes and where daily life for both adults and students is organized in ways which foster commitment among its members' (1988: 2). As Selznick further explains, its function 'is to regulate, discipline, and especially to channel self-regarding conduct, thereby binding it so far as is possible, to comprehensive interests and ideals', and its favoured form 'is the small, intimate, person-centered structure where solidarity is most effective and most genuine . . . where persons are created and nurtured, where they become situated beings and implicated selves' (1992: 369).

These conceptions of schools as communities begin to indicate the ways in which they might provide students with the social capital that, in the past, schools could more safely assume was being provided to their students through some combination of their immediate families and the networks of relationships available in the lives of students outside their immediate families. Social capital consists of the norms, obligations and trust that are developed among people through such relationships (Coleman 1987), and the sense of stability, security and positive self-concept typically engendered in individual children who participate in such relationships. Social capital thereby offers many of the personal and social prerequisites for successful mastery of the challenges provided by the school's curriculum. Claims Gamoran, 'when such relations are flourishing, social capital can serve as a resource supporting the cognitive and social development of young people' (1996: 2). The social capital provided through community in school has been cited by many as the explanation for apparent achievement of students in some types of schools (for example Coleman and Hoffer 1987; Wehlage *et al.* 1989; Bryk *et al.* 1993b), especially for students from disadvantaged backgrounds.

Implications for leadership

To sum up, several forces shaping the evolution of schools warrant more attention to inclusivity in the design of future schools. In this context, inclusivity is a broad category of values encompassing such related values important to reflect in school leadership as:

1 *Caring and respect for others*: As Starratt explains, caring requires 'fidelity to persons, a willingness to acknowledge their right to be who they are, an openness to encountering them in their authentic individuality, a loyalty to the relationship . . . This value is grounded in the belief that the integrity of human relationships should be held sacred' (1991: 195). Walker (1995) coded such words as compassion, generosity and dignity as instances of this value.
2 *Participation*: This encompasses Hodgkinson's (1978) values of consensus. It also reflects the concerns for freedom, equality and social justice in schools rooted in Dewey's concept of the democratic school and given expression currently, for example, in Giroux's (1992) concept of leader as transformative intellectual.

School as high reliability organization (HRO)

While much has been written about the appropriateness of school as community, a conception of school as a highly reliable organization has not yet received much consideration. This image has some of its roots in earlier research on effective schools, especially the work of Stringfield (1992, 1995), who has spearheaded the effort to apply to schools high reliability ideas originally developed in non-school organizations.

Like efforts to develop more 'effective' schools (for example Mortimore *et al.* 1988), the motivation for exploring how schools could become more reliable can be traced to concerns about the development of basic skills. This concern is focused especially on those young students either not well served by traditional school practices or enrolled in schools where the context has seemed to erode the systematic use of such practices. Under such circumstances, students' development of reading skills, in particular, is retarded and so, as a consequence, is their opportunity to master other aspects of the school curriculum that depend on the application of such skills. Early failures in the development of reading skills, then, often cascade into increasingly serious problems in a broad range of school achievements.

Stringfield uses hydroelectrical power grids and air traffic control systems as examples of HROs to demonstrate some of the characteristics that schools would need to acquire in order to be more reliable. HROs of this sort accomplish their goals more or less *all of the time* and the failure to do so would be considered a disaster by the public. According to Stringfield, this public perception is a critical pre-condition for the emergence of HROs and, until quite recently, the public has not considered failure to learn to read to be such a disaster.

Evidence is mounting, however, that this perception is changing. One such piece of evidence is the persistence of calls for school reform, calls that have been sustained now in North America since at least 1983 when *A Nation at Risk* was first published (National Commission on Excellence in Education 1983). Calls for school reform, while common throughout this century, have never persisted for more than a few months to several years at a time. Stringfield argues (personal communication) that the reason for this persistence is growing public awareness of the significant negative financial consequences of a failure to successfully complete school for both individuals (for example, reduced lifelong income, unemployment) and for society (reduced tax revenues, increased welfare and unemployment insurance costs). So the perception-of-disaster pre-condition to support the emergence of schools as HROs would appear to be at least in the formative stages.

From the dozen or more attributes associated with HROs (Stringfield 1995), one example serves to illustrate one of the small but significant changes that would be required of a traditional school for it to qualify as an

HRO. HROs are alert to surprises or lapses. The experience of HROs is that small failures can cascade into major system failures and so such failures are monitored carefully. In contrast, in the context of schools, there is compelling evidence that dropping out of high school can be predicted reasonably accurately from student levels of classroom participation as early as Grade 3 (Lloyd 1978). Yet schools rarely conceive of Grade 3 students' off-task behaviour as a potential future disaster and so rarely either track it very closely or take extraordinary steps to reduce it.

Application to schools of the full set of HRO characteristics would result in an organization with many of the structural features of a traditional school but with, for example: more flexible, varied and task-dependent sets of professional relationships; greater commitment by staff to a clearer and more precisely focused set of goals; much greater attention to evidence about the effects of selected teaching practices; and meticulous attention to the maintenance of the equipment and technology considered important for achieving the instructional purposes of the school.

Implications for leadership

As a broad category of values, efficient reliability encompasses such specific values important to reflect in school leadership practices as:

1 *Equity*: In this context equity means equal access to knowledge on the part of students rather than equal access to educational resources. The goals of a high reliability school will only be achieved through inequitable distributions of those resources (some children will need much more of those resources than others).
2 *Knowledge*: In this case the knowledge of greatest concern is about the effectiveness of educational practices used by the school in accomplishing the purposes for which they are intended, in the context in which they are used.
3 *Dependability*: Almost a synonym for reliability, valuing dependability means rewarding people for unfailingly implementing the practices that the school judges to be most effective for its purposes.
4 *Persistence*: This value recognizes that to be reliable in accomplishing outcomes as complex as those addressed by schools will often require recognizing the failure of initial attempts to accomplish some of those goals and being willing to change one's approach and try again, perhaps many times.

School as learning organization

In a future context of declining resources, escalating expectations and turbulent environments, schools will need to be designed so that changing is considered an ordinary activity rather than an extraordinary event. At the heart of an organization's capacity to change is the individual and collective learning of its members (for example Peterson *et al.* 1996). Appreciation of the importance of such learning has given rise to a venerable body of research on collective or 'organizational-learning' processes in non-school organizations (for a comprehensive review of this literature see Cousins 1995). More recent literature has popularized some of these ideas in the concept of the 'learning organization' (Senge 1990; Watkins and Marsick 1993).

According to Fiol and Lyles, 'Organizational learning means the process of improving actions through better knowledge and understanding' (1985: 203). A learning organization has been defined as 'a group of people pursuing common purposes (individual purposes as well) with a collective commitment to regularly weighing the value of those purposes, modifying them when that makes sense and continuously developing more effective and efficient ways of accomplishing those purposes' (Leithwood and Aitken 1995: 63).

Morgan's (1986) use of the brain as a metaphor for the organization is a productive way of quickly glimpsing the promise of the learning organization. Bureaucracies, he notes, behave 'with brains'; those at the top of the hierarchy think on behalf of the organization (they are the organization's brains) and transmit messages to those lower in the hierarchy about what to do. Learning organizations, in contrast, behave 'as brains'; responsibility for thinking is widely distributed throughout the organization. As their environments become more complex, less predictable and demand more rapid responses, organizations with brains become overloaded with problems that they cannot possibly have enough information or processing power to solve. Organizations behaving as brains, in contrast, are able to take full advantage of the information collection and problem-solving capacities residing in each of their members, many of whom will be interacting with those environments on a daily basis.

The principal challenge facing those designing schools as learning organizations is to determine the organizational conditions that foster individual and collective learning and to build these conditions into the school. Attention has only recently been devoted to discovering what these conditions might be. Leithwood *et al.* (1995), for example, report that such conditions include: a widely shared vision of what the school is trying to accomplish; a professional culture that encourages considerable collaboration among staff on matters of teaching and learning with strong norms of continuous professional growth; structures that allow for frequent interaction and authentic participation in key decisions in the school; and policies and resources that support professional learning initiatives.

An image of future schools as learning organizations (or 'adaptive learning environments' to use the term of Aspin *et al.* 1994: 196) is particularly attractive because it does not require especially accurate predictions about the circumstances that future schools will face or the practices that would be most functional in response. The only prediction required is that schools will face a steady stream of complex problems, a prediction that places a premium on continuous improvements in school staff's individual and collective problem-solving capacities.

Implications for leaders' values

As a category of values associated with schools as learning organizations, generativity (a propensity to produce new ideas), encompasses at least such specific values as:

- *Openness to new ideas*: Learning is fostered as organizational members discard preconceived beliefs about where useful ideas might come from.
- *Tolerance for divergent points of view*: Too much consensus leads to groupthink (Janis 1983). Learning organizations need just enough consensus to carry out their work and no more.
- *Tolerance for strategic failure*: Valuing failure as a source of learning rather than something to be avoided is a productive value in relation to issues where mistakes do not create disasters for the organization (Sitkin 1996).
- *Questioning of basic assumptions*: Argyris and Schön (1978) refer to this as 'double loop' learning.
- *Speculative thinking*: Encourages people to imagine plausible future states, anticipate the challenges that those future states may create, and prepare to address them rather than simply responding or adapting to them when they arise.
- *Personal mastery*: As Senge (1990) defines it, personal mastery values the effort of individual members of the organization to become as skilled and knowledgeable as possible about how to carry out their individual responsibilities in the organization as well as how to contribute to collective efforts.
- *Interconnectedness*: Senge's (1990) fifth discipline, interconnectedness or systems thinking, encourages organizational members to appreciate the complex nature of the relationships among different aspects of the organization.

Toward a comprehensive image of future schools

The three images of future schools that have been described are based on quite different assumptions; each image, nevertheless, contains a partial solution to the dilemmas future schools are likely to face, and a synthesis of these images is both possible and desirable.

To illustrate some of the differences in these three images, consider how they differ in their assumptions about human learning, motivation and organizational mission and goals. With respect to learning, a community image of organization is based on developmentalist views of the sort reflected, for example, in Piagetian theory. Members of the community, it is assumed, learn what they need to know and be able to do 'naturally' and relatively effortlessly from participation in a suitable community setting, much as developmentalists believe children learn in unstructured ways from a stimulating educational setting (Scardamalia and Bereiter 1989).

HROs, on the other hand, reflect an information-processing view of learning, one in which there are clear learning goals and a set of powerful procedures available for their achievement; systematic development by individuals of the skills required to use such procedures is one of the central tasks of organizational members. Finally, learning organizations assume that: learning and problem solving is both an individual and a collective act (Leithwood *et al.* 1996a); such learning is often aimed at unclear goals; and knowledge is socially constructed through interactions among the cognitive resources of individual members as they work towards making sense of new problems and information (Saavedra and Anderson 1996).

The three images of future schools also vary considerably in their assumptions about human motivation. Using Maslow's (1954) needs hierarchy as an illustration, schools as communities most obviously fill people's affiliation needs. HROs appear to address people's achievement needs most directly, whereas self-actualization needs are most obviously met within the context of a learning organization.

As a final illustration of just how different are the assumptions underlying the three images of future schools, consider the most likely mission and goals each type of organization would be capable of realizing. With their overriding concern for inclusion and diversity, schools designed as communities are most likely to view *equity* as their mission and place considerable emphasis on social–emotional goals; the main instrument for change is likely to be organizational members' commitments to students, and to the school and its mission.

A widely distributed version of *excellence* appears the most obvious mission to be addressed by HROs along with a core set of traditional goals for schools; goals included in McGregor's concept of 'gateway achievements' (1994: 26).

Continuous quality improvement would be a likely contender for the primary mission of the learning organization. Although 'quality' is eventually judged in terms of service to students, first in the order of business are the processes used to provide such service and the capacities needed by organizational members to refine and implement increasingly effective processes. Continuous improvement, although not ignoring the improvement of processes designed to develop gateway achievements, would be focused especially on higher order, more complex student outcomes; those for which well codified processes do not already exist.

These examples of different assumptions underlying the three images of future schools illustrate two important points. First, and most obviously, these three images really do represent fundamentally different school designs. Less obviously, but central to the purposes of this chapter, there is an important sense in which all of these assumptions can be justified at some point in time, for some people, in some contexts. Consider just the assumptions about human learning for example: although these assumptions are quite different, each reflects quite closely the nature of learning under some circumstances.

Developmentalist assumptions reflect the ways in which most people learn a first language and the informal and implicit way in which tacit knowledge is acquired in most domains of practice. Information processing assumptions, on the other hand, describe reasonably well the cognitive processes associated with learning well codified, explicit knowledge and skill. And constructivist conceptions of learning are useful in understanding how people make sense of situations in which significant amounts of interpretation are required of them and where there are multiple possible 'correct answers'.

The same general case made for the appropriateness of each of the three perspectives on learning can also be made for the alternative sources of human motivation and the different organizational missions and goals that were described. This suggests that a synthesis of the three images of schools, described separately to this point, offers a comprehensive and potentially workable design for future schools. *School-as-community* acts as a foundation for the organization by providing the psychological stability and sense of mutual trust required for organizational members to be willing to risk making changes in their practices. *School-as-HRO* offers the conditions to ensure that students achieve the basic capacities or gateway achievements that parents and the wider community have always expected, and continue to expect, schools to develop. Finally, *school-as-learning organization* works to accomplish those ambitious and/or novel student outcomes for which schools have not, as yet, developed reliable and effective practices. Both 'school-as-HRO' and 'school-as-learning organization' build on the foundation provided by 'school-as-community'.

School change and implications for leadership

The problem of imagining the design of future schools includes the problem of how they will get to be future schools. Future schools, however much we may wish them to, will not spring into existence full blown on, say, 1 January 2000. Rather, they will evolve into something different from, but connected to, today's schools, on a broken front, over a very unpredictable timeline and without any sense of ever completing that evolution. Most likely, as Davis argues, this evolution will involve a long series of 'marginal improvements' (1996: 201).

Such incremental approaches to change are quite inconsistent with current calls for 'systemic' change (Epps 1994), 'bold plans for school restructuring' (Stringfield *et al.* 1996), 'break-the-mould schools' (Cooperman 1994), and radical 'restructuring' (Bast and Walberg 1994). Incremental approaches to change neither spark the imagination of educational reformers nor offer much leverage to policy makers. As much as we may wish that we are entering a brave new world in which many things (including schools) will somehow behave differently, the wisest bet is that incrementalism will prevail; it will prevail as the most accurate description of how schools will change over the next 20 years just as it is the most accurate description of how they have changed over the past 50 years. This is the case for at least four reasons.

First, there is no evidence of significant non-incremental change having occurred in schools in the past. Indeed, most evidence suggests that at least a five-year period of time has been required for changes considerably less ambitious than the comprehensive and systemic reforms currently being proposed by many advocates and school critics (Fullan 1992). Some might argue 'that was then and this is now' – reform is considered more urgent than ever before. But preliminary evidence from one of the most recent, ambitious and heavily funded initiatives, the New American Schools, for example, offers no reason to think that things are going to be different in this respect (Bodily 1996).

A second reason why it is safe to assume that schools will evolve incrementally is that most non-regulatory types of changes proposed for schools require significant new learning on the part of teachers and administrators. Contemporary understandings of how such learning occurs suggests that it is an unavoidably messy and protracted process in which existing cognitive resources are used to construct new understandings and further develop one's repertoire of practices. Or as Aspin *et al.* explain in their argument for an evolutionary approach to change, 'future growth in knowledge has to stand on the shoulders of past cognitive achievements' (1994: 208). Shortcuts do not exist, although we now have a fairly robust body of knowledge about effective ways of supporting professional learning (Ruohotie and Grimmett 1996).

A third reason for assuming that schools will evolve gradually has to do with their location, largely within the 'institutional' as opposed to 'technical' sector of organizations. As Meyer and Scott (1983) and others point out, organizations fall primarily in the institutional sector when they have ambiguous and contested goals, and uncertain techniques or procedures for accomplishing their goals. Institutional sector organizations must also take account of the interests of multiple legitimate stakeholders when establishing their goals and procedures. In the case of schools, these include, for example, parents, students, business representatives and other members of the wider community, universities, special interest groups and, of course, teachers themselves.

Unlike most other employee groups, teachers begin being socialized into their professional roles when they first enter school at the age of 6 or 7. A significant proportion are persuaded to become teachers because they like the idea of school as they experienced it; they like doing what they understand their own teachers to be doing. Furthermore, length of experience in the role 'also socializes people to accept conventional definitions of good work and worthy activities' (Hart 1995b: 180). So both the pre-professional experiences of teachers and the significant average length of tenure of the current pool of teachers create deeply rooted sources of resistance to rapid acceptance of new school designs that significantly alter the teachers' traditional role. Such resistance is likely to be overcome only gradually as teachers have opportunities to understand, experiment with and find satisfaction in new ways of working with their students.

So organizations residing largely in the institutional sector, as schools do, must negotiate what they will do. Forging agreements on what changes will be made is a highly political process. And it involves not only the stakeholders who consume the services of the organization and provide the financial resources for such services, but also those stakeholders who provide the services and, as a consequence, are most crucial in determining what the nature of those services will be.

This strategy for both survival and change in institutional sector organizations is markedly different from the strategy used by organizations, such as many private businesses, residing largely in the technical sector. Given a much less contested set of goals and many fewer competing stakeholder interests to consider, such organizations can decide what they will do based on their understanding of what works most efficiently to accomplish their goals. So the present design of most schools, unlike many private enterprises, is 'overdetermined'. There are many interests to be satisfied before a significant change in their design can be even adopted, much less implemented.

A final reason for assuming gradual evolution of schools takes as its premise not its inevitability but its desirability. Incremental approaches, as Davis explains, avoid the debilitating and, finally, destructive 'rhetoric of excess' that has typically accompanied previous reform efforts: 'Willingness to seek and to accept marginal change is not acceptance of second- or third-best ... [it is] not minimal, not superficial, not trivial ... Marginal

improvements in education are actual, real, practical improvements . . .
Marginal improvements do not deny the nature of the boundaries of their
context' (1996: 204).

Given the improbability of non-incremental or revolutionary change,
future school designs must be ones that we 'can get to from here'; they must
be images of organizations whose main features are capable of growing out
of the seeds of today's school designs. This does not mean that future schools
should not be dramatically different from today's schools; undoubtedly they
must and will. But brave new visions of schools only establish directions
towards which to strive. The small changes that will take place in gradually
moving in those directions will always appear, by comparison with the
visions, to be relatively small – perhaps even trivial. From this perspective,
success means eventually having these seemingly trivial changes add up to
something worthwhile. Quite probably this will not be what was originally
envisioned because the experience of trying to get there will teach us about
a better place to go.

Acknowledging the authenticity and robustness of practices and organizational features potentially resulting from incremental change processes
makes it imperative that we respect the durability of today's schools. Popular perceptions notwithstanding, it also means that we recognize just how
remarkably effective schools have been in meeting the ambiguous, slippery
and wildly ambitious expectations of their many masters, in comparison
with the effectiveness of almost any other social institution. We would be
sadly remiss if we did not systematically build on the hard-won lessons in
organizational design available to be learned from schools in their relatively
short histories.

This adds up to a case for valuing what Argyris (1982) has labelled 'single
loop' learning (detecting and correcting errors without questioning underlying assumptions), or what Weick (1991) refers to as 'exploitation learning', especially since there is some evidence that repeated cycles of such
learning periodically lead to bold leaps forward in understanding and practice. The position also ascribes considerable importance to 'double loop'
(Argyris and Schön 1978) or 'exploration learning' (Weick 1991) in the
course of engaging in such improvement.

Legions of people are unprepared to acknowledge the durability and
effectiveness of schools to which we allude. But this chapter, and indeed the
book, assumes this positive perspective towards schools without further
justification. To be clear, however, this perspective in no way denies the existence of some pretty awful schools. Nor does this position deny the need for
major efforts to improve.

Implications for leaders' values

Three sets of values underly incremental orientations to change and are an important part of the value system of those who would exercise leadership for incremental change.

Carefulness and a constructively critical perspective

This set of values fosters incrementalism by eschewing premature initiatives and initiatives that have not been developed to the point where their implications for practice are clear. Such values give rise to demands that the claims made for new initiatives be demonstrated under real-school conditions before adoption; they encourage an open-minded but dispassionately sceptical attitude towards the claims of current reformers about the consequences of their favourite 'change of the month'.

Respect for the capacities and commitments of past and current educators

This set of values manifests itself in a willingness to build on the insights about how to educate large numbers of children that are embedded in the collective memories and structures of existing school organizations and educational practices. At the minimum, these insights take account of the imperatives in schools that many reformers are neither aware of nor interested in – for example, what it actually feels like at 3:30 in the afternoon of a normal day when a serious planning meeting is scheduled, having: had a planning meeting with your teaching partner for 45 minutes before the beginning of classes; taught, entertained, mothered and nursed 32 8-year-olds (two of whom are physically handicapped) for the past six hours; dealt with several disasters on the playground at recess; spent your half-hour lunch period organizing the next cross-country team meeting; and your 30-minute 'preparation' period talking to five parents on the phone about how their children's lack of sleep at night is interfering with their learning at school.

Continuous improvement

This value encourages one to build on the existing strengths of the school, and to use those strengths as a means of responding to initiatives for change. Such a value would, for example, give rise to the use of the existing skills of teachers in computer technology to make more manageable aspects of the new student assessment system based on the development of student portfolios.

Continuous improvement is an antidote for the sense of being overwhelmed and confused that is fuelled by excessively turbulent environments such as those currently faced by schools. A continuous improvement value encourages the seizing of as much local control as central mandates and regulations allow, the determination of manageable priorities for change that make local sense, and systematic, focused initiatives for the improvement of schools through achieving such priorities.

Summary and conclusion

From the consideration of clearly independent images of future schools has emerged a more comprehensive image: the school as *high reliability learning community*. This image responds well to four requirements or criteria that we have asserted to be critical in the design of future schools. Such schools should be inclusive, efficient and effective, and adaptable. They should also be capable of growing out of the design of today's schools, since the most likely process through which future schools will develop is an incremental one.

The seeds of high reliability are clearly evident in many of today's schools, and especially in those that have responded to research evidence concerning effective teaching strategies and the correlates of effective schools. Stringfield (1995) reviews evidence about specific school programmes as well as school-wide initiatives in support of this claim. Evidence of existing schools with well developed community features can be found in Sergiovanni (1994) and recent evidence reported by Louis and Kruse (1995). Leithwood *et al.* (1995), Sharrat (1996) and Leonard (1996) report significant amounts of organizational learning in selected schools responding to major policy initiatives.

The high reliability learning community, then, appears to be a plausible design for future school organizations because it addresses quite directly the forces for change currently impinging on schools and because it takes into account critical constraints on the implementation of school change. To create and sustain such a school design requires the practices of stakeholders in the school, especially the practices of those offering leadership, to be governed by a complex array of values, which we have identified in this chapter.

Such values, we think, have never been more important to school leaders as they face the swampy problem of moving their present schools towards a defensible vision of future schools. As we argued in Chapter 7, values are substitutes for knowledge in the swamp. Transformational leaders understand their importance; they are the leadership tools of postmodern organizations.

REFERENCES

Achilles, C.M. (1992) The leadership enigma is more than semantics, *Journal of School Leadership*, 1(1): 59–65.

Allison, D.J. (1996) Problem finding, classification and interpretation: in search of a theory of administrative problem processing, in K. Leithwood (ed.) *The International Handbook of Educational Leadership and Administration*. Dordrecht: Kluwer.

Allison, D.J. and Allison, P.A. (1993) Both ends of a telescope: experience and expertise in principal problem solving, *Educational Administration Quarterly*, 29(3): 302–22.

Anderson, J.R. (1983) *The Architecture of Cognition*. Cambridge, MA: Harvard University Press.

Anderson, P. (1989) *Great Quotations from Great Leaders*. Lombard, IL: Great Quotations Inc.

Argyris, C. (1982) *Reasoning, Learning, and Action*. San Francisco, CA: Jossey-Bass.

Argyris, C. and Schön, D.A. (1978) *Organizational Learning: A Theory of Action Perspective*. Reading, MA: Addison-Wesley.

Aspin, D.N., Chapman, J.D. and Wilkinson, V.R. (1994) *Quality Schooling: A Pragmatic Approach to Some Current Problems, Topics, and Issues*. London: Cassell.

Atkinson, N.J. and Wilmore, B.E. (1993) The management profile: identification of the management and leadership skills of school administrators, *Journal of School Leadership*, 3(5): 566–78.

Avolio, B.J. and Bass, B.M. (1988) Transformational leadership, charisma, and beyond, in J.G. Hunt, B.R. Baliga, H.P. Dachler and C.A. Schriesheim (eds) *Emerging Leadership Vistas*. Lexington, MA: Lexington Books.

Bandura, A. (1986) *Social Foundations of Thought and Action*. Englewood Cliffs, NJ: Prentice-Hall.

Barth, R.S. (1981) The principal as staff developer, *Boston University Journal of Education*, Spring: 144–61.

Bascia, N. (1997) Invisible leadership: teachers' union activity in schools, *Alberta Journal of Educational Research*, XLIII(2/3): 69–85.

Bass, B.M. (1981) *Stogdill's Handbook of Leadership, Chapter 4: Leadership Traits, 1904–1947*. New York: The Free Press.

Bass, B.M. (1985) *Leadership and Performance Beyond Expectations*. New York: The Free Press.

Bass, B.M. (1988) *The Multifactor Leadership Questionnaire, Form 5 (revised)*. Centre for Leadership Studies, State University of New York at Binghampton, New York, USA.

Bass, B.M. and Avolio, B.J. (1993) Transformational leadership: A response to critiques, in M.M. Chemers (ed.) *Leadership theory and research: Perspectives and directions*. San Diego: Academic Press.

Bass, B.M. and Avolio, B.J. (eds) (1994) *Improving Organizational Effectiveness Through Transformational Leadership*. Thousand Oaks, CA: Sage.

Bast, J. and Walberg, H. (1994) Free market choice: Can education be privatized?, in C.E. Finn Jr and H. Walberg (eds) *Radical Education Reforms*. Berkeley, CA: McCutchan.

Bates, R. (1993) On knowing: cultural and critical approaches to educational administration, *Educational Management and Administration*, 21(3): 171–6.

Battersby, D. (1987) Is there a place for 'craft theory' in educational administration?, *Educational Management and Administration*, 15(1): 63–6.

Beck, L.G. and Murphy, J. (1993) *Understanding the Principalship: Metaphorical Themes 1920s–1990s*. New York: Teachers College Press.

Bennis, W. (1959) Leadership theory and administrative behavior: the problem of authority, *Administrative Science Quarterly*, 4(1): 259–60.

Bennis, W. and Nanus, B. (1985) *Leaders: The Strategies for Taking Charge*. New York: Harper and Row.

Benson, N. and Malone, P. (1987) Teachers' beliefs about shared decision making and work alienation, *Education*, 107(3): 244–51.

Berliner, D. (1988) *The Development of Expertise in Pedagogy*. Charles W. Hunt Memorial Lecture. New Orleans, LA.

Berliner, D. and Biddle, B. (1996) *The Manufactured Crisis: Myths, Fraud, and the Attack on America's Public Schools*. New York: Addison-Wesley.

Berman, P. and McLaughlin, M.W. (1977) *Federal Programs Supporting Educational Change, Volume VII: Factors Affecting Implementation and Continuation*. Santa Monica, CA: Rand.

Blake, R.R. and Mouton, J.S. (1964) *The Managerial Grid*. Houston, TX: Gulf.

Blase, J. (1984) Teacher coping and school principal behaviors, *Contemporary Education*, 22(2): 173–91.

Blase, J. (1986) A quantitative analysis of sources of teacher stress: consequences for performance, *American Educational Research Journal*, 23(1): 13–40.

Blase, J. and Greenfield, W. (1985) How teachers cope with stress: how administrators can help, *The Canadian Administrator*, 25(2): 1–5.

Blase, J., Dedrick, C. and Strathe, M. (1986) Leadership behavior of school principals in relation to teacher stress, satisfaction and performance, *Journal of Humanistic Education and Development*, 24(4): 159–71.

Boal, K.B. and Bryson, J.M. (1988) Charismatic leadership: a phenomenological and structural approach, in J.G. Hunt, B.R. Baliga, H.P. Dachler and C.A. Schriesheim (eds) *Emerging Leadership Vistas*. Lexington, MA: Lexington Books.

Bodily, S. (1996) Lessons learned: RAND's formative assessment of NAS's phase 2 demonstration effort, in S. Stringfield, S. Ross and L. Smith (eds) *Bold Plans for School Restructuring: The New American Schools Designs*. Mahwah, NJ: Lawrence Erlbaum.

Bolman, L.G. and Deal, T.E. (1991) *Reframing Organizations: Artistry, Choice, and Leadership*. San Francisco, CA: Jossey-Bass.

Bolman, L.G. and Deal, T.E. (1994) Looking for leadership: another search party's report, *Educational Administration Quarterly*, 30(1): 77–96.

Bransford, J.D. (1993) Who ya gonna call? Thoughts about teaching problem solving, in P. Hallinger, K. Leithwood and J. Murphy (eds) *Cognitive Perspectives on Educational Leadership*. New York: Teachers College Press.

Bredeson, P.V. (1988) Perspectives on schools: metaphors and management in education, *Journal of Educational Administration*, 26(3): 293–310.

Bredeson, P.V. (1993) Letting go of outlived professional identities: a study of role strain for principals in restructured schools, *Educational Administration Quarterly*, 29(1): 34–68.

Brightman, H.J. (1988) *Group Problem Solving: An Improved Managerial Approach*. Georgia State University, Atlanta: College of Business Administration.

Brissie, J.S., Hoover-Dempsey, K.V. and Bassler, O.C. (1988) Individual, situational contributors to teacher burnout, *Journal of Educational Research*, 82(2): 106–12.

British Columbia Ministry of Education (1989) *Year 2000: A Curriculum and Assessment Framework for the Future*. Victoria, BC: British Columbia Ministry of Education.

Brookfield, S.D. (1984) Self-directed adult learning: a critical paradigm, *Adult Education Quarterly*, 35(2): 59–71.

Brookover, W.B., Schweitzer, J., Schneider, C., Flood, P. and Wisenbaker, J. (1978) Elementary school social climate and school achievement, *American Educational Research Journal*, 15(2): 301–18.

Brown, J.S., Collins, A. and Duguid, P. (1989) Situated cognition and the culture of learning, *Educational Researcher*, 18(1): 32–42.

Bryk, A.S. (1988) Musings on the moral life of schools, *American Journal of Education*, 96(2): 256–90.

Bryk, A.S. and Driscoll, M.E. (1988) *The High School as Community: Contextual Differences and Consequences for Students and Teachers*. Madison, WI: National Centre on Effective Secondary Schools, University of Wisconsin-Madison.

Bryk, A.S., Easton, J.Q., Kerbow, D., Rollow, S.G. and Sebring, P.A. (1993a) *A View from the Elementary Schools: The State of Reform in Chicago*. Chicago, IL: The Consortium on Chicago School Research.

Bryk, A.S., Lee, V.E. and Holland, P.B. (1993b) *Catholic Schools and the Common Good*. Cambridge, MA: Harvard University Press.

Bryman, A. (1992) *Charisma and Leadership in Organizations*. Newbury Park, CA: Sage.

Buck, J.T. (1989) *Transformational Leadership Behaviors of Exemplary Texas Superintendents*. Ann Arbor, MI: UMI Dissertation Services.

Bullock, A. and Thomas, H. (1997) *School at the Centre*. London: Routledge.

Burns, J.M. (1978) *Leadership*. New York: Harper & Row.

Byrne, B.M. (1994) Burnout: testing of the validity, replication and invariance of causal structure across elementary, intermediate, and secondary teachers, *American Educational Research Journal*, 31(3): 645–73.

Caldwell, B.J. (1992) The principal as leader of the self-managing school in Australia, *Journal of Educational Administration*, 30(3): 6–19.

Chapman, J. (1996) A new agenda for a new society, in K. Leithwood, J. Chapman, D. Corson, P. Hallinger and A. Hart (eds) *International Handbook of Educational Leadership and Administration*. Dordrecht: Kluwer.

Chase, A.M. (1992) *School Level Factors Predicting Teachers' Sense of Professional Engagement, Efficacy, Commitment, and Job Satisfaction: An Application of Structural Equation Modelling*. Boston, MA: Harvard Graduate School of Education.

Cheng, Y.C. (1991) Leadership style of principals and organizational process in secondary schools, *Journal of Educational Administration*, 29(2): 25–37.

Cherniss, C. (1988) Observed supervisory behavior and teacher burnout in special education, *Exceptional Children*, 54(5): 449–54.

Chi, M.T.H., Feltovich, P.J. and Glaser, R. (1981) Categorization and representation of physics problems by experts and novices, *Cognitive Science*, 5(2): 121–52.

Clark, C.M. (1988) Is there a place for 'craft theory' in educational administration? Yes, but not in the way Battersby suggests, *Educational Management and Administration*, 16(1): 65–8.

Clark, K.E. and Clark, M.B. (eds) (1990) *Measures of Leadership*. West Orange, NJ: Leadership Library of America.

Clune, W.H. and White, P.A. (1988) *School-based Management: Institutional Variation, Implementation, and Issues for Further Research*. New Brunswick, NJ: Eagleton Institute of Politics, Center for Policy Research in Education.

Cohen, M.D. (1996) Individual learning and organizational routine: emerging connections, in D. Cohen and L.G. Sproull (eds) *Organizational Learning*. Thousand Oaks, CA: Sage.

Cohen, M.D. and Bacdayan, P. (1996) Organizational routines are stored as procedural memory: evidence from a laboratory study, in M.D. Cohen and L.S. Sproull (eds) *Organizational Learning*. Thousand Oaks, CA: Sage.

Cohen, M.D., McLaughlin, M. and Talbert, J. (eds) (1993) *Teaching for Understanding: Challenges for Policy and Practice*. San Francisco, CA: Jossey-Bass.

Coleman, J.S. (1987) Families and schools, *Educational Researcher*, 16(6): 32–8.

Coleman, J.S. and Hoffer, T. (1987) *Public and Private High Schools: The Impact of Communities*. New York: Basic Books.

Coleman, M. (1996) The management style of female headteachers, *Educational Management and Administration*, 24(2): 163–74.

Coleman, P. and LaRocque, L. (1990) *Struggling to be Good Enough: Administrative Practices and School District Efforts*. London: Falmer Press.

Conger, J.A. and Kanungo, R.N. (1987) Towards a behavioral theory of charismatic leadership in organizational settings, *Academy of Management Review*, 12(4): 637–47.

Conley, D.T. (1993) *Roadmap to Restructuring: Policies, Practices and the Emerging*

Visions of Schooling. University of Oregon, Eugene: ERIC Clearinghouse of Educational Management.

Connors, L.J. and Epstein, J.L. (1994) *Taking Stock: Views of Teachers, Parents, and Students on School, Family, and Community Partnerships in High Schools*, report no. 25, August. John Hopkins University, Baltimore, MD: Center on Families, Communities, Schools, and Childrens' Learning.

Cook, S.D.N. and Yanow, D. (1996) Culture and organizational learning, in M.D. Cohen and L.S. Sproull (eds) *Organizational Learning*. Thousand Oaks, CA: Sage.

Cooper, M. (1988) Whose culture is it anyway?, in A. Lieberman (ed.) *Building a Professional Culture in Schools*. New York: Basic Books.

Cooperman, S. (1994) The new American schools development corporation, in C.E. Finn Jr and H. Walberg (eds) *Radical Education Reforms*. Berkeley, CA: McCutchan.

Cousins, J.B. (1995) Understanding organizational learning for educational leadership and school reform. Unpublished paper, University of Ottawa.

Cowan, D.A. (1986) Developing a process model of problem recognition, *Academy of Management Review*, 11: 763–76.

Cowan, D.A. (1988) Executives' knowledge of organizational problem types: applying a contingency perspective, *Journal of Management*, 14: 513–27.

Cowan, D.A. (1990) Developing a classification structure of organizational problems: an empirical investigation, *Academy of Management Journal*, 33: 366–90.

Cowan, D.A. (1991) The effect of decision-making styles and contextual experience on executives' descriptions of organizational problem formulation, *Journal of Management Studies*, 28(5): 463–83.

Crookall, P.S. (1989) *Leadership in the Prison Industry*. Unpublished PhD dissertation, University of Western Ontario, London, Ontario.

Cunningham, W.G. and Gresso, D.W. (1993) *Cultural Leadership*. Boston, MA: Allyn & Bacon.

Cunningham, W.J. (1983) Teacher burnout – solutions for the 1980s: a review of the literature, *The Urban Review*, 15(1): 37–49.

Cusack, B.O. (1993) Political engagement in the restructured school: the New Zealand experience, *Educational Management and Administration*, 21(2): 107–14.

Dannetta, V. (1996) Factors influencing secondary school teachers' commitment. University of Toronto: qualifying research paper, unpublished.

Darling, S.K. (1990) *A Study to Identify and Analyze the Relationship Between (1) Transformational Leadership and Collaboration, and (2) Transactional Leadership and Collaboration in Selected Minnesota Elementary Schools*. Ann Arbor, MI: UMI Dissertation Services.

Darling-Hammond, L. and Sclan, E. (1992) Policy and supervision, in C. Glickman (ed.) *Supervision in Transition: The 1992 ASCD Handbook*. Alexandria, VA: Association for Supervision and Curriculum Development.

David, J.L. (1989) Synthesis of research on school-based management, *Educational Leadership*, 46(8): 45–53.

Davidson, G. (1992) Beyond direct instruction: educational leadership in the elementary school classroom, *Journal of School Leadership*, 2(3): 280–8.

Davies, L. (1987) The role of the primary school head, *Educational Management and Administration*, 15(1): 43–7.

Davis Jr, O.L. (1996) The pursuit of marginal improvements, *Journal of Curriculum and Supervision*, 11(3): 201–4.

Day, D. and Lord, R. (1992) Expertise and problem categorization: the role of expert processing in organizational sense making, *Journal of Management Studies*, 29(1): 35–48.

Deal, T. and Peterson, K. (1990) *The Principal's Role in Shaping School Culture*. Washington, DC: US Department of Education, Office of Educational Research and Improvement.

Deal, T. and Peterson, K. (1991) Instrumental and expressive aspects of school improvement. Paper presented to the Annual Meeting of the International Congress on School Effectiveness and School Improvement, Cardiff, Wales, January.

Deal, T.E. and Peterson, K.D. (1994) *The Leadership Paradox: Balancing Logic and Artistry in Schools*. San Francisco, CA: Jossey-Bass.

de Gues, A.P. (1996) Planning as learning, in K. Starkey (ed.) *How Organizations Learn*. London: International Thomson Business Press.

Deluga, R.J. (1991) The relationship of leader and subordinate influencing activity in naval environments, *Military Psychology*, 3(1): 25–39.

Dillard, C.B. (1995) Leading with her life: an African-American feminist (re)interpretation of leadership for an urban high school principal, *Educational Administration Quarterly*, 31(4): 539–63.

Downton Jr, J.V. (1973) *Rebel Leadership*. New York: Free Press.

Duignan, P.A. and MacPherson, R.J.S. (1993) Educative leadership: a practical theory, *Educational Administration Quarterly*, 29(1): 8–33.

Duke, D. (1987) *School Leadership and Instructional Improvement*. New York: Random House.

Duke, D. (1996) The normative context of organizational leadership. Paper presented to the Toronto conference, Ontario Institute for Studies in Education, 2–4 October.

Duke, D. and Leithwood, K. (1994) *Functions of School Leadership: A Review*, technical report prepared for the Connecticut State Board of Education, Leadership Standards Project.

Duke, D., Showers, B. and Imber, M. (1980) Teachers and shared decision making: The costs and benefits of involvement, *Educational Administration Quarterly*, 16: 93–106.

Dunning, G. (1993) Managing the small primary school: the problem role of the teaching head, *Educational Management and Administration*, 21(2): 79–89.

Dwyer, D.C. (1984) The search for instructional leadership: routines and subtleties in the principal's role, *Educational Leadership*, 41(5): 32–8.

Egan, O. and Archer, P. (1985) The accuracy of teachers' ratings of ability: a regression model, *American Educational Research Journal*, 22(1): 25–34.

Eisenstat, R.A. and Cohen, S.G. (1991) Summary: top management groups, in J.R. Hackman (ed.) *Groups that Work (and Those that Don't)*. San Francisco, CA: Jossey-Bass.

Epps, E.G. (1994) Radical school reform in Chicago: how is it working?, in C.E. Finn Jr and H. Walberg (eds) *Radical Education Reforms*. Berkeley, CA: McCutchan.

Evers, C.W. and Lakomski, G. (1991) *Knowing Educational Administration*. Oxford: Pergamon Press.

Farber, B. and Miller, J. (1981) Teacher burnout: a psycho-educational perspective, *Teachers College Record*, 83(2): 235–43.

Fenech, J.M. (1994) Managing schools in a centralized system: headteachers at work, *Educational Management and Administration*, 22(2): 131–40.

Fernandez, C.F. and Vecchio, R.P. (1997) Situational leadership theory revisited: a test of an across-jobs perspective, *The Leadership Quarterly*, 8(1): 67–84.

Fiedler, F.E. and Garcia, E. (1987) *New Approaches to Leadership: Cognitive Resources and Organizational Performance*. New York: Wiley.

Fieman-Nemser, S. and Floden, R.E. (1986) The cultures of teaching, in M.C. Wittrock (ed.) *Handbook of Research on Teaching*. New York: Macmillan.

Finn, J.D. (1989) Withdrawing from school, *Review of Educational Research*, 59(2): 117–43.

Finn, J.D. and Cox, D. (1992) Participation and withdrawal among fourth-grade pupils, *American Educational Research Journal*, 29(1): 141–62.

Fiol, C.M. and Lyles, M.A. (1985) Organizational learning, *Academy of Management Review*, 10(4): 803–13.

Firestone, W. and Rosenblum, S. (1988) Building commitment on urban high schools, *Educational Evaluation & Policy Analysis*, 10(4): 285–99.

Firestone, W. and Wilson, B.L. (1985) Using bureaucratic and cultural linkages to improve instruction: the principal's contribution, *Educational Administration Quarterly*, 21(2): 7–30.

Floden, R.E., Porter, A.C., Alford, L.E. *et al.* (1988) Instructional leadership at the district level: a closer look at autonomy and control. *Educational Administration Quarterly*, 24(2): 96–124.

Ford, M. (1992) *Motivating Humans: Goals, Emotions and Personal Agency Beliefs*. Newbury Park, CA: Sage.

Foster, W. (1986) *The Reconstruction of Leadership*. Victoria, Australia: Deakin University Press.

Friedman, I.A. and Farber, B. (1992) Professional self-concept as a predictor of teacher burnout, *Journal of Educational Research*, 86(1): 28–35.

Fuhrman, S.H. (1993) *Designing Coherent Education Policy: Improving the System*. San Francisco, CA: Jossey-Bass.

Fullan, M. (1991) *The New Meaning of Educational Change*. Toronto: OISE Press.

Fullan, M. (1992) *Successful School Improvement*. Toronto: OISE Press.

Fullan, M. (1993) *Change Forces: Probing the Depths of Educational Reform*. London: Falmer Press.

Fullan, M. and Hargreaves, A. (1991) *What's Worth Fighting For? Working Together for Your School*. Toronto: Ontario Public School Teachers Federation.

Gagné, E.D. (1985) *The Cognitive Psychology of School Learning*. Boston, MA: Little, Brown.

Gamoran, A. (1996) Student achievement in public magnet, public comprehensive, and private city high schools, *Educational Evaluation and Policy Analysis*, 18(1): 1–18.

Geltner, B.B. and Shelton, M.M. (1991) Expanded notions of strategic instructional leadership: the principal's role with student support personnel, *Journal of School Leadership*, 1(4): 338–50.

Gephart, R.P., Thatchenkery, T.J. and Boje, D.M. (1996) Conclusion: reconstructing organizations for future survival, in D.M. Boje, R.P. Gephart and T.J. Thatchenkery (eds) *Postmodern Management and Organization Theory*. London: Sage.

Gioia, D.A. (1986) Conclusion: the state of the art in organizational social cognition, in H.P. Sims Jr, D.A. Gioia *et al.* (eds) *The Thinking Organization*. San Francisco, CA: Jossey-Bass.

Giroux, H.A. (1992) Educational leadership and the crisis of democratic government. *Educational Researcher*, 21(4): 4–11.

Glaser, R. and Chi, M.T.H. (1988) Overview, in M.T.H. Chi, R. Glaser and M. Farr (eds) *The Nature of Expertise*. Hillsdale, NJ: Lawrence Erlbaum.

Goldberger, S. and Kazis, R. (1996) Revitalizing high schools: what the school-to-career movement can contribute, *Phi Delta Kappan*, 77(8): 547–54.

Goldring, E.B (1990) Elementary school principals as boundary spanners: their engagement with parents, *Journal of Educational Administration*, 28(1): 53–62.

Greenfield, T. (1991) Re-forming and re-valuing educational administration: whence and when cometh the phoenix?, *Educational Management and Administration*, 19(4): 200–17.

Greenfield, W.D. (1995) Toward a theory of school administration: the centrality of leadership, *Educational Administration Quarterly*, 31(1): 61–85.

Greeno, J.G. (1978) A study of problem solving, in R. Glaser (ed.) *Advances in Instructional Psychology, Volume 1*. Hillsdale, NJ: Lawrence Erlbaum.

Greeno, J.G. (1980) Trends in the theory of knowledge for problem solving, in D. Tuma and R. Feif (eds) *Problem Solving and Education*. New York: Wiley.

Griffin, G. (1995) Influences of shared decision making on school and classroom activity: conversations with five teachers, *The Elementary School Journal*, 96(1): 29–45.

Gronn, P. (1996) From transactions to transformations: a new world order in the study of leadership, *Educational Management and Administration*, 24(1): 7–30.

Gurley, W. (1996) It's the end of the net as we know it, *Fortune*, 133(8): 181–2.

Hackman, J.R. (1991) Introduction: work teams in organizations: an orienting framework, in J.R. Hackman (ed.) *Groups That Work (and Those That Don't)*. San Francisco, CA: Jossey-Bass.

Hallinger, P. (1992) The evolving role of American principals: from managerial to instructional to transformational leaders, *Journal of Educational Administration*, 30(3): 35–48.

Hallinger, P. and Heck, R. (1996) Reassessing the principal's role in school effectiveness: a review of empirical research 1980–1995, *Educational Administration Quarterly*, 32(1): 5–44.

Hallinger, P. and McCary, C. (1990) Developing the strategic thinking of instructional leaders, *Elementary School Journal*, 91(2): 89–107.

Hallinger, P. and Murphy, J. (1985) Assessing the instructional management behavior of principals, *Elementary School Journal*, 86(2): 217–47.

Hallinger, P., Leithwood, K. and Murphy, J. (eds) (1993) *Cognitive Perspectives on Educational Leadership*. New York: Teachers College Press.

Halpin, A.W. (1957) The observed leader behavior and ideal leader behavior of aircraft commanders and school superintendents, in R.M. Stogdill and A.E. Coons (eds) *Leader Behavior: Its Description and Measurement*. Columbus, OH: Bureau of Business Research, Ohio State University.

Hambrick, D.C. and Brandon, G.L. (1988) Executive values, in D. Hambrick (ed.) *The Executive Effect: Concepts and Methods for Studying Top Managers.* London: JAI Press.

Hamilton, D., Ross, P., Steinbach, R. and Leithwood, K. (1996) Differences in the socialization experiences of promoted and aspiring school administrators, *School Leadership,* 6(4): 346–67.

Handy, C. (1996) The new language of organizing and its implications for leaders, in F. Hesselbein, M. Goldsmith and R. Beckhard (eds) *The Leader of the Future.* San Francisco, CA: Jossey-Bass.

Hannay, L.M. and Denby, M. (1994) Secondary school change: The role of department heads. Paper presented to the Annual Meeting of the American Educational Research Association, New Orleans, LA, 4–8 April.

Hargreaves, A. (1990) Individualism and individuality: reinterpreting the teacher culture. Paper presented to the Annual Meeting of the American Educational Research Association, Boston, MA, 16–20 April.

Hargreaves, A. and Fullan, M. (1998) *What's Worth Fighting For Out There?* Toronto: Ontario Public School Teachers' Federation.

Hargreaves, A. and Macmillan, R. (1992) Balkanized secondary schools and the malaise of modernity. Paper presented to the Annual Meeting of the American Educational Research Association, San Francisco, CA, 20–24 April.

Harrison, J.W. and Lembeck, E. (1996) Emergent teacher leaders, in G. Moller and M. Katzenmeyer (eds) *Every Teacher is a Leader: Realizing the Potential of Teacher Leadership.* San Francisco, CA: Jossey-Bass.

Hart, A.W. (1993) Reflection: an instructional strategy in educational administration, *Educational Administration Quarterly,* 29(3): 339–63.

Hart, A.W. (1995a) Reconceiving school leadership: emergent views, *The Elementary School Journal,* 96(1): 9–28.

Hart, A.W. (1995b) The impact of mathematics and computer technology on the core assumptions and practices of teaching, in S. Bacharach and B. Mundell (eds) *Images of Schools.* Thousand Oaks, CA: Corwin Press.

Harvey, C.W. (1986) How primary heads spend their time, *Educational Management and Administration,* 14(1): 60–8.

Hayes, J. (1980) Teaching problem-solving mechanisms, in D. Tuma and R. Feif (eds) *Problem Solving and Education.* New York: Wiley.

Hayes, J. (1981) *The Complete Problem Solver.* Philadelphia, PA: Franklin Institute Press.

Hayes, D. (1995) The primary head's tale: collaborative relationships in a time of rapid change, *Educational Management and Administration,* 23(4): 233–44.

Heald-Taylor, G. (1991) An investigation of the relationship among school goal setting procedures, school goal consensus and the cohesiveness of a school's culture. Unpublished doctoral dissertation, The Ontario Institute for Studies in Education, Toronto.

Hedberg, B. (1981) How organizations learn and unlearn, in P.C. Nystrom and W.H. Starbuck (eds) *Handbook of Organizational Design, Volume 1: Adapting Organizations to their Environments.* New York: Oxford University Press.

Heller, H., Clay, R. and Perkins, C. (1993) The relationship between teacher job satisfaction and principal leadership style, *Journal of School Leadership,* 3(1): 74–86.

Helm, C.M. (1989) *Cultural and Symbolic Leadership in Catholic Element-ary Schools: An Ethnographic Study*. Ann Arbor, MI: UMI Dissertation Services.

Hersey, P. and Blanchard, K.H. (1977) *Management of Organizational Behavior*, 3rd edn. Englewood Cliffs, NJ: Prentice-Hall.

Herzberg, F. (1959) *The Motivation to Work*, 2nd edn. New York: Wiley.

Hess, G.A. Jr (1995) *School-based Management after Five Years in Chicago: The Partnership of Parents, Community and Education*. Chicago, IL: Chicago Panel on School Policy.

Hipp, K.A. and Bredeson, P.V. (1995) Exploring connections between teacher efficacy and principals' leadership behaviors, *Journal of School Leadership*, 5(2): 136–50.

Hodgkinson, C. (1978) *Towards a Philosophy of Administration*. Oxford: Basil Blackwell.

Hodgkinson, C. (1991) *Educational Leadership: The Moral Art*. Albany, NY: SUNY Press.

House, J.S. and Wells, J.A. (1978) Occupational stress, social support, and health, in A. McLean, G. Black and M. Colligan (eds) *Reducing Occupational Stress: Proceedings of a Conference*, publication 78-140. Washington, DC: National Institute of Occupational Safety and Health.

House, R.J. and Mitchell, T.R. (1974) Path–goal theory of leadership, *Journal of Contemporary Business*, 3(4): 81–97.

Howell, J.M. and Avolio, B.J. (1991) Predicting consolidated unit performance: Leadership ratings, locus of control and support for innovation. Paper presented to the 51st Annual Meeting of the Academy of Management, Miami, FL.

Hoy, W.K. and Brown, B.L. (1988) Leadership behavior of principals and the zone of acceptance of elementary teachers, *Journal of Educational Administration*, 26(1): 23–38.

Huberman, M. (1988) Teacher careers and school improvement, *Journal of Curriculum Studies*, 20(2): 119–32.

Huberman, M. (1993) Burnout in teaching careers, *European Education*, 25(3): 47–69.

Hunt, J.G. (1991) *Leadership: A New Synthesis*. Newbury Park, CA: Sage.

Hunt, J.G., Baliga, B.R., Dachler, H.P. and Schriesheim, C.A. (eds) (1988) *Emerging Leadership Vistas*. Lexington, MA: Lexington Books.

Hutchins, E. (1991) Organizing work by adaptation, *Organization Science*, 2(1): 14–39.

Imber, M. and Neidt, W. (1990) Teacher participation in school decision making, in P. Reyes (ed.) *Teachers and their Workplace*. Newbury Park, CA: Sage.

Janis, I.L. (1983) *Groupthink*, 2nd edn. Boston, MA: Houghton Mifflin.

Jantzi, D. and Leithwood, K. (1996) Toward an explanation of teachers' perceptions of transformational school leadership, *Educational Administration Quarterly*, 32(4): 312–538.

Jaques, E. (1986) The development of intellectual capability: a discussion of stratified systems theory, *Journal of Applied Behavioral Science*, 22(4): 361–83.

Johnston, J. (1986) Gender differences in teachers' preferences for primary school leadership, *Educational Management and Administration*, 14(3): 219–26.

Johnston, J. and Pickersgill, S. (1992) Personal and interpersonal aspects of effective team-oriented headship in the primary school, *Educational Management and Administration*, 20(4): 239–48.

Kagan, D. (1988) Teaching as clinical problem solving: a critical examination of the analogy and its implications. *Review of Educational Research*, 58(4): 482–505.

Kasl, E., Marsick, V.J. and Dechant, K. (1997) Teams as learners, *Journal of Applied Behavioral Science*, 33(2): 227–46.

Kelsey, J.G.T. (1993) Learning from teaching: problems, problem formulation, and the enhancement of problem-solving capability, in P. Hallinger, K. Leithwood and J. Murphy (eds) *Cognitive Perspectives on Educational Leadership*. New York: Teachers College Press.

Kendrick, J.A. (1988) *The Emergence of Transformational Leadership Practice in a School Improvement Effort: A Reflective Study*. Ann Arbor, MI: UMI Dissertation Services.

King, M.I. (1989) *Extraordinary Leadership in Education: Transformational and Transactional Leadership as Predictors of Effectiveness, Satisfaction and Organizational Climate in K-12 and Higher Education*. Ann Arbor, MI: UMI Dissertation Services.

Kirby, P.C., King, M.I. and Paradise, L.V. (1992) Extraordinary leaders in education: understanding transformational leadership, *Journal of Educational Research*, 85(5): 303–11.

Kleine-Kracht, P. (1993) Indirect instructional leadership: an administrator's choice, *Educational Administration Quarterly*, 29(2): 187–212.

Kmetz, J.T. and Willower, D.J. (1982) Elementary school principals' work behavior, *Educational Administration Quarterly*, 18(4): 1–29.

Knowles, M. (1980) *The modern practice of adult education: from pedagogy to androgogy*, 2nd edn. New York: The Adult Education Company.

Kofman, F. and Senge, P. (1995) Communities of commitment: the heart of learning organizations, *Organizational Dynamics*, 22(2): 5–22.

Koh, W.L.K. (1990) *An Empirical Validation of the Theory of Transformational Leadership in Secondary Schools in Singapore*. Ann Arbor, MI: UMI Dissertation Services.

Kouze, J. and Posner, B. (1996) Seven lessons for leading the voyage to the future, in F. Hesselbein, M. Goldsmith and R. Beckhard (eds) *The Leader of the Future*. San Francisco, CA: Jossey-Bass.

Kowalski, J. and Oates, A. (1993) The evolving role of superintendents in school-based management. *Journal of School Leadership*, 3(4): 380–90.

Kushman, J.W. (1992) The organizational dynamics of teacher workplace commitment: a study of urban elementary and middle schools, *Educational Administration Quarterly*, 28(1): 5–42.

Lampert, M. (1990) When the problem is not the question and the solution is not the answer: mathematical knowing and teaching, *American Educational Research Journal*, 27(1): 29–64.

Lave, J. and Wenger, E. (1994) *Situated Learning: Legitimate Peripheral Participation*. Cambridge: Cambridge University Press.

Leach, D.J. (1984) A model of teacher stress and its implications for management, *Journal of Educational Administration*, 22(2): 157–72.

Lees, K.A. (1995) Advancing democratic leadership through critical theory, *Journal of School Leadership*, 5(3): 220–30.

Leinhardt, G. (1988) Situated knowledge and expertise in teaching, in J. Calderhead (ed.) *Teachers' Professional Learning*. London: Falmer Press.

Leinhardt, G. (1991) What research on learning tells us about teaching, *Educational Leadership*, April: 20–5.

Leithwood, K. (1990) The principals' role in teacher development, in B. Joyce (ed.) *Changing School Culture Through Staff Development*. Alexandria, VA: Association of Supervision and Curriculum Development.

Leithwood, K. (1992) The move towards transformational leadership, *Educational Leadership*, 49(5): 8–12.

Leithwood, K. (1994) Leadership for school restructuring, *Educational Administration Quarterly*, 30(4): 498–518.

Leithwood, K. (1995) Cognitive perspectives on school leadership, *Journal of School Leadership*, 5(2): 115–35.

Leithwood, K. and Aitken, R. (1995) *Making Schools Smarter: A System for Monitoring School and District Progress*. Thousand Oaks, CA: Corwin Press.

Leithwood, K. and Duke, D. (in press) A century's quest to understand school leadership, in J. Murphy and K. Louis (eds) *Handbook of Research on Educational Administration*. San Francisco, CA: Jossey-Bass.

Leithwood, K. and Hallinger, P. (1993) Cognitive perspectives on educational administration: an introduction, *Educational Administration Quarterly*, 29(3): 296–301.

Leithwood, K. and Jantzi, D. (1990) Transformational leadership: how principals can help reform school cultures, *School Effectiveness and School Improvement*, 1(4): 249–80.

Leithwood, K. and Jantzi, D. (1997) Explaining variation in teachers' perceptions of principals' leadership: a replication. *Journal of Educational Administration*, 35(4): 312–31.

Leithwood, K. and Steinbach, R. (1991) Indicators of transformational leadership in the everyday problem solving of school administrators, *Journal of Personnel Evaluation in Education*, 4(3): 221–44.

Leithwood, K. and Steinbach, R. (1995) *Expert problem solving*. Albany, NY: SUNY Press.

Leithwood, K., Begley, P. and Cousins, B. (1990) The nature, causes and consequences of principals' practices: an agenda for future research, *Journal of Educational Administration*, 28(4): 5–31.

Leithwood, K., Dart, B., Jantzi, D. and Steinbach, R. (1991a) *Building Commitment for Change: A Focus on School Leadership*. Final report for year two of the research project 'Implementing the Primary Program', prepared for the British Columbia Ministry of Education.

Leithwood, K., Jantzi, D. and Dart, B. (1991b) Toward a multi-level conception of policy implementation processes based on commitment strategies. Paper presented to the Fourth International Congress on School Effectiveness, Cardiff, Wales.

Leithwood, K., Begley, P. and Cousins, B. (1992a) *Developing Expert Leadership for Future Schools*. London: Falmer Press.

Leithwood, K., Dant, B., Jantzi, D. and Steinbach, R. (1992b) *Fostering Organizational Learning: A Study of British Columbia's Intermediate Developmental Site Initiatives*. Victoria, BC: British Columbia Ministry of Education.

Leithwood, K., Steinbach, R. and Begley, P. (1992c) Socialization experiences:

becoming a principal in Canada, in G. Hall and F. Parkay (eds) *Becoming a Principal*. Boston, MA: Allyn and Bacon.

Leithwood, K., Cousins, B. and Gérin-Lajoie, D. (1993a) *Years of Transition, Times for Change: A Review and Analysis of Pilot Projects Investigating Issues in the Transition Years, Volume 2: Explaining Variations in Progress*. Toronto: Final report of research to the Ontario Ministry of Education.

Leithwood, K., Dart, B., Jantzi, D. and Steinbach, R. (1993b) *Fostering Organizational Learning: A Study in British Columbia's Intermediate Developmental Sites, 1990–1992*. Final report for year three of the research project 'Implementing the Year 2000 Policies', prepared for the British Columbia Ministry of Education.

Leithwood, K., Dart, B., Jantzi, D. and Steinbach, R. (1993c) *Building Commitment for Change and Fostering Organizational Learning*. Final report for phase four of the research project 'Implementing British Columbia's Education Policy', prepared for the British Columbia Ministry of Education.

Leithwood, K., Steinbach, R. and Raun, T. (1993d) Superintendents' group problem-solving processes, *Educational Administration Quarterly*, 29(3): 364–91.

Leithwood, K., Jantzi, D. and Fernandez, A. (1994) Transformational leadership and teachers' commitment to change, in J. Murphy and K. Louis (eds) (in press), *Reshaping the Principalship*. Newbury Park, CA: Corwin Press.

Leithwood, K., Jantzi, D. and Steinbach, R. (1995) An organizational learning perspective on school responses to central policy initiatives, *School Organization*, 15(3): 229–52.

Leithwood, K., Chapman, J., Corson, D., Hallinger, P. and Hart, A. (eds) (1996a) *International Handbook of Educational Leadership and Administration*. The Netherlands: Kluwer.

Leithwood, K., Tomlinson, D. and Genge, M. (1996b) Transformational school leadership, in K. Leithwood, J. Chapman, D. Corson, P. Hallinger and A. Hart (eds) *International Handbook of Educational Leadership and Administration*. The Netherlands: Kluwer.

Leithwood, K., Haskell, P. and Jantzi, D. (1997a) Leadership and school effects: A case study. Paper presented to the Annual Meeting of the University Council for Educational Administration, Orlando, FL, October.

Leithwood, K., Jantzi, D., Steinbach, R. and Ryan, S. (1997b) Distributed leadership in secondary schools. Paper presented to the Annual Meeting of the American Educational Research Association, Chicago, March.

Leithwood, K., Menzies, T., Jantzi, D. and Leithwood, J. (1997c) Teacher burnout: a critical challenge for leaders of restructuring schools, in M. Huberman and R. van den Berg (eds) *Teacher Burnout*. The Netherlands: Kluwer.

Leithwood, K., Steinbach, R. and Ryan, S. (1997d) Leadership and team learning in secondary schools, *School Leadership and Management*, 17(3): 303–25.

Leonard, L. (1996) Organizational learning and the initiation of school councils. Unpublished PhD dissertation, University of Toronto.

Lesourd, S., Tracz, S. and Grady, M.L. (1992) Attitude toward visionary leadership, *Journal of School Leadership*, 2(1): 34–44.

Lieberman, A., Saxl, E.R. and Miles, M.B. (1988) Teacher leadership: ideology and practice, in A. Lieberman (ed.) *Building a Professional Culture in Schools*. New York: Basic Books.

Little, J. (1982) Norms of collegiality and experimentation, *American Educational Research Journal*, 19(3): 325–40.

Little, J.W. (1995) Contested ground: the basis of teacher leadership in two restructuring high schools, *The Elementary School Journal*, 96(1): 47–63.

Lloyd, D. (1978) Prediction of school failure from third-grade data, *Educational and Psychological Measurements*, 38(4): 1193–200.

Lord, R.G. and Maher, K.J. (1993) *Leadership and Information Processing*. London: Routledge.

Louis, K. and Kruse, S. (1995) *Professionalism and Community*. Thousand Oaks, CA: Corwin Press.

Louis, K. and Miles, M. (1990) *Improving the Urban High School*. New York: Teachers College Press.

Louis, K.S. and King, J. (1993) Professional cultures and reforming schools: does the myth of Sisyphus apply?, in J. Murphy and P. Hallinger (eds) *Restructuring Schooling*. Newbury Park, CA: Corwin Press.

Louis, K.S. and Smith, B. (1991) Restructuring, teacher engagement and school culture: perspectives on school reform and the improvement of teachers' work, *School Effectiveness and School Improvement*, 2(1): 34–52.

MacDonald, B. (1991) Critical introduction: from innovation to reform – a framework for analysis, in J. Rudduck, *Innovation and Change*. Toronto: OISE Press.

Machiavelli, N. (1981) The Prince, tr. G. Bull. London: Penguin (first published 1513).

Malen, B., Ogawa, R.T. and Krantz, J. (1990) What do we know about school-based management? A case study of the literature – a call for research, in W.H. Clune and J.F. Witte (eds) *Choice and Control in American Education, 2: The Practice of Choice, Decentralization, and School Restructuring*. New York: Falmer Press.

March, J. (1991) Exploration and exploitation in organizational learning, *Organization Science*, 2(1): 71–87.

Maslach, C. and Jackson, S.E. (1981) A scale measure to assess experienced burnout: the Maslach burnout inventory, *Journal of Occupational Behavior*, 2: 99–113.

Maslow, A.H. (1954) *Motivation and Personality*. New York: Harper.

Mathews, D. (1997) The lack of a public for public schools, *Phi Delta Kappan*, June: 740–3.

Mazur, P.J. and Lynch, M.D. (1989) Differential impact of administrative, organizational and personality factors on teacher burnout, *Teaching and Teacher Education*, 5(4): 337–53.

McGregor, E.B. (1994) Economic development and public education: strategies and standards, *Educational Policy*, 8(3): 252–71.

McLaughlin, M.W. and Talbert, J.E. (1993) Introduction: new visions of teaching, in D. Cohen, M. McLaughlin and J. Talbert (eds) *Teaching for Understanding: Challenges for Policy and Practice*. San Francisco, CA: Jossey-Bass.

McNeil, D. and Frieberger, P. (1993) *Fuzzy Logic: The Discovery of Revolutionary Computer Technology and How it is Changing our World*. New York: Simon & Schuster.

Mehan, H. (1984) Institutional decision-making, in B. Rogoff and J. Lave (eds) *Everyday Cognition: Its Development in Social Context*. Cambridge, MA: Harvard University Press.

Mehlinger, H.D. (1996) School reform in the information age, *Phi Delta Kappan*, 77(6): 400–7.

Menzies, T.V. (1995) Teacher commitment in colleges of applied arts and technology: sources, objects, practices and influences. Unpublished PhD dissertation, University of Toronto.

Meyer, J.W. and Scott, W.R. (1983) Centralization and the legitimacy problems of local government, in J.W. Meyer and W.R. Scott (eds) *Organizational Environments: Ritual and Rationality*. Beverly Hills, CA: Sage.

Milstein, M.M., Golaszewski, T.J. and Duquette, R.D. (1984) Organizationally based stress: what bothers teachers, *Journal of Educational Research*, 77(5): 293–7.

Mohrman, S.A. and Mohrman, A.M. (1995) *Designing Team-based Organizations: New Forms for Knowledge Work*. San Francisco, CA: Jossey-Bass.

Mohrman, S.A., Wohlstetter, P. (1994) *School-based Management: Organizing for High Performance*. San Francisco, CA: Jossey-Bass.

Mojkowski, C. and Fleming, D. (1988) *School-site Management: Concepts and Approaches*. Andover, MA: Regional Laboratory for the Educational Improvement of the Northeast and Islands.

Moorhead, R. and Nediger, W. (1991) The impact of values on a principal's daily activities, *Journal of Educational Administration*, 29(2): 5–24.

Morgan, G. (1986) *Images of Organization*. Beverly Hills, CA: Sage.

Morgan, G. (1993) *Imaginization: The Art of Creative Management*. Newbury Park, CA: Sage.

Mortimore, P., Sammons, P., Stoll, L., Lewis, D. and Ecob, R. (1988) *School Matters: The Junior Years*. Somerset, UK: Open Books Publishing.

Mott, P.E. (1972) *The Characteristics of Effective Organizations*. New York: Harper and Row.

Mowday, R., Steers, R. and Porter, L. (1979) The measurement of organizational commitment, *Journal of Vocational Behavior*, 14(2): 224–47.

Mumford, M.D. and Connelly, M.S. (1991) Leaders as creators: leader performance and problem solving in ill-defined domains, *Leadership Quarterly*, 2(4): 289–315.

Murphy, J. (1991) *Restructuring Schools: Capturing and Assessing the Phenomena*. New York: Teachers College Press.

Murphy, J. and Beck, L.G. (1995) *School-based Management as School Reform: Taking Stock*. Thousand Oaks, CA: Corwin Press.

Murphy, J. and Hallinger, P. (1992) The principalship in an era of transformation, *Journal of Educational Administration*, 30(3): 77–88.

Myers, E. and Murphy, J. (1995) Suburban secondary school principals' perceptions of administrative control in schools, *Journal of Educational Administration*, 33(3): 14–37.

Nanus, B. (1992) *Visionary Leadership*. San Francisco, CA: Jossey-Bass.

National Commission on Excellence in Education (1983) *A Nation at Risk: The Imperative of Educational Reform*. Washington, DC: US Government Printing Office.

Neck, C.P. and Manz, C.C. (1994) From groupthink to teamthink: toward the creation of constructive thought patterns in self-managing work teams, *Human Relations*, 47(8): 929–52.

Newell, A. (1975) Discussion of papers by Robert M. Gagné and John R. Hayes, in

B. Kleinmuntz (ed.) *Problem Solving: Research, Method, and Theory.* Huntington, NY: Robert E. Kreiger.

Newell, A. and Simon, H. (1972) *Human Problem Solving.* Englewood Cliffs, NJ: Prentice-Hall.

Newell, A., Rosenblum, P. and Laird, J. (1990) Symbolic architectures for cognition, in M. Posner (ed.) *Foundations of Cognitive Science.* Cambridge, MA: MIT Press.

Ng, E. (1992) Children and elderly people: sharing public income resources, *Canadian Social Trends,* 25(Summer): 12–15.

Nias, J., Southworth, G. and Campbell, P. (1989) *Staff Relationships in the Primary School.* London: Cassell.

Oderkirk, J. (1994) Marriage in Canada: changing beliefs and behaviors, 1600–1990. *Canadian Social Trends,* 33(Summer): 2–7.

Oderkirk, J. and Lochhead, C. (1992) Lone parenthood: gender differences, *Canadian Social Trends,* 27(Winter): 15–19.

Ogawa, R. (1993) The institutional sources of educational reform: the case of school-based management. Presented to the Annual Meeting of the American Educational Research Association, Atlanta, 12–16 April.

Orr, D.R. (1990) *An Expectancy Theory Investigation of School Superintendent Job Performance.* Ann Arbor, MI: UMI Dissertation Services.

Peterson, P.L., McCarthey, S.J. and Elmore, R. (1996) Learning from school restructuring, *American Educational Research Journal,* 33(1): 119–53.

Podsakoff, P.M., MacKenzie, S.B., Moorman, R.H. and Fetter, R. (1990) Transformational leaders' behaviors and their effects on followers' trust in leader, satisfaction, and organizational citizenship behaviors, *Leadership Quarterly,* 1(2): 107–42.

Polanyi, J. (1967) *The Tacit Dimension.* Garden City, NY: Doubleday.

Prestine, N. (1993) Feeling the ripples, riding the waves: making an essential school, in J. Murphy and P. Hallinger (eds) *Restructuring Schooling.* Newbury Park, CA: Corwin Press.

Reavis, C. and Griffith, H. (1993) *Restructuring Schools: Theory and Practice.* Lancaster, PA: Technomic Publishing Co.

Reid, E.J. (1991) The elementary school principal as facilitator of adult learning. Unpublished PhD dissertation, Ontario Institute for Studies in Education, Toronto.

Reilly, D.H. (1993) Educational leadership: a new vision and a new role within an international context, *Journal of School Leadership,* 3(1): 9–20.

Reitman, W. (1965) *Cognition and Thought.* New York: Wiley.

Reitzug, U.C. (1994) Diversity, power and influence: multiple perspectives on the ethics of school leadership, *Journal of School Leadership,* 4(2): 197–222.

Reitzug, U.C. and Reeves, J.E. (1992) Miss Lincoln doesn't teach here: a descriptive narrative and conceptual analysis of a principal's symbolic leadership behavior, *Educational Administration Quarterly,* 28(2): 185–219.

Reyes, P. (1990) Organizational commitment of teachers, in P. Reyes (ed.) *Teachers and their Workplace.* Newbury Park, CA: Sage.

Roberts, N.C. (1985) Transforming leadership: a process of collective action, *Human Relations,* 38(11): 1023–46.

Rogoff, B. (1984) Introduction: thinking and learning in context, in B. Rogoff and J. Lave (eds) *Everyday Cognition: Its Development in Social Context*. Cambridge, MA: Harvard University Press.

Rogoff, B. and Lave, J. (1984) *Everyday Cognition: Its Development in Social Context*. Cambridge, MA: Harvard University Press.

Rosenholtz, S. (1989) *Teachers' Workplace*. New York: Longman.

Rossmiller, R.A. (1992) The secondary school principal and teachers' quality of work life, *Educational Management and Administration*, 20(3): 132–46.

Rost, J.C. (1991) *Leadership for the 21st Century*. New York: Praeger.

Roueche, J., Baker, G. and Rose, R. (1989) *Shared Vision: Transformational Leadership in American Community Colleges*. Washington, DC: The Community College Press.

Rowan, B. (1990) Commitment and control: alternative strategies for the organizational design of schools, *Review of Research in Education*, 16: 353–92.

Rubinstein, M.F. (1975) *Patterns of Problem Solving*. Englewood Cliffs, NJ: Prentice-Hall.

Rumelhart, D.E. (1990) The architecture of mind: a connectionist approach, in M. Posner (ed.) *Foundations of Cognitive Science*. Cambridge, MA: MIT Press.

Ruohotie, P. and Grimmett, P. (eds) (1996) *Professional Growth and Development: Direction, Delivery, and Dilemmas*. Tampere, Finland: Career Development Finland Ky.

Russell, D.W., Altemaier, E. and VanVelzen, D. (1987) Job-related stress, social support and burnout among classroom teachers, *Journal of Applied Psychology*, 72(2): 269–74.

Saavedra, E.R. and Anderson, G.L. (1996) Transformative learning in organizational settings. Paper presented to the Annual Meeting of the American Educational Research Association, New York City, 8–12 April.

Sandelands, L. and St. Clair, L. (1993) Toward an empirical concept of group, *Journal for the Theory of Social Behavior*, 23(4): 423–57.

Sashkin, M. and Sashkin, M. (1990) Leadership and culture-building in schools: Quantitative and qualitative understandings. Paper presented to the Annual Meeting of the American Educational Research Association, Boston, MA, 16–20 April.

Savery, L.K., Soutar, G.N. and Dyson, J.D. (1992) Ideal decision-making styles indicated by deputy principals, *Journal of Educational Administration*, 30(2): 18–25.

Scardamalia, M. and Bereiter, C. (1986) Research on written composition, in M. Wittrock (ed.) *Handbook of Research on Teaching*. New York: Macmillan.

Scardamalia, M. and Bereiter, C. (1989) Conceptions of teaching and approaches to core problems, in M.C. Reynolds (ed.) *Knowledge Base for the Beginning Teacher*. Oxford: Pergamon Press.

Schein, E.H. (1985) *Leadership and Organizational Culture*. San Francisco, CA: Jossey-Bass.

Scherer, M. (1996) On our changing family values: a conversation with David Elkind, *Educational Leadership*, 53(7): 4–9.

Schlansker, B. (1987) A principal's guide to teacher stress, *Principal*, 66(5): 32–4.

Schlecty, P. (1990) *Schools for the 21st Century*. San Francisco, CA: Jossey-Bass.

Schoenfeld, A.H. (1989) Ideas in the air: speculations on small group learning, environmental and cultural influences on cognition and epistemology, *International Journal of Educational Research*, 13(1): 71–88.

Schön, D. (1983) *The Reflective Practitioner*. San Francisco, CA: Jossey-Bass.

Schwenk, C.R. (1988) The cognitive perspective on strategic decision-making, *Journal of Management Studies*, 25(1): 41–56.

Scribner, S. (1984) Studying working intelligence, in B. Rogoff and J. Lave (eds) *Everyday Cognition: Its Development in Social Context*. Cambridge, MA: Havard University Press.

Scribner, S. (1986) Thinking in action: some characteristics of practical thought, in R.K. Wagner and R. Sternberg (eds) *Practical Intelligence: Nature and Origins of Competence in the Everyday World*. Cambridge: Cambridge University Press.

Seltzer, J. and Bass, B.M. (1990) Transformational leadership: beyond initiation and consideration, *Journal of Management*, 16(4): 693–703.

Selznick, P. (1992) *The Moral Commonwealth: Social Theory and the Promise of Community*. Berkeley, CA: University of California Press.

Senge, P.M. (1990) *The Fifth Discipline*. New York: Doubleday.

Senge, P. (1996) Leading learning organizations: the bold, the powerful, and the invisible, in F. Hesselbein, M. Goldsmith and R. Beckhard (eds) *The Leader of the Future*. San Francisco, CA: Jossey-Bass.

Sergiovanni, T.J. (1989) Mystics, neats and scruffies: informing professional practice in educational administration, *Journal of Educational Administration*, 27(2): 7–21.

Sergiovanni, T.J. (1994) *Building Community in Schools*. San Francisco, CA: Jossey-Bass.

Shamir, B. (1991) The charismatic relationship: alternative explanations and predictions, *Leadership Quarterly*, 2(2): 81–104.

Shank, R. and Abelson, R. (1977) *Scripts, Plans, Goals, and Understanding*. Hillsdale, NJ: Lawrence Erlbaum.

Sharratt, L. (1996) The influence of electronically available information on the stimulation of knowledge use and organizational learning in schools. Unpublished PhD dissertation, University of Toronto.

Shedd, J. and Bacharach, S. (1991) *Tangled Hierarchies: Teachers as Professionals and the Management of Schools*. San Francisco, CA: Jossey-Bass.

Sheppard, B. (1996) Exploring the transformational nature of instructional leadership, *Alberta Journal of Educational Research*, XLII(4): 325–44.

Showers, C. and Cantor, N. (1985) Social cognition: a look at motivated strategies, *Annual Review of Psychology*, 36: 275–305.

Silins, H.C. (1992) Effective leadership for school reform, *The Alberta Journal of Educational Research*, 38(4): 317–34.

Silins, H.C. (1994a) *The Relationship Between Transformational and Transactional Leadership and School Improvement Outcomes*. Adelaide: The Flinders University of South Australia.

Silins, H.C. (1994b) *Analyzing Leadership and its Components: What Makes the Difference?* Adelaide: The Flinders University of South Australia.

Silins, H.C. and Leithwood, K. (1994) *The Relative Impact of Factors Influencing*

Student Outcomes in the Transition Years. Adelaide: The Flinders University of South Australia.

Simon, H. (1993) Decision making: Rational, nonrational, and irrational, *Educational Administration Quarterly*, 29(3): 392–411.

Sims Jr, H.P. and Lorenzi, P. (1992) *The New Leadership Paradigm: Social Learning and Cognition in Organizations.* Newbury Park, CA: Sage.

Singer, M.S. (1985) Transformational vs. transactional leadership: a study of New Zealand company managers, *Psychological Reports*, 57(1): 143–6.

Sirotnik, K. (1994) Curriculum: overview and framework, in M.J. O'Hair and S. Odell (eds) *Educating Teachers for Leadership and Change.* Thousand Oaks, CA: Corwin Press.

Sirotnik, K. and Kimball, K. (1996) Preparing educators for leadership: in praise of experience, *Journal of School Leadership*, 6(2): 180–201.

Sitkin, S.B. (1996) Learning through failure: The strategy of small losses, in M.D. Cohen and L.S. Sproull (eds) *Organizational Learning.* Thousand Oaks, CA: Sage.

Skalbeck, K.L. (1991) *Profile of a Transformational Leader: A Sacred Mission.* Ann Arbor, MI: UMI Dissertation Services.

Smith, C.A., Organ, D.W. and Near, J.P. (1983) Organizational citizenship behavior: its nature and antecedents, *Journal of Applied Psychology*, 68: 653–63.

Smith, F.J. (1976) The index of organizational reaction (IOR), *JSAS Catalogue of Selected Documents in Psychology: Volume 6, MS no. 1265.* Washington, DC: American Psychological Association.

Smith, J.G. (1989) *The Effect of Superintendent Leader Behavior on Principal Work Motivation.* Ann Arbor, MI: UMI Dissertation Services.

Smith, W.F. and Andrews, R.L. (1989) *Instructional Leadership: How Principals make a Difference.* Alexandria, VA: Association for Supervision and Curriculum Development.

Smylie, M. and Brownlee-Conyers, J. (1992) Teacher leaders and their principals: exploring the development of new working relationships, *Educational Administration Quarterly*, 28(2): 150–84.

Smylie, M.A. (1990) Teacher efficacy at work, in P. Reyes (ed.) *Teachers and their Workplace.* Newbury Park, CA: Sage.

Smylie, M.A. and Crowson, R.L. (1996) Working within the scripts: building institutional infrastructure for children's service coordination in schools. *Educational Policy*, 10(1): 3–21.

Smylie, M.A. and Denny, J.W. (1990) Teacher leadership: tensions and ambiguities in organizational perspective, *Educational Administration Quarterly*, 28(2): 150–84.

Spangler, W.D. and Braiotta, L. (1990) Leadership and corporate audit committee effectiveness, *Group and Organizational Studies*, 15(2): 134–57.

Stalhammar, B. (1994) Goal-oriented leadership in Swedish schools, *Educational Management and Administration*, 22(1): 14–25.

Starratt, R.J. (1991) Building an ethical school: a theory for practice in educational leadership, *Educational Administration Quarterly*, 27(2): 185–202.

Steinbach, R., Leithwood, K. and Gleue, K. (1996) Struggling to manage distributed leadership. Paper presented to the Annual Meeting of the American Educational Research Association, New York, 8–12 April.

Stern, G.C. and Steinhoff, C.R. (1965) *College Characteristics Index*. Skaneateles, NY: FAAX Corporation.

Sternberg, R. and Caruso, O.R. (1985) Practical modes of knowing, in E. Eisner (ed.) *Learning and Teaching the Ways of Knowing*. Chicago, IL: University of Chicago Press.

Stevens, J., Beyer, J. and Trice, H. (1978) Assessing personal, role and organizational predictors of managerial commitment, *Academy of Management Journal*, 21(3): 380–96.

Stringfield, S. (1992) Research on high reliability organizations: implications for school effects research, policy, and educational practice. Paper presented to the International Congress for School Effectiveness and Improvement. Victoria, British Columbia, January 2–5.

Stringfield, S. (1995) Attempting to enhance students' learning through innovative programs: the case for schools evolving into high reliability organizations, *School Effectiveness and School Improvement*, 6(1): 67–96.

Stringfield, S., Ross, S. and Smith, L. (1996) *Bold Plans for School Restructuring*. Mahwah, NJ: Lawrence Erlbaum.

Tarter, C., Hoy, W. and Bliss, J. (1989) Principal leadership and organizational commitment: The principal must deliver, *Planning and Changing*, 20(3): 131–40.

Taylor, D.L. and Bogotch, I.E. (1994) School level effects of teachers' participation in decision making, *Educational Evaluation and Policy Analysis*, 16(3): 302–19.

Thomas, H. and Pruett, M. (1993) Introduction to the special issue: perspectives on theory building in strategic management, *Journal of Management Studies*, 30(1): 3–10.

Tuettemann, E. and Punch, K.F. (1992) Psychological distress in secondary teachers: research findings and their implications, *Journal of Educational Administration*, 30(1): 42–54.

Uwazurike, C.N. (1991) Theories of educational leadership: implications for Nigerian educational leaders, *Educational Management and Administration*, 19(4): 259–63.

Van Lehn, K. (1990) Problem solving and cognitive skill acquisition, in M.I. Posner (ed.) *Foundations of Cognitive Science*. Cambridge, MA: MIT Press.

Vandenberghe, R. (1992) The changing roles of principals in primary and secondary schools in Belgium, *Journal of Educational Administration*, 30(3): 20–34.

Vandenburghe, R. and Staessens, K. (1991) Vision as a core component in school culture. Paper presented to the Annual Meeting of the American Educational Research Association, Chicago, 3–7 April.

Voss, J.F. and Post, T.A. (1988) On the solving of ill-structured problems, in M.T.H. Chi, R. Glaser and M.J. Farr (eds) *The Nature of Expertise*. Hillsdale, NJ: Lawrence Erlbaum.

Vygotsky, L.S. (1978) *Mind in Society: The Development of Higher Psychological Processes*. London: Harvard University Press.

Wagner, R.K. (1987) Tacit knowledge in everyday intelligent behavior, *Journal of Personality and Social Psychology*, 52(6): 1236–47.

Wagner, R.K. and Sternberg, R. (1986) Tacit knowledge and intelligence in the everyday world, in R.K. Wagner and R. Sternberg (eds) *Practical Intelligence: Nature and Origins of Competence in the Everyday World*. Cambridge, UK: Cambridge University Press.

Walberg, H.J. (1984) Improving the productivity of America's schools, *Educational Leadership*, 41(8): 19–27.

Walker, K.D. (1995) Perceptions of ethical problems among senior educational leaders, *Journal of School Leadership*, 5(6): 532–64.

Walker, W.G. (1989) Leadership in an age of ambiguity and risk, *Journal of Educational Administration*, 27(1): 7–17.

Ward, J.G. (1994) Reconciling educational administration and democracy, in N. Prestine and P. Thurston (eds) *Advances in Educational Administration*. Middlesex, UK: JAI Press.

Wasley, P.A. (1991) *Teachers as Leaders: The Rhetoric of Reform and the Realities of Practice*. New York: Teachers College Press.

Watkins, K.E. and Marsick, V.J. (1993) *Sculpting the Learning Organization*. San Francisco, CA: Jossey-Bass.

Weber, M. (1947) *The Theory of Social and Economic Organization*, tr. A.M. Henderson and T. Parsons, T. Parsons (ed.). New York: Free Press.

Webster's Seventh New Collegiate Dictionary (1971) Toronto: Thomas Allen & Sons.

Wehlage, G.G., Rutter, R.A., Smith, G.A., Lesko, N. and Fernandez, R.R. (1989) *Reducing the Risk: Schools as Communities of Support*. London: Falmer Press.

Weick, K.E. (1979) *The Social Psychology of Organizing*, 2nd edn. Reading, MA: Addison-Wesley.

Weick, K.E. (1991) The nontraditional quality of organizational learning, *Organizational Science*, 2(1): 116–24.

Weick, K.E. and Roberts, K.H. (1996) Collective mind in organizations: heedful interrelating on flight decks, in M.D. Cohen and L.S. Sproull (eds) *Organizational Learning*. Thousand Oaks, CA: Sage.

Weiss, A.M. (1996) System 2000: if you build it, can you manage it? *Phi Delta Kappan*, 77(6): 408–15.

Wertsch, J.V., Minick, N. and Arns, F.J. (1984) The creation of context in joint problem solving, in B. Rogoff and J. Lave (eds) *Everyday Cognition: Its Development in Social Context*. Cambridge, MA: Harvard University Press.

Westley, F. (1990) Middle managers and strategy: microdynamics of inclusion, *Strategic Management Journal*, 11: 337–51.

Whitaker, K.S., McGrevin, C. and Granier, A. (1991) Know thyself: a prerequisite for educational leaders, *Journal of School Leadership*, 1(2): 168–75.

Whitaker, T. (1995) Informal teacher leadership: the key to successful change in the middle school, *NASSP Bulletin*, January: 76–81.

White, P. (1992) Teacher empowerment under 'ideal' school-site autonomy. *Evaluation and Policy Analysis*, 14(1): 69–84.

Willower, D.J. (1994) Dewey's theory of inquiry and reflective administration, *Journal of Educational Administration*, 32(1): 5–22.

Wohlstetter, P. (1990) *Experimenting with Decentralization: The Politics of Change*. University of Oregon: Eric Document Reproduction Service No. ED337861.

Wohlstetter, P. and McCurdy, K. (1991) The link between school decentralization and school politics, *Urban Education*, 25(4): 391–414.

Wohlstetter, P. and Mohrman, S.A. (1993) *School-based Management: Strategies for Success*. New Brunswick, NJ: Rutgers University.

Wohlstetter, P. and Odden, A. (1992) Rethinking school-based management policy and research, *Educational Administration Quarterly*, 28(4): 529–49.

Wolbers, M. and Woudenberg, C. (1995) Teachers' commitment to change. Unpublished PhD dissertation, University of Toronto.

Yammarino, F.J. and Bass, B.M. (1990) Transformational leadership and multiple levels of analysis, *Human Relations*, 43(10): 275–95.

Yukl, G. (1989) *Leadership in Organizations*, 2nd edn. Englewood Cliffs, NJ: Prentice-Hall.

Yukl, G. (1994) *Leadership in Organizations*, 3rd edn. Englewood Cliffs, NJ: Prentice-Hall.

INDEX